D0340795

Hillary's Scheme

Hillary's Scheme

Inside the Next Clinton's Ruthless Agenda to Take the White House

CARL LIMBACHER
WITH NEWSMAX.COM

Published by Crown Forum, New York, New York, a Member of the Crown Publishing Group, a division of Random House, Inc.
www.randomhouse.com

Printed in the United States of America

Library of Congress Cataloging-in-Publication Data
Limbacher, Carl.
Hillary's scheme : inside the next Clinton's ruthless agenda to take the White House / Carl Limbacher and NewsMax.com.
p. cm.
Includes bibliographical references and index.
1. Clinton, Hillary Rodham. 2. Presidents' spouses—United States—Biography. 3. Women legislators—United States—Biography. 4. Presidential candidates—United States—Biography. 5. Presidents—United States—Election. 6. Political campaigns—United States. 7. United States—Politics and government—2001- 8. United States—Politics and government—1993–2001. 9. Political corruption—United States. I. Title.
E887.C55 L56 2003
973.931'092—dc21 2003001132

ISBN 0-7615-3115-7
10 9 8 7 6 5 4 3 2 1
First Edition

For Louise, Allison, and Carl

Contents

Introduction

> *"The order of succession to the presidency in this poor benighted country may well be Bush-Clinton-Bush-Clinton."*
> —Dick Morris to NewsMax.com, May 2002

The year 2003 began with startling prospects for New York's junior senator, opportunities that were almost unimaginable just weeks before. Former vice president Al Gore had dominated Democratic Party presidential preference polls for most of 2002. But in all the surveys in which her name had been included—regional polls taken by New York's Marist College or Connecticut's Quinnipiac University or national polls like Gallup or Zogby International—former first lady Hillary Clinton routinely ran a strong second to Gore. Gore usually managed to draw between 30 and 40 percent in these surveys, with Mrs. Clinton running about 10 to 15 points behind. Meanwhile, other prospective candidates—rising political stars like John Kerry, Joe Lieberman, and John Edwards, who were regularly touted by the experts as the party's best hope to beat George Bush in 2004—almost never attracted more than single-digit support.

Gore Withdraws

Then it happened. On December 15, 2002, Gore stunned the political world by announcing that he would not seek a much anticipated rematch against President Bush in 2004. Overnight, Hillary Clinton rocketed to the top of the two major polls of Democratic Party presidential prospects, attracting 30 percent support in a *Time*/CNN survey and 40 percent backing in a Gallup poll. In both surveys, more Democrats backed Clinton than her two nearest competitors, Kerry and Lieberman, combined. The first presidential spouse to hold elective office in U.S. history was suddenly her party's front-runner for the 2004 presidential nomination. A week later, Hillary Clinton was named "the most admired woman in America" in a separate CNN survey, edging out even current first lady Laura Bush.

Throughout the early months of 2003, Mrs. Clinton continued to top presidential surveys of Democrats, drawing 42 percent support in one February Quinnipiac survey. In her home state of New York, 50 percent of Democrats wanted her to run—a greater percentage than all the other Democrats combined when undecided voters were figured in.

The Big Question

Will Hillary run in 2004 when the plan has always been for her to make her move in 2008? And if she does, can she win? My answer to those two questions, as someone who has covered both Bill and Hillary Clinton for years as a reporter for the online news Web site NewsMax.com, will likely surprise Democrats—and perhaps shock Republicans into a new awareness of the dangers that lie ahead. Because the short answer to both questions is yes and yes. Her denials to the contrary, Hillary Clinton is considering a presidential run against George W. Bush in 2004 because she knows that year's election may be her last, best hope to reclaim the White House.

After the attacks of September 11, 2001, most observers acknowledged that Bush's superb performance dispelled any doubts about his strength of character, his resolve, and his leadership. His stirring words—delivered from Ground Zero just a few days after the twin symbols of America's economic dominance collapsed in a cloud of debris that made Lower Manhattan look as if it had been the target of a nuclear strike—rallied a shaken nation and will remain among the most memorable ever uttered by a U.S. president. Burned into the American psyche forever is the now famous quote: "I can hear you. The world can hear you. And the people who knocked these buildings down will hear from all of us soon." It was Bush's shout-out to a firefighter who complained that the president couldn't be heard. The off-the-cuff response from a president not known for his spontaneous eloquence became the most memorable phrase uttered by any leader since FDR pronounced the attack on Pearl Harbor "a day that will live in infamy."

That day Senator Clinton, not yet a year in office, was among the dignitaries who crowded the small paths carved through the Ground Zero rubble where the president would walk. A witness told NewsMax that Bush was mobbed by firefighters and rescue workers anxious to show support for the nation's leader in a moment of national crisis. "They couldn't wait to shake his hand. And they did the same with Giuliani and Pataki—even Schumer, too," he said, referring to the Republican governor and mayor as well as the state's senior senator, a Democrat. "But when her turn came the guys just folded their arms and wouldn't shake her hand. I'm no fan of Hillary," the source added. "But even I felt bad for her." The episode didn't make the newspapers, but it spoke volumes about the nation's disdain for her husband's legacy in the immediate aftermath of September 11.

The White House knew that the nation's near unanimous support for Bush in those weeks of September and October 2001 wouldn't last forever, but they bet—correctly as it turned out—that the tragedy that took 3,000 lives would color American politics for the foreseeable future. The battle of the 2002 midterm election, the White House decided, would be waged on national security issues. Now, with both houses of Congress as well as the presidency in GOP hands, all that goes right—along with anything that does not—will be credited to George Bush.

The Gulf War Lesson

Unlike his son, George Herbert Walker Bush did not have the same sweeping control over the government when he was president. And yet with his Gulf War victory over Iraq in March 1991—just twenty months before the 1992 election—Bush Sr.'s approval ratings hit a stratospheric 91 percent. He was considered so politically invincible that most Democrats thought it was a waste of time to challenge him. Even New York governor Mario Cuomo, whose stirring speech to the 1984 Democratic Convention had turned him into a presidential contender and whose Depression-era rhetoric would have been perfect for the burgeoning recession that was then just a flicker on the national radar screen, decided not to get in the race.

Enter Bill Clinton, whose sordid private life and sorry military record—he dodged three separate draft notices and finally reneged on a pledge to serve in the reserves—made him his party's perfect sacrificial lamb. "[Clinton] would get opened up like a soft peanut," predicted then Senator Bob Kerrey, after abandoning his own bid for the White House in 1992.[1] No way could this Arkansas unknown—whose only previous moment in the national spotlight came during a speech to the 1988 Democratic convention that went on so long they had to get out the hook—beat the man who led America to victory in the Persian Gulf and whose own military record as a World War II pilot shot down over the Pacific qualified him as a war hero.

Yet it happened. When the Democratic Party looked destitute in 1991 and 1992 and Bush Sr.'s popularity was at least as high as his son's was in the wake of September 11, the team of Clinton and Clinton decided to get into the race. From there they managed not only to get themselves elected, but also to hold on to the White House longer than any other Democratic administration since FDR's.

Déjà Vu 1992?

For the Bush family, 2004 could be shaping up as déjà vu all over again. By the fall of 2002, Democrats like New Jersey Senator Jon Corzine had begun referring to "the worst economic environment we've had in 50 years"—an unmistakable echo of Bill Clinton's 1992 campaign mantra that under Bush Sr. Americans were suffering "the worst economy in 50 years."[2] Then after the midterm election, the dismissal of top Bush administration economic officials Paul O'Neill and Lawrence Lindsey had Democrats crowing over what looked like an admission that the president's economic policies had been an abject failure.

In 1991 and 1992, Bush Sr. at least had the afterglow of the Iraq war victory to cushion the blow of a souring economy. Today, the international horizons are a good deal more clouded. Another Al Qaeda attack on U.S. soil—especially one that could be tied to Bush's decision to leave U.S. immigration policy and border controls virtually unchanged since September 11—would be met by a chorus of congressional critics arguing that the president had deliberately left America vulnerable. If the next attack comes with a Saudi pedigree, previous assurances that the Saudis have been "reliable allies in the war on terror" delivered by senior administration officials like Colin Powell and Condoleezza Rice, not to mention Bush himself, will look particularly ridiculous. In that case the president would be vulnerable to charges that he put his own family's long-standing relationship with Riyadh royalty ahead of U.S. national security interests. And any U.S. attack on Iraq that ends up with terrorists retaliating on American soil will have the media blaming Bush for putting American civilian populations in harm's way instead of protecting them.

Instinctively, most Democrats seem to understand that Bush indeed will be vulnerable in 2004. Unlike 1991, a year out from the New Hampshire primary there is no shortage of ambitious Democrats seeking to challenge Bush in 2003; among them are John Kerry, Joe Lieberman, Dick Gephardt, Al Sharpton, Howard Dean, and Bob Graham. That's a lot of high-powered political talent competing for the chance to be the Democratic Party's sacrificial lamb in 2004.

The Risks of Waiting

Another factor Hillary has to consider: Waiting until 2008 entails substantial career risks. What if, for instance, another Democrat beats Bush in 2004? Mrs. Clinton's year of choice, 2008, would have to go by the boards unless she wanted to lead a political insurrection against a president of her own party—or go the third-party route herself. By not making the run in 2004 against Bush, she may end up having to wait until 2012 if the Democrat who beats Bush wins a second term. By then Hillary Clinton would be at retirement age, sixty-five, just four years younger than Ronald Reagan when he sought the White House in 1980 amidst catcalls from Democrats that he was too old for the job.

Also arguing for a Hillary presidential bid sooner rather than later is the Democratic Party itself, still in the grip of Clinton-era apparatchiks. The Democratic National Committee's top message people, Maria Cardona and Jennifer Palmieri, are former Clintonistas. Cardona was the widely quoted spokeswoman for the Clinton INS during the Elian Gonzalez fiasco. Palmieri worked in the White House before becoming one of Clinton's postpresidential spokeswomen. In fact, in June 2001, both the ex-president and former first lady ordered Terry McAuliffe, whom they had handpicked to run the DNC six months earlier, to hire Palmieri as DNC spokeswoman after party officials initially balked.[3] (She has since moved on to join the campaign of presidential hopeful, Senator John Edwards, who had reportedly been consulting with Bill Clinton throughout much of 2002.)

Still, the Clinton influence didn't help much when it came to the 2002 midterm election debacles, when the party's hard-won control of the Senate evaporated overnight.

Many rank-and-file Democrats blamed McAuliffe. No wonder. He made Florida governor Jeb Bush Democratic Party enemy number one and diverted precious financial resources into a campaign to defeat him. Despite the Clinton moneyman's best efforts, Governor Bush beat his opponent Bill McBride by a 13-point landslide. And Democrats around the country were left grousing that the cash wasted in the McBride effort might have been better spent to save Democratic senators like Jean Carnahan and Walter Mondale, who went down to defeat in close races where the extra funds might have made the difference.

Still, McAuliffe wasn't fired. And that's because, in targeting the Bush family, he was merely following the orders of Bill and Hillary Clinton, who still control the party's fund-raising apparatus through Mr. McAuliffe, despite their own Election Day debacle. Most of the candidates they campaigned for around the country also went down to defeat. But when independent observers suggested the 2002 election results showed it was time for the former first couple to relinquish their leadership role, elected Democrats themselves would have none of it. Typical was the reaction of New York Representative Gary Ackerman: "I've been with President Clinton as recently as a week or so ago and he's still one of the most popular drawing cards you could have anywhere in the country, probably second only to President Bush," the New York Democrat boasted to a New York radio interviewer a few days after the election. "He attracts huge, huge crowds, very enthusiastic."[4] Translation: The Clintons won't be giving up control of the Democratic Party anytime soon.

Democrats Held Hostage

In truth, they probably couldn't afford to—not if Hillary Clinton ever wants to sit in the Oval Office herself. That's another reason why 2008 looks increasingly problematic for Hillary. Six years is a long time to hold a national political party hostage to your ambitions. And McAuliffe isn't likely to be able to maintain his grip on the party beyond the 2004 election, especially if his candidate loses, forcing the Clintons to step aside and let somebody else run the show. Even if a Democrat wins, it's bad news for Mrs. Clinton's presidential designs. By 2012, there will have been too much water under the bridge for Americans to remember much about the Clintons beyond Monica Lewinsky and impeachment.

Hillary Clinton seemed to understand this when, in late November 2002, just after her party's downfall at the polls, she stuck a finger in the eye of Gore's presidential hopes at a time when he was going through a very public soul-searching over his political future. Gore and his wife Tipper were in the midst of their high-profile book tour, a kind of second-family listening tour that was widely understood to be a vehicle to test the appeal of another Gore presidential bid.

As the vice president who had proclaimed on the day of Mr. Clinton's impeachment that he thought his boss would go down in history as "one of the greatest presidents ever," Gore was owed a significant debt of loyalty. And despite rumors about continuing resentments left over from the Monica Lewsinky case, as well as Gore's decision not to give Mr. Clinton a high-profile role in his 2000 presidential campaign, Hillary had no problem offering a full-throated endorsement for a Tipper senatorial bid when the ex–second lady voiced an interest in March 2002. "I talked to her this morning," Hillary told the *New York Daily News* after Tipper floated the idea. "I called her and told her I'd heard this, and that if, after careful consideration, she decided to do this, I'd be fully behind her. I think she's a wonderful person, and I'd be delighted to campaign for her."[5]

That's a far cry from the support Tipper's husband got from Hillary Clinton just before Thanksgiving, when Clinton repeatedly refused to endorse Gore for a 2004 run during an appearance on Chris Matthews's *Hardball.*

MATTHEWS: If former Vice President Al Gore seeks the Democratic nomination and announces it this coming January as he said he will make an announcement one way or the other, will you support his candidacy?

CLINTON: I'm a very good friend of Al Gore and Tipper Gore and I'm going to wait and see whether he decides to run. I think that has to be his decision. It's so personal and I'm going to support whoever the Democratic nominee is.

MATTHEWS: If I had a really, really good friend—as you've described Al Gore to me—a really, really good friend, and he was telling me I think I'm going to run for president. I'll announce in January . . .

CLINTON: He hasn't said that to me.

MATTHEWS: But if he did announce, I'd say "I'm with you" beforehand. I wouldn't wait and say, "Well, if you run I'll be with you." You'll say, "I'm with you, buddy, all the way." What have you said to him?

CLINTON: He hasn't talked to me about it . . .

MATTHEWS: . . . OK. Come January 6 or so, when I think he's going to make his announcement—will you support him then?

CLINTON: You know, I'm going to Hawaii.

MATTHEWS: But you will—as he will make a decision—you will make a decision whether to endorse him at that point.

CLINTON: No. You know, Chris, I don't endorse in Democratic primaries.[6]

Clinton's unexpected refusal to offer Gore any measure of support should have sent shock waves through the political press. What would it have cost her, after all, to repay her debt of loyalty to Gore with an endorsement—even if, in the end, another candidate had picked up steam and supplanted the ex–vice president as the front-runner? The answer, of course, is nothing—unless that other candidate turned out to be Hillary Clinton herself, which would have made the early Gore endorsement look like a premeditated act of political sabotage. Whether coincidence or not, twenty-five days after Mrs. Clinton openly repudiated another Gore presidential bid, the former vice president withdrew from the race.

Hillary Positioned

As the only Democratic candidate with 100 percent name recognition and a ready-to-go coast-to-coast fund-raising operation—as a candidate who has been piling up IOUs raising cash for other candidates—Hillary Clinton knows she won't have to toil like the others in the political vineyards more than a year ahead of time, building up her profile and introducing herself to the world of Democratic Party high rollers. They're already in her corner, ready to loosen the purse strings the moment she gives the word. Unless some other candidate catches fire between now and the convention—an unlikely proposition given the competition—Clinton can wait almost until the last minute, snap her fingers, and scarf up the nomination.

Meanwhile, she can bide her time and leave her options open. If the economy turns around, if victory in Iraq returns Bush to 80 percent approval ratings, if North Korea suddenly decides to dump its nuclear arsenal into the sea, Mrs. Clinton can step back and remind everyone that she always said she wouldn't run in 2004. But if the victory in Iraq leads to months of troublesome occupation and the economy doesn't improve, Hillary will be ready.

A Cautionary Tale

Hillary's Scheme is a cautionary tale, written especially for those who insist the Clinton era is over. Political pros and pundits alike have eagerly accepted the White House's mantra that it's "time to move on" merely because George Bush was able to deny the Clintons the vindication of installing their own successor. But with November 2004 fast approaching, each passing week offers compelling new evidence to the contrary. In fact, Bill and Hillary have set up a White House in exile, a kind of "disloyal opposition" that includes everything from criticizing the president in wartime—sometimes from foreign soil in Mr. Clinton's case—to trying to blame his economic policy for September 11.

Hillary's Scheme is the first book to examine in any detail the Clintons' plan to return to power, offering an unprecedented look into the minds and hearts of America's number one power couple. Like no other Clinton book, *Hillary's Scheme* details the tactics employed by the most ruthless political team since John and Robert Kennedy, strategies that have kept the press at bay and the public in the dark about Bill and Hillary's sordid personal histories and rampant abuses of power.

But it also explores the failed political strategies of the Bush White House and the Republican Party—the withering timidity of Bush's "new tone" that all but guarantees the Clintons a serious shot at reclaiming the White House. Having failed to vanquish Bill and Hillary by January 20, 2001, the Bush Republicans bet the farm that the ex-president and his wife would disappear into the woodwork after a short period. They were wrong. Whether GOP strategists come to appreciate in time the significance of that critical miscalculation will determine whether Dick Morris was right when he predicted last year that Hillary Clinton will succeed George Bush as the next president of the United States of America.

CHAPTER ONE

The Clintons' Long Goodbye

"Whatever happens, I think I can speak for all of us. We are profoundly grateful. You've got a senator over here who will be a voice for you."

—Bill Clinton to supporters upon leaving the White House, January 20, 2001

"I left the White House, but I'm still here. We're not going anywhere."[1]

Those were the words of ex-president Bill Clinton on January 20, 2001, delivered even before newly elected president George W. Bush was finished with his inaugural address. For some, Clinton's remarks sounded less like a promise that he wasn't about to vanish from the scene altogether than like the ring of a pledge, the political equivalent of General Douglas MacArthur's famous vow after being vanquished in the Philippines—"I shall return."

The new president had arrived, but the old one was refusing to leave the stage. Traveling to Maryland's Andrews Air Force Base after handing the White House keys to the Bush family, the forty-second president and his freshly minted senator-wife had arranged to be greeted by 2,500 well-wishers who had ostensibly gathered to express their gratitude for eight years of peace, prosperity, and political success. For news viewers at home it was a bizarre scene. TV coverage of the Bush inauguration was not only interrupted by continuing reports on the Clintons' activities, but cable news stations also offered intermittent split-screen coverage of the ex-president's speech as he competed with his successor for the national spotlight. Though no longer entitled to the perks of office, the former first couple had managed to commandeer a military honor guard for the reception, which offered a twenty-one gun salute to "Citizen Clinton."

"I would like to thank the honor guard and the representatives of all the military services behind us for rendering honors to me this one last time on this important day in our country's life," the ex-president began. After noting that he had no intention of "going anywhere," Clinton consoled those in the Andrews hangar, some of whom were visibly upset at the prospect of his departure, with the thought that their work together would continue. "That's the only thing I ask of any of you. If you really believe in what we did these last eight years, you do not have to be in the position of power in government to advance those causes. And the celebration we mark today is ordained under a Constitution in which the people are supposed to be in the driver's seat."

Citizen Clinton took a final opportunity to remind the crowd of the successes of his administration, remarking somewhat wistfully, "I want all of you to know that I feel, as John Podesta did. We walked out of the Oval Office for the last time today about 10:30, and—no, no about 10:00—and he was tearing up a little bit. He just looked, he said, 'We did a lot of good. We did a lot of good. We did a lot of good.'" The assemblage erupted in cheers as the man who had planned for almost all of his adult life to take the White House drank in the acclaim for one last time. Clinton then directed the spotlight toward his wife and proclaimed, "Whatever happens, I think I can speak for all of us. We are profoundly grateful. You've got a senator over here who will be a voice for you."

For Republicans who heralded the election of George W. Bush as the ultimate deliverance from the Clinton co-presidency's eight years of wall-to-wall scandal, unbridled moral turpitude, and the dangerous erosion of America's national security, the scene was disconcerting, to say the least.

And it wasn't over. After the Andrews ceremony, the Clintons climbed aboard the jet that served as Air Force One while he was in office and flew to New York's John F. Kennedy International Airport. This time, in a scene that was not covered by the television networks, Hillary Clinton took the spotlight. With Mr. Clinton and their daughter Chelsea at her side, Senator Clinton told the smaller airport gathering, "We are so glad to see all of you and happy to be here. For eight years this president and administration put people first." That same phrase, "Putting People First," also adorned the seal on the lectern from which she spoke.[2] In the twilight of that cold January afternoon, few people remembered those words as the unofficial slogan of her husband's presidential primary campaign. In the intervening eight years, the former first couple had been, at times, far less cryptic about their intentions, at least according to those who claim familiarity with private comments.

When, Not If

"Former President Clinton speaks about his wife's run for the presidency as a matter of 'when,' not 'if,' say people who have discussed it with him," reported the Associated Press in 2002, adding, "Several of her associates said she is eyeing 2008 as the year to run."[3] But rumors swirled that Mrs. Clinton had no intention of waiting that long. Chicago gossip columnist Michael Sneed noted in December 2001 that "Former first lady Hillary Clinton is warming up to the idea of a presidential race in 2004. Stay tuned."[4]

Was she really? Senator Clinton has protested repeatedly that nothing could be further from the truth. "I have no intention of running for president," she insisted to *Meet the Press* host Tim Russert a few days after the Sneed report. "I do not intend to do that. But what I do intend to do is, you know, to be the best senator I can be, which is what I'm trying to do to the best of my ability every single day."[5] Still, while Democratic party insiders say that 2008 makes the most sense for Hillary's White House run, even Democratic National Committee Chairman Terry McAuliffe, who served as chief fund-raiser for the William Jefferson Clinton Presidential Library Foundation and who also floated a multimillion-dollar loan to help the Clintons buy their Chappaqua, New York, mansion, was unwilling to bet against a 2004 Clinton candidacy.

"I feel pretty safe saying—making a Shermanesque statement here—that Hillary Rodham Clinton will not run for president in 2004," he said initially during an interview on the same show seven months before Mrs. Clinton's appearance. In fact it was "guaranteed," said McAuliffe, that she wouldn't make a White House run so soon.

But when host Tim Russert asked, "If she does, will you contribute a million dollars to the Boys & Girls Club of America?" McAuliffe was unwilling to put his money where his mouth was.

"Wow," McAuliffe sighed as he pondered his "guarantee." "Tim, in fairness, I would like to check with my lovely wife, Dorothy, before I make such a statement," he finally answered.[6]

Hillary in 2004?

Republicans could indeed face their political bête noir—another Clinton bid for the White House—a lot sooner than most now think. While Beltway pundits have long predicted that Mrs. Clinton's best chance to recapture the presidency won't come until 2008, when neither party will have the advantage of incumbency, the man who tried to halt her political rise with his own campaign for Senate isn't sure she'll be that patient. "If the economy falters and President Bush's approval numbers soften during the course of the next six or nine months, I would not be shocked if she pivoted on that and became a candidate," said former Long Island congressman Rick Lazio.[7] As the only person to face the former first lady in a race for elective office, the up-and-coming conservative has particularly good credentials on the issue of Mrs. Clinton's formidability as a candidate.

> "If the economy falters and President Bush's approval numbers soften during the course of the next six or nine months, I would not be shocked if she pivoted on that and became a candidate."
>
> —*Clinton Senate opponent Rick Lazio*

While almost all polls had New York's 2000 Senate race too close to call right down to the wire, Lazio and the rest of his state awoke that November 8 morning to the news that a political star had been born, delivered via a 12-point landslide that no one had predicted. Victory for Hillary was not only historic, making her the first presidential spouse ever to win elective office in her own right, but it also gave the Clintons a new lease on their political lives. It kept alive the prospect that one day, like General MacArthur, they would return to reclaim what was, they believed, rightfully theirs—wrested from them by that bit of constitutional quirkiness, the Twenty-Second Amendment.

Hillary's win instantly created worldwide speculation about another Clinton presidential campaign. "Defeat would have meant early retirement," reported Britain's *Economist* three days after the vote. "Now Mrs. Clinton can plausibly dream that she will one day return to the White House as more than a guest."[8] The London *Telegraph* echoed similar sentiments. Stateside, members of something called "The Hillary Clinton Fan Club" abandoned plans to disband, vowing instead to remain intact lest the first lady–senator decided to make her move.

Hillary's Senate Opponent Predicts Her Future

Would Hillary really consider making her move as early as 2004? "I would imagine that she will look at the opportunities," former congressman Lazio predicts. "Then she [will be able to] see how things unfold and what the economy looks like over the course of the year and whether anybody emerges as a clear front-runner." While the Long Island Republican believes that Hillary's master plan is to serve out her full Senate term before running for the White House in 2008, a continuing Democratic Party leadership vacuum may force her hand.

"I think in all likelihood nobody is going to emerge as a clear front-runner during the course of the next year. It will be a process that behooves candidates who have name recognition, the ability to raise a lot of money and organizational strength [to run]. And if you look at who fits that bill, she's got to be one of maybe two or three people that can mount a challenge in a relatively quick time. And having Terry McAuliffe as chairman of the party is helpful to her as well."

Whether she runs in 2004 or 2008, Lazio has no doubt about Senator Clinton's ultimate goal. "I think she has the ambition to run for president. I think that she is a person who plans into the future with respect to her own career. For example, they were polling five years before she ran [for Senate] as to which state she would run in. So this is somebody who sets a personal objective. And I think her long-term personal objective is to run for the presidency and be back in the White House."

But can she win?

Allies Warned of Scandal Trouble

Consider what even some of her fans first said when the prospect of her running for Senate first cropped up in late 1998.

"For your sake, I hope you don't run," one-time Clinton presidential aide George Stephanopoulos advised from the pages of *Newsweek*. "You'd be a terrific senator, but the campaign wouldn't be a walkover, and being in the Senate may not be the worthiest use of your talents. . . . You have to prepare for the worst. Whitewater billing records, cattle futures, the travel office and Castle Grande will all be back. Sure, you've answered all the allegations. But that's not going to stop the Republicans—and the *New York Post*—from weighing in again."[9]

James Carville, Stephanopoulos's war-room partner from the Clinton 1992 campaign, was reportedly not too keen on the idea of the first lady seeking New York's Senate seat either, at least not at first. "If you're determined to run for the Senate, wait at least until 2002, in some other state," he reportedly advised.[10] Big-time media fan, CBS anchorman Dan Rather also suggested she sit the race out. "Is Hillary Rodham Clinton really going to run for the Senate? Anybody who says it's a cinch doesn't know Hillary Clinton. She is many things, but a fool is not one of them," he cautioned.[11]

Clinton defenders had much to be concerned about. Despite Republican losses in that year's midterm elections, the House of Representatives had just voted by an overwhelming margin to hold full-scale impeachment hearings into her husband's attempted cover-up of his affair with Monica Lewinsky.

And while the aura of victimhood had begun to settle over Hillary Clinton's image as a political wife done wrong by her wayward husband, it was by no means clear in late fall 1998 that the impeachment probe would stop with Monicagate. House investigators were still actively probing allegations that the Clinton political attack machine, with Hillary at the helm, had hired private detectives to intimidate women who claimed to have experienced not just consensual affairs with Bill but, instead, actual sexual assaults and, in one case, a brutal rape. If a full investigation revealed that Hillary had been even an unwitting accomplice to covering up credible charges of sexual brutality, her political future would be toast.

"Is Hillary Rodham Clinton really going to run for the Senate? . . . She is many things, but a fool is not one of them."
—*CBS News anchorman Dan Rather*

Conservatives had expected all the Clinton scandals to be laid bare. Some argued that Bill Clinton should get the same rough treatment Richard Nixon got when impeachment probers came after him for Watergate. As a twenty-six-year-old staffer on the House Watergate committee, Hillary Diane Rodham had argued that the thirty-seventh president shouldn't be allowed to have a lawyer and that any review of his "crimes" not be limited to mere violations of the law but instead get to the heart of his fitness for office. Associates remembered her attitude toward Nixon as something of a jihad. One who worked with Clinton researching Nixon's misdeeds said she regarded him as "evil."

"Her opinion of him was more a result of the McGovern campaign and those kinds of issues," Watergate prober Tom Bell told Clinton biographer David Maraniss. "I saw him as evil because he was screwing with the Constitution. She came at it with more preconceived ideas than I did. She saw the work as absolutely the most important thing in the world. I saw it as important but also a job. To her it may have been more of a mission."[12]

Luckily for Mrs. Clinton, when it came to her husband's misdeeds, GOP congressional leaders had little tolerance for such prosecutorial zeal, and so the allegations involved in Travelgate, Filegate, Chinagate, the raft of IRS audits launched against political opponents, and the Whitewater land-deal cover-up were shunted aside. Her husband's impeachment probers would end up focusing on the one scandal that Hillary could have had no role in, the act of having sex with Monica Lewinsky. The GOP's timidity worked strongly to Mrs. Clinton's advantage. Though lead House impeachment counsel David Schippers gathered reams of testimony from Kathleen Willey and Juanita Broaddrick, who both accused Clinton of sexual assault, Republican House and Senate leaders, mindful of mainstream media polls showing President Clinton's job approval well above 60 percent, were anxious to get the entire Sexgate imbroglio behind them.

In the midst of these turgid political crosscurrents, Harlem congressman Charles Rangel floated the idea of Hillary replacing retiring New York Senator Daniel Patrick Moynihan. The flamboyant Democrat described how he broached the idea of "Senator Hillary" for Long Island's *Newsday* in January 1999, saying he had "made pitches" to the first lady about her making a bid to run for Moynihan's seat. "She says 'Tell me more.' . . . She smiles. She does very little talking, but she listens." He says he told both Bill and Hillary there is plenty of support, money, and "an easy glide path in the primary." While others react negatively to the idea, Rangel proclaimed, "She would be a winning candidate."[13]

Three days before Rangel's revelation, *Meet the Press* host Tim Russert revealed what then Senator Robert Torricelli had told him off the air before his appearance on the show. "Here's a little mini-bombshell," Russert announced. "Senator Robert Torricelli of New Jersey, who heads the Senate Campaign Committee, told me before the program that if he had to guess, he believes that Hillary Rodham Clinton will run for the United States Senate seat from New York being opened by the retirement of Daniel Patrick Moynihan, which means Mrs. Clinton would have to establish residency in New York before the end of the president's term."[14]

Twenty-three months later, it was still far from certain that Hillary's gamble would pay off. On election eve, pollster John Zogby, one of the few to correctly call the popular vote trend for Gore, told Fox News Channel's Bill O'Reilly, "Lazio has been closing the gap since last Thursday." Monday's tracking poll showed Mrs. Clinton with a 2-point lead, he explained. But she was losing ground steadily in the final hours before the voting began Tuesday morning.

New Yorkers made Hillary Clinton the first presidential spouse elected senator in U.S. history—and they did it by giving her a 12-point landslide.

Former White House insider Dick Morris concurred, telling O'Reilly that unless the first lady reached 51 percent support—which hadn't happened—Rick Lazio would win the race. "Hillary is basically running against herself," Morris said. "And whenever you run against yourself you're going to lose. . . . It's incredibly close," the former Clinton adviser added. "But I still think Lazio will pull it out."[15]

The next day New Yorkers made Hillary Clinton the first presidential spouse elected senator in U.S. history—and they did it by giving her a 12-point landslide.

CHAPTER TWO

Decoding Hillary's Denials

"I am very intent on doing everything I can as a senator for New York and I'm going to support whoever our nominee is because I think we need a good debate."

— Hillary Clinton to NewsMax, January 24, 2003.[1]

Senator Clinton has insisted repeatedly that she'll serve out her six-year term as New York's junior senator, which would seem to rule out a White House bid in 2004. But she's usually careful to leave herself plenty of wiggle room for 2008. And political wags have factored her denials into their own predictions that another Clinton presidential campaign is at least five years away.

But Clinton herself has, at different times, removed herself from presidential consideration at any point in the future and—during her pre-Senate days—once told a roomful of reporters that she wouldn't seek elective office of any kind—ever.

In April 2002, for instance, the *New York Post* asked Mrs. Clinton point-blank, "So, Senator Clinton, are you ruling out a run for president not just in 2004, but in 2008 and beyond?"

"Yes," Hillary replied, without equivocation.[2]

And just five years before Clinton launched the famous listening tour that laid the groundwork for her victorious Senate campaign, she went even further with gossip columnists Liz Smith, Cindy Adams, Jeannie Williams, and Linda Stasi. Smith recounted the episode for a column *Newsday* headlined the next day, "Hillary Says: No! I'll Never Run!"

"She had joined the kaffeeklatsch (sans coffee) without any ceremony—just as if she were 'one of the girls,'" Smith said, describing the somewhat improbable scene. After making small talk about everything from AIDS to Elvis, the discussion turned to politics.

"When asked about the Whitewater problem, Mrs. Clinton seemed to dismiss it with a wave of her hand. She said. 'It's now in someone else's ballpark. It will be taken care of.' Would she campaign for her brother, Hugh Rodham, who is about to run for office in Florida?

"She hesitated and said, 'I am not sure he has decided yet to do it, but if he does, I'll help him any way I can.'

"Would she ever run for office herself? She gave a very definite 'NO!'" Smith revealed.[3]

Following Bill's Lead

The first lady turned senator wouldn't be the first Clinton to profess allegiance to the state she was elected to serve—and then jump ship when the time looked right. Here's how the late John Robert Starr, managing editor of the *Arkansas Democrat-Gazette* in 1990, recalled Bill Clinton's pledge to serve out his full four-year term on the eve of his reelection to a fifth term as governor.

"I didn't want to support Clinton in 1990, and I told him so," Starr explained in a column he wrote for his own paper in

1998. "Clinton's absences from the statehouse were such a problem that, when he begged for my support in his sixth race for governor on the grounds that his education program would die if he were not in office to protect it, I made him promise not only that he'd not run for president, but that he'd stay in Little Rock and do the work of the governor."[4]

Clinton's desperate plea for the *Democrat-Gazette*'s endorsement came two days before the election, when the polls were turning against him. "You need to endorse me. I'm at 50 percent and dropping like a rock," complained the candidate, in a tone of voice that Starr recalled as "panicky." Reluctantly, the editor rewrote the paper's election-eve editorial and endorsed Clinton.

Starr wasn't the only Arkansan to be duped by Clinton's "serve out my full term" promise. During one 1990 campaign debate against challenger Sheffield Nelson, Clinton was asked if he would take the pledge not to run for the White House in 1992. "You bet!" the soon-to-be presidential candidate shot back.

The very public denial deeply worried top Clinton aides at the time.

"You're not going to like this," campaign staffer Gloria Cabe warned Frank Greer, the Washington media consultant who had been recruited by Clinton in preparation for his national run. "Clinton just took himself out of the '92 race," she told him.[5]

Greer later told Clinton biographer David Maraniss that he was devastated at the news. "I died a thousand deaths. I thought perhaps [the White House run] wasn't going to happen."

But on May 6, 1991, just six months after he took the pledge, the noncandidate showed up at the Democratic Leadership Council convention in Cleveland. He delivered a stirring address on national themes that left no doubt about his intentions.

"The buzz in Washington . . . was that the Cleveland speech had established Clinton as a serious national figure who seemed to have a clear idea of what he wanted to do as president," Maraniss observed.

John Starr finally realized he'd been completely duped. He later complained, "I kept my part of the bargain. It should be understandable that I got upset when he didn't keep his."

Ironically, a mere two days after the Cleveland DLC speech, Clinton revealed what he really wanted to do once he got to the White House. Just before he gave a speech to the Governor's Quality Conference at Little Rock's Excelsior Hotel, he had his bodyguard summon to his hotel room a dark-haired young woman from the reception desk. Her name was Paula Corbin Jones.

In September 1991, less than ten months after he gave his word both publicly and privately that he wasn't running, Bill Clinton officially announced his presidential bid. If she follows her husband's example, Mrs. Clinton can keep issuing denials throughout most of 2003 before bowing to "unforeseen circumstances."

Indeed, Mrs. Clinton's presidential ambitions are so widely acknowledged that her denials not only ring hollow, but also sometimes seem downright laughable. One such episode came in July 2001, during an address before Washington, D.C.'s National Press Club, where Mrs. Clinton slipped and began to refer to herself as president of the United States.

"I have said that I'm not running and I'm having a great time being pres—being a first-term senator."

—*Hillary Clinton*

Responding to the requisite questions about her White House plans, Hillary told the gathering, "I have said that I'm not running and I'm having a great time being pres—being a first-term senator." As the crowd chortled at the gaffe, Clinton warned, "You guys are going to get me into a lot of trouble."[6]

What won't give Senator Clinton trouble is obtaining the Democratic nomination, with poll after poll going back to the 2000 presidential race indicating that the only Democrat more popular among party faithful would have been former vice president Al Gore, had he stayed in the race.

Hillary as Democratic Front-Runner

Even before Al Gore dropped out of the race in mid-December 2002, Clinton was running a strong second in her party's presidential sweepstakes. Gallup/CNN/*USA Today* conducted one typical survey in August 2001. It showed 34 percent of Democrats backing Gore, with Hillary drawing 21 percent support. Gore's ex–running mate, Senator Joe Lieberman, usually placed third in the late 2002 surveys. The rest of the Democrat pack—Senator John Kerry, Senator John Edwards, Senator Tom Daschle, and Representative Dick Gephardt—seldom managed to garner more than single-digit support. A September 2002 Zogby poll showed that left-wing long shot Reverend Al Sharpton had as much support as almost any of the second-tier Democrats.

Al Gore's mid-December withdrawal from the race hit the Democratic Party like a political earthquake, catapulting Hillary Clinton to the front of the pack despite nearly two years' worth of her assertions that a 2004 White House run was absolutely out of the question.

A Gallup survey taken a week after Gore withdrew found that a full 40 percent of Democrats named Senator Clinton as their number one choice to challenge President Bush next year. Clinton's nearest contenders—Lieberman and Kerry—tied at a mere 13 percent each. Days later, a *Time*/CNN poll found that 30 percent of Democrats wanted Clinton to run for president in 2004—she again outpaced all others in the race. In late December a Fox News Dynamics survey gave Clinton her lowest rating yet, showing just 21 percent of Democrats behind a 2004 run. Still, that support was more than any other Democrat could garner in the Fox poll.

In late January 2003, an NBC News/*Wall Street Journal* survey found that 39 percent of Democrats backed Hillary for a

White House run, more than the number who supported her three nearest competitors combined. In February a Quinnipiac University poll found Clinton's Democratic Party support had risen nationwide to 42 percent, its highest number yet. Interestingly, Quinnipiac also found that for the first time, support for a "Hillary for President" campaign in 2004 had topped 50 percent among Democrats in her home state of New York. The same poll found that a majority of New Yorkers of both parties—54 percent—now intended to back the Democratic presidential candidate, whoever it was. Only 36 percent planned to back President Bush. In the months after September 11, Bush's approval rating topped 80 percent even in Clinton's home state.

Hillary's Ultimate Presidential Denial

I caught up to Senator Clinton one Friday afternoon in January 2003, the same day results from the NBC News/*Wall Street Journal* presidential survey were released. The exchange, which took place during an interview she granted to WLIE-NY radio host Mike Siegel, went like this:

NEWSMAX: Senator Clinton, you are once again tops in a presidential poll. The NBC/*Wall Street Journal* poll has you at 39 percent among Democrats, dwarfing every other Democratic candidate in the race. You've said you won't run in 2004. You say you have no plans for 2008. Would you accept a draft in 2004?

CLINTON: No. You know, I am very intent on doing everything I can as a senator for New York, and I'm going to support whoever our nominee is because I think we need a good debate.[7]

As Clinton topped one poll after another among Democrats, she continued to trail Bush whenever the two were paired in national surveys. But an October 2002 *Newsweek* survey actually gave her a better chance of winning the White House back for her party than Mr. Gore, who was still in the race at the time. While Democrats and Democratic-leaning voters still preferred Gore to Hillary by a slim margin of 25 to 23 percent, voters of both parties told *Newsweek* that they'd reelect Bush over Gore by a margin of 58 to 36 percent. Hillary would also lose by a landslide—56 to 36 percent—but Bush's margin of victory would diminish by two points.

Clearly, with Gore out of the race, the Democratic Party's presidential nomination is Hillary Clinton's for the asking. But whether she'll accept even a draft—and in January she told me she would not—will depend not on her previous pledges not to run, but on whether it appears that President Bush can be beaten.

Eight Years for Bill, Eight for Hill

"There is not a doubt in my mind that she will run for president: in 2004 if she sees a chance, certainly in 2008," said pollster John Zogby in December 2002. "What she has done in New York, where a majority is now on her side, she could do in any state. Don't underestimate her."[8]

By late 2002 it had become a foregone conclusion that Hillary Clinton would seek the White House before the decade was out. "The order of succession in this poor benighted country may well be Bush-Clinton-Bush-Clinton,"[9] the Clintons' ace political guru Dick Morris predicted to NewsMax, describing the goal that Clinton insiders have mostly kept to themselves. The ex-president's comment earlier in the year that yet another Clinton presidential campaign was a matter of "when, not if" only underscored what most Clinton watchers had long regarded as an inevitability. Insiders, however, knew that the idea of installing Hillary in the Oval Office didn't just materialize after she won her Senate race. In fact, among those who know the Clintons best, Hillary's ambition to become the first American to hold the title "Madam President" has long been an open secret.

"Eight years of Bill, eight years of Hill, that was the dream," Hillary privately confided to Linda Bloodworth-Thomason way back in 1992. Thomason said she regarded Mrs. Clinton's presidential prediction as her "private slogan."[10] There were other manifestations early on that Mrs. Clinton intended to pick up where her husband left off.

"As far back as 1993, there were printed signs all over her office, proclaiming 'In The White House, Hillary 1996,' according to Judicial Watch President Tom Fitton, who says he garnered the info from White House whistleblower Sheryl Hall.[11]

> "Eight years of Bill, eight years of Hill, that was the dream."
> — *Linda Bloodworth-Thomason*

As they were working to make the first part of Mrs. Clinton's private slogan come true, Mr. Clinton confided to *Vanity Fair* writer Gail Sheehy, "It doesn't bother me that people see her and get excited and say she could be president, too."

"So after eight years of Bill Clinton?" Sheehy inquired.

"Eight years of Hillary Clinton. Why not?" the then candidate offered.[12]

Still, most political experts agree with Morris, who said Hillary could win the White House only if she waits till 2008, when she won't have to face George Bush.

"I think that 2004 is too soon for her," he observed in May 2002. "She knows Bush is likely to be re-elected, and I think she needs to run against someone who isn't an incumbent."[13] Putting himself in the role of advising Hillary's campaign instead of Bill's, Morris said the key for turning the senator into a president is timing.

"She needs to run after a period where the nation is bored with Republican leadership," he recommended. "We're now in a period of great energy with the war on terror. But I think that's going to last only through 2004 and 2005. Then the next three years you're going to see not much happening at the federal level."

Mrs. Clinton will be able to capitalize on the political lethargy, the top political consultant said. "One of the problems Republicans always have is that they don't really believe in government doing a whole lot. They don't want to make a lot of new proposals because they don't believe in them." According to Morris, "people may well welcome her sense of activism and her energy" after two or three years of Republican inactivity.

Meanwhile, he predicted, the Clintons will use the 2004 race to clear out the backlog of presidential hopefuls, such as John Kerry, Joe Lieberman, John Edwards, and especially Al Gore. "They'll run, and they'll lose," he said. "And it's very hard once you lose a presidential race to run again and be successful."

At that point Senator Clinton will be able to step over the political corpses and grab the nomination, said the former White House insider. "Hillary will clearly be the Democratic Party front-runner when she runs in 2008." But that was before Gore rocked the political world in December 2002 by announcing that he wouldn't seek the White House in 2004. The move turned Mrs. Clinton into her party's front-runner four years ahead of schedule.

The numbers were impressive. By late winter 2003, no fewer than five nationally recognized surveys showed Senator Clinton with more support than any announced 2004 candidate. In surveys including her name, no Democratic Party rival has yet to garner even 20 percent support.

But the chief obstacle to the Clintons' deciding whether to try to fulfill their eight-plus-eight dream now or wait until

2008 continued to be the perception that Bush, buoyed by September 11 and the war in Iraq, will be impossible to defeat.

But how accurate is that perception? Will the war on terrorism continue to inoculate Bush against the kind of political attacks that sank his father's reelection bid? Or will memories of September 11 begin to fade and complications from a long-term boots-on-the-ground commitment in the Middle East begin to cloud Bush's political horizons?

Hillary as Underdog

Even before Mrs. Clinton made her intentions to run for Senate clear in early 1999, polls forecast an uphill battle against the presumed Republican nominee, Rudolph Giuliani, then New York City mayor. In December 1998, for instance, as her husband's impeachment battle generated a spike of sympathy for Hillary as the aggrieved party in the Monica Lewinsky scandal, a Zogby International poll gave Giuliani a 46 to 41 point edge. Seven months later, Giuliani had widened his lead over the then first lady to 10 points in the same survey.

But as Mrs. Clinton kept pounding away at the mayor's autocratic style, Giuliani's numbers began to dip, while, predictably, the press ignored her own record of abuse of power. Clinton was particularly adept at playing the race card after two controversial city police shootings of unarmed African Americans, one of which she publicly referred to as a "murder."

"At just the moment when a real leader would have reached out and tried to heal the wounds, [Giuliani] has chosen divisiveness," Hillary told a Harlem audience after the second shooting. "I want to engage in the politics of reconciliation, not revenge and retribution. I want to be known by who I lift up, not who I push down."[14] Though New York City police shootings had actually declined under Giuliani, along with the city's murder rate, which had plummeted from 2,100 annually to less than 700, Mrs. Clinton was able to turn the mayor's crime-fighting record into a political liability.

The press, which had remained deferential about the Clintons' private life throughout the campaign, suddenly pounced on Giuliani over rumors that he was seeing another woman as his long-troubled marriage to journalist Donna Hanover deteriorated further. It made no difference to reporters covering the race that Rudy and Hanover had been separated for months. Or that there was no court record—as with Clinton and the Paula Jones case—forcing Giuliani's private life into the public arena. Even the staid *New York Times* covered the story of the mayor's dalliance with relish, although neither of the principal parties involved had admitted to anything beyond friendship. Columnist Gail Collins kicked off the *Times'* sleaze-fest under the headline, "The Rudy Chronicles":

"In the most discussed political development of the week, we learned that the mayor's new very good friend is a Manhattan resident who met him at a parent-teacher gathering," wrote the *Times'* scribe. "She has been seen in his company at events ranging from New Year's Eve at Times Square to town hall meetings in the outer boroughs. The voters may be willing to leave Mr. Giuliani alone on this one, but if his companion is willing to sit through town halls, it sounds pretty serious."[15]

> "If Hillary and her hitmen were not investigating Giuliani's private life, it would be the first time that the Clintons did not try to collect dirt to smear their political opponents."
>
> *—Dick Morris*

Dick Morris suspected that Hillary's campaign had set Giuliani up, reminding readers of his *New York Post* column that the Clintons were experts in leaking secrets to the press to dirty up political opponents. "If Hillary and her hitmen were not investigating Giuliani's private life, it would be the first time that the Clintons did not try to collect dirt to smear their political opponents," the one-time top White House aide argued. "In almost all their campaigns and scandals, the Clintons hire investigators (in 1992, they even paid for them with federal campaign funds) to find ammunition to use their adversaries' private lives against them. Woman after woman has been demonized by their secret police—usually on orders from Hillary—and [these women] have had their past dragged through the mud and leaked to the press to discredit their accounts of the president's sexually predatory practices."[16]

The attacks on Giuliani began to take their toll. By mid-May, Mrs. Clinton had finally edged into the lead by just under three points, 42.3 percent to 39.6 percent. Statistically the race was still a dead heat. But gone were any concerns that Hillary Clinton's own personal baggage would prevent her from becoming the first of the first ladies to win elective office in her own right. Four days after the May 15 poll, the New York City mayor announced that a recently diagnosed case of prostate cancer was forcing him to withdraw from the race.

When Rick Lazio stepped into the race, the early polls showed him maintaining Giuliani's levels of support. But he remained behind for almost the rest of the race. And even those surveys ultimately underestimated the Clinton campaign juggernaut, which roared across the finish line on Election Day with 12-point blowout.

Before Giuliani-Lazio, Bush Sr.

Could Hillary Clinton repeat her come-from-behind win against the Giuliani-Lazio tag team with an upset against President Bush in 2004? Conventional wisdom says no. But the numbers suggest otherwise. Bush's approval rating, which skyrocketed into the 90 percent range nationally in the aftermath of September 11, 2001, had settled into the 60s a little more than a year later. And it's not clear that victory over Iraq would give him the kind of bounce that would last until he faced the voters again. The Gulf War victory in March 1991 netted Bush Sr. 90 percent job approval ratings, which had all but evaporated just a year later.

By November 1991, just eight months after Bush Sr.'s positive approval ratings had broken all previous records, the bottom had dropped out, with a poll by the Times Mirror Center for the People & the Press giving the president a 55 percent positive job approval rating. Two months later, the same survey showed the slide continuing, with only 46 percent of those responding giving Bush a thumbs-up. A Gallup survey a month later had even worse news for the White House, with just 39 percent of respondents giving the president who had led America to its first decisive wartime win since 1945 a positive job approval rating.

Another number that sent shock waves through the White House at the time was the dwindling percentage of people who wanted to see Bush Sr. reelected. A comparable poll taken the previous June, when Bush Sr.'s post–Gulf War approval rating was still soaring, showed that 52 percent wanted him reelected no matter which candidate the Democrats nominated. By December 1991, Bush's reelect number had plummeted to just 35 percent, with 46 percent saying they wanted someone else.

Bush Trending Down, Clinton Up

The current President Bush may have some cause for concern in that department, with two late 2002 polls showing surprisingly poor reelect numbers despite approval ratings that were hovering, at the time, in the 60–65 percent range. A November 2002 *New York Times* poll had President Bush's reelect number down to just 32 percent. And while most independent observers consider the *Times* number too low to be accurate, a Fox News Dynamics poll taken the same month found that just 44 percent wanted the current president reelected.

"It is interesting that despite these high approval ratings, only 44 percent of the public say that they will vote to re-elect Bush," said Opinion Dynamics President John Gorman. "Of course, whatever reservations people may have about re-electing him, the other questions indicate that the Democrats don't currently have a candidate capable of making the race competitive."[17]

Maybe not. Then again, Mrs. Clinton's own job approval numbers in New York have been trending up fairly consistently. After just a month in office in February 2001, with the Pardongate scandal heating up and stories about the Clintons trashing the White House on their way out spicing up the news, Mrs. Clinton's positive job approval numbers bottomed out to a low of 38 percent of New Yorkers surveyed by Quinnipiac University. By the end of her second year in office, after she had donned the mantle to become her party's chief critic of a popular president, 57 percent of her constituents said they thought she was doing a good job.

In the same December 2002 poll, 51 percent of New Yorkers gave Bush a positive rating, about 10 percent less than the nation as a whole and down from 85 percent a month after the September 11 attacks. But in a Marist College survey the same week, Bush's job approval rating among New Yorkers was tied with Clinton's 57 percent positive rating in the Quinnipiac poll. A January 2003 Siena College survey found that 52 percent of New Yorkers gave Bush a thumbs-up, reflecting a steady decline since September 11. In a theoretical matchup between Clinton and Bush, the Texas Republican managed to edge out the former first lady among New Yorkers 48 to 45 percent, according to the December 2002 Quinnipiac poll—this, despite a Marist survey the same week where 59 percent of New York Democrats said they didn't want Hillary to seek the White House.

But how would Hillary fare in a national face-off with Bush, especially in some of those "red states" where the president won walking away? An October 2002 Gallup survey found that Clinton would do at least as well as Gore would have, had he stayed in the race and captured his party's nomination. She would still get trounced, 55 to 40 percent. But in the same survey Gore lost to Bush, 54 to 39 percent.

Media Testimonials

Plainly, the press will play the key role in determining whether a 2004 Hillary for President campaign is viable, just as they did for Mrs. Clinton's Senate campaign. And that's likely good news for those who would like to return to the Clinton era sooner rather than later. *CBS Evening News* anchorman Dan Rather, for instance, is an unabashed admirer of Mrs. Clinton, who changed his mind on Hillary's election prospects after her 2000 Senate win and has more recently advised her to seek the White House in 2004. Recall Rather's obsequious comments about Hillary to Bill Clinton, when he and his then TV partner Connie Chung interviewed the new president in 1993.

"If we could be one one-hundredth as great as you and Hillary Rodham Clinton have been together in the White House, we'd take it right now and walk away winners."

—CBS News anchorman Dan Rather

"I think you two will be great together," President Clinton told the news team. While Chung stayed mercifully silent, a fawning Rather blurted out:

"If we could be one one-hundredth as great as you and Hillary Rodham Clinton have been together in the White House, we'd take it right now and walk away winners." Rather ended the interview by telling Mr. Clinton, "God bless you. Thank you very much. And tell Mrs. Clinton we respect her and we're pulling for her."[18]

The CBS newsman began pulling for Hillary to become president as early as February 2002, when, in a bit of prescient speculation, Rather predicted that Democrats would turn to the former first lady if Gore dropped out.

"If not Gore, then who else for the Democrats?" Rather told talk radio host Don Imus. "Who could develop a national name, a core of people who are willing to work for you and people who are willing to give money for you? If Hillary Clinton were prepared to run this next time around, she might be such a person."[19]

And Rather is far from alone. Beth Harpaz, who covered Clinton's Senate campaign for the Associated Press, saw fit to include this tidbit in her own campaign memoir, *The Girls in the Van*. Attending the White House Christmas party with her husband after Hillary was elected, Harpaz recalled introducing him to the soon-to-be senator. After she offered her own perfunctory congratulations, the reporter's spouse told Clinton, "Beth would never say this but we're thrilled that you won."[20]

Whenever she chooses to seek the White House, whether it be in 2004 or later, Hillary Clinton will undoubtedly have the Rathers and the Harpazes and most of the rest of the press in her corner. And President Bush, in the same dynamic that ended his father's presidency, will not.

CHAPTER THREE

Old Friends: Hillary Is Running

"She's waiting, biding her time, and then she's going to be drafted into the race."
—Former Clinton appointee Larry Nichols

While Washington's pundit class continues to insist that Hillary Clinton won't make her run for the White House until 2008, it's worth noting that some of the people who know her best think otherwise. After Al Gore's withdrawal from the race in December 2002, when Senator Clinton shot to the top of one Democratic Party presidential preference poll after another, I caught up to a few of them and asked whether they believed Hillary Clinton would keep her word and serve out her six-year term as New York's senator.

"We've been through this before, haven't we with Bush/Clinton?" said Meredith Oakley, longtime columnist for the *Arkansas Democrat-Gazette* and author of her own Clinton biography, *On the Make*. "Anything could happen; you know

93 percent today. Dead last tomorrow, but yes I think she could be nominated. And yes I think it's a somewhat long shot and yes I think she could be elected with the right things coming together because the Clintons have built a very good, eager, and solid and dedicated machine over the years."[1]

But did Oakley agree with most of her fellow pundits that Hillary Clinton couldn't get elected till at least 2008? "Not necessarily, but it depends; there's so much time there for things to go wrong. She is not her husband, who is . . . very good at what he does. But she is finally learning now that she is out from under, under his shadow. Now that she's not having to help carry him, she's finally learning."

Oakley noted that for much of their public life together, Mrs. Clinton was "abysmal" at politics. "She didn't understand them, didn't know how to play the game, and was too arrogant to learn." But now, said the newspaper scribe, Hillary doesn't have to worry about Bill anymore. "She's out there actually involved in the governmental and political process and she's learning fast because she's very smart, very smart."

One big obstacle Oakley sees is Senator Clinton's personal aloofness, an innate inability to communicate warmth. "Hillary is by and large not as well liked as Bill. And he has always had a built-in negative of 42–43 percent." Clinton's lack of likability is so pronounced among those over whom she reigned as Arkansas' first lady for twelve years that she wouldn't be able to carry the state, Oakley predicts. "But then Bill barely carried Arkansas in both his presidential elections," she noted.

Intriguingly, Senator Clinton has built a political operation separate and apart from that of her husband, whose home-state supporters she kept at arm's length during her run for the Senate in 2000. "The old Arkansas travelers, the friends of Bill's," recalled Oakley, "they wanted to go and campaign for her and she did not invite them. She did not make them welcome. And in the process she offended some of those people who were still high on Clintonmania, who had gone all over the country for Bill in two elections. . . . She didn't want Arkansans up there campaigning for her."

But Hillary may not be averse to mimicking her husband in extricating herself from her promise to New Yorkers that she won't run for president in 2004. Oakley recalled how Mr. Clinton did it.

"He came back to Arkansas from a meeting in Seattle and made a big production of going around the state to ask the people of Arkansas if it was OK if he broke his promise not to run for another office," the top columnist recalled. "Well, what he did was he made three or four stops in Arkansas to handpicked groups of his people. Most of the events were closed to the press, but press got into a few of them. And what they found out was that there was no such thing as him asking the people to release him from his promise; it didn't happen. He lied. He broke his promise."

"But," added a jaded Oakley, "So what else is new; he always does it."

Whistleblower Predicts: She's Running

Pioneer Clinton whistleblower Larry Nichols was even more blunt about Hillary's promise not to run in 2004. Don't believe it for a minute, the old Arkansas hand told NewsMax, just days after Mrs. Clinton topped her fourth presidential survey of Democrats. Nichols has a fair amount of experience on the inside of the Clinton political operation, having helped Bill get elected and reelected to five terms as governor. He was later rewarded with a high-level appointment to the Arkansas Development and Finance Authority.

"She's waiting, biding her time, and then she's going to be drafted into the race," said the man whose 1990 lawsuit introduced the name Gennifer Flowers to Arkansans as one member of a veritable harem of women he claimed Clinton was using state funds to maintain.[2]

As to Hillary, said Nichols, "She's using a trick we used with Bill a million times. We always had him 'drafted.'" Nichols said Clinton operatives in Arkansas would use rigged polls to make it seem as if Bill had grassroots support behind whatever he wanted to do as governor, up to and including running for president. Nichols recalled how, nine years before Hillary promised New Yorkers she would serve out her term as Senator, Bill managed to extract himself from the same promise made to Arkansans, a pledge that would have kept him in the Arkansas governor's mansion two years past the 1992 presidential election.

> "She's waiting, biding her time, and then she's going to be drafted into the race."
>
> —*Clinton critic Larry Nichols*

"In the 1990 campaign, I asked the moderator of a debate in Fayetteville to ask Bill if he wasn't just going to use the governor's job as a platform to run for president," Nichols recalled. As planned, he made the promise that he wouldn't run for the White House. "That was in November—and by January, he hardly set foot in the governor's office anymore. He was out running for president."

Like columnist Oakley, Nichols recalled how Clinton operatives staged a series of town hall meetings with the help of his supporters in the Democratic Party. "He'd tell the crowds that he was being called on to run for president, but instead he was determined not to give up being governor," Nichols recalled. "But then he'd always add the qualification that he'd only leave if they thought he could do more for Arkansas as president of the United States. . . . So he went around to twenty or so of his handpicked places and, of course, they all said, 'Go, Bill, go!'"

Whitewater Stonewaller Endorses Hillary

Senator Clinton's former Whitewater business partner is probably one of those Arkansas backers whom she didn't want campaigning for her in New York. Nevertheless, Susan McDougal sees her old scandal chum as someone whom Americans would be lucky to have as their president and is encouraging her to make the run.

"I think she makes a great senator from the state of New York," she told me in January. "I don't know anyone who would fight harder for the things she believes in, and she certainly represents her state well. I agree with her politics. So go Hillary!"[3]

McDougal had been equally enthusiastic about Mrs. Clinton's 2000 Senate run, offering a somewhat macabre endorsement in a conversation we had in July of that year. "I mean, she's a scary woman. You should have her," urged the Whitewater convict whom Mr. Clinton would later pardon. "She'll go after what she believes in, and I doubt that anyone could stand up to her. . . . I would vote for her."[4]

A few days after her "Hillary for President" endorsement, I caught up to McDougal again and asked whether, as her former business partner, she could assure Americans that Senator Clinton could be trusted with the awesome powers of the presidency.

McDougal insisted that she could. "I think they can trust her, yes." But the former Whitewater witness quickly shifted the subject from Mrs. Clinton's integrity to her overwhelming ambition, saying, "I think she is one of the most focused, the most driven, most goal-oriented women I have ever known." McDougal added that anyone who believed in Mrs. Clinton's politics couldn't ask for a stronger advocate. "That is why I say, 'Go, Hillary.' Because I certainly believe in her politics." Then, returning to the subject of Hillary's character, the one-time

Whitewater witness, said, "Trust is not something that I would tend to say people would have a problem with. . . . I've never had a problem trusting her." In fact, said McDougal, during their Whitewater dealings together, she found Mrs. Clinton to be "brutally truthful and straightforward—crazily so." She explained, "Once she gets something in her mind that, that's the way it is, she is going to be absolutely honest about it."[5]

Thumbs Down from a Law School Classmate

Of course, not everybody who knew Senator Clinton way back when thinks she's ready to challenge President Bush in 2004. "If she runs for president, it will be the best thing the Republican Party will ever experience," said John Doggett, a Dallas attorney who went to Yale Law School with Mrs. Clinton.[6]

Doggett said the Clintons are still too scandal-scarred for Hillary to make a run that soon. "Because of all the things that happened at the end of the Clinton presidency, the people just said, 'Oh what the hell, they're on their way out, let's ignore it.'" But if she were to launch her bid for the White House less than four years later, Doggett predicts, the postpresidential scandals would dog Senator Clinton's campaign.

"If she runs for president, it will be the best thing the Republican Party will ever experience."
—*Yale Law School classmate John Doggett*

"The Marc Rich pardon, that was criminal; that would be part of the campaign. As would the looting of the White House, taking of gifts that were given to the Clintons as president and first lady, the White House furniture that was shipped to their New York house—that would all be part of the campaign." So would any of her husband's suspected ongoing sexual "indiscretions," the Clinton classmate said.

"So I would be very surprised, given all that, to see Hillary running in 2004."

The Divorce Option

But Doggett did foresee one scenario that would signal Mrs. Clinton's intention to make the run in 2004. "Now if Hillary were to divorce Bill, then everything changes. In that event, there would be some people who say, 'Well she finally saw the light.'"

"Now if she divorced him," the Dallas attorney continued, "Hillary would probably claim that she was tired of putting up with all his crap. That's the only scenario that I think would give her reasonable chance to get the Democratic nomination."

CHAPTER FOUR

"New Tone" or Political Surrender?

"I think what we learned today is that President Bush was in the loop on trading arms for hostages. He denied it. He'll say anything to stay in office."
—Hillary Clinton, criticizing the first President Bush four days before the 1992 election

In almost every survey taken since he assumed the powers of the presidency, Americans by overwhelming margins say they trust President George W. Bush. And undoubtedly, the sense that, after eight long years, America finally has a leader with integrity and character proved indispensable in the weeks and months after the September 11 attacks.

When some of Bush's more wild-eyed critics on the left tried to suggest that he had known Al Qaeda was about to pounce—or even worse—that his family had somehow profited from their attacks, the notion was dismissed out of hand by almost every sane American. Bush's very lack of guile and shortage of clever verbal skills, with none of his predecessor's facile ability to lie about matters both public and public, were precisely the characteristics that told the nation its president was the right man for that time of national crisis and self-doubt.

But while Bush's straightforward, no-nonsense governing style served both him and the nation well in the weeks and months after September 11, it has never been tested against the Clintons' strategy of the never-ending campaign, where every move is calculated for its political advantage and the concept of winning at all costs reigns supreme. Bush may be far and away the better president and still be no match for a soon-to-be resurrected Clinton war room that made mincemeat out of his father eleven years ago.

Bush's Missed Opportunities

In Bush's first two and a half years in office, the White House political team has either failed to pursue or otherwise declined to capitalize on a short list of issues that could make the president vulnerable in the next election. The economy, for instance, is likely to be the ripest target for Democrats in 2004. And Hillary herself hasn't been at all shy about making comparisons between the go-go Clinton economy and the mess she and her husband left Bush after the bubble burst.

"The [Bush] administration is not just attempting to reverse the last eight years of progress and prosperity, they want to reverse the last 50 or 60 years," said Clinton, less than three months after becoming New York's junior senator. "It's not just trying to turn back the clock on the Clinton administration; they want to turn back the clock on the Roosevelt administration," she added. Criticism of Bush's economic performance, especially in contrast with the Clinton years, was a recurring theme for the first lady turned senator, and she kept it up right through the 2002 midterm elections.[1]

"I didn't support the large tax cut because I thought that it was based on phony arithmetic," she complained two months before the election. "There's no way that you could make the numbers work." Then she took a slap at the Reagan-era boom. "We've seen this before. This is what was done in the 1980s and it took about eight years to get out of the deficit ditch and to get a surplus so that we could be prepared for rainy days and even terrible tragedies like what happened to us on September 11."[2]

It's an easy bet that if Bush's latest round of tax cuts aren't enough to turn the economy around, Hillary will turn up the heat on comparisons with the administration she ran with her husband. And then there's the time-lag factor.

Even if the economy were headed in the right direction by late 2003, the results might not be apparent for more than a year. The Reagan tax cuts, for instance, were passed in March 1981, just two months after he took office. But they didn't begin to affect the stock market until August 1982, fifteen months later. Unemployment remained in double-digit territory through most of 1983.

Apply the same timetable to the Bush economy, and it's easy to see how any impending recovery could get lost in Democrat demagoguery. The same kind of delay doomed Bush Sr.'s reelection bid, when economic growth didn't show up in government reports until two months after Clinton had won the White House. They bolstered their slogan, "It's the economy, stupid!" with the bogus claim that Bush Sr. had given America "the worst economy in 50 years." Predictably, the media did nothing to set the record straight.

Clinton Economic Statistics

As Mrs. Clinton launched a full-court press to undermine the Bush tax cuts and even discredit the Reagan boom in the first two years of the Bush presidency, the White House seemed almost uninterested in responding. GOP spinmeisters, for instance, have left virtually intact the myth that the Clinton years were an era of unprecedented prosperity. Only once, in July 2002, did President Bush openly criticize the Clinton economic record, complaining that the late 1990s were a "binge" that had left the economy with "a hangover."

Still, no one in the White House saw the public relations value of evidence that emerged just a week after Bush offered his "binge" remarks, new numbers from the Commerce Department suggesting that the Clinton administration had cooked the books to give the false impression the economy was still booming right up until the election. Clinton-Gore statisticians, according to the Commerce Department's July 2002 report, wildly overstated figures on corporate profits in 1999 and 2000.

Noted columnist Robert Novak at the time: "The Commerce Department's painful report last week that the national economy is worse than anticipated obscured the document's startling revelation. Hidden in the morass of statistics, there is proof that the Clinton administration grossly overestimated the strength of the economy leading up to the 2000 election."[3]

Starting in 1999, as the report by Commerce's Bureau of Economic Analysis made clear, before-tax business profits were overstated by a factor of 10 percent. As the presidential election drew closer, that discrepancy skyrocketed to nearly 30 percent.

The bogus figures enabled Clinton's would-be successor, Al Gore, to paint himself the rightful heir to "the longest economic boom in American history"—when in fact the economy had been heading into the tank for two years. Clinton undersecretary of commerce Rob Shapiro dismissed the notion that the distorted figures represented any kind of scandal, insisting to Novak that the agency's Bureau of Economic Analysis is "the most non-political, non-partisan agency in the government."

Just days before the devastating Commerce Department statistics emerged, Senator Hillary Clinton fired back at Bush for his "binge" remarks, telling the Democratic Leadership

Council in New York: "I am reminded of what Abraham Lincoln once said, when his commanders complained about Ulysses S. Grant's binges. 'Find out,' he said, 'what brand of whiskey Grant drinks because I'm going to send a barrel to each of my generals.'"[4]

A Bumbling White House Political Operation

The White House political team, led by the inimitable Karl Rove, is supposed to have mastered the high art of media spin, timing and creating the right perception. But time and again, Bush has found himself in awkward, politically damaging situations that were easily avoidable—the kind of predicaments that will have to be better defended once Hillary's media SWAT team is poised to strike.

Bush has found himself in awkward, politically damaging situations that were easily avoidable—the kind of predicaments that will have to be better defended once Hillary's media SWAT team is poised to strike.

On July 9, 2002, for instance, after months of media reports on corporate bankruptcies linked to cooked books and executive malfeasance, Bush traveled to Wall Street to give a speech that was supposed to calm markets that had been sliding for weeks. But even though stocks worldwide had plunged precipitously the night before—usually a good indicator that Wall Street would be down at least during the morning trading session—the White House went ahead with the speech.

Predictably, as the president spoke, markets began to slide, leaving the distinct impression that traders thought his comments were making things worse. The next day, newspapers were filled with reports like the one in the *New York Daily News,* which began, "President Bush brought his bully pulpit to Wall Street yesterday, hoping to boost financial markets roiled by months of corporate scandals, but investors sent the Dow skidding another 178 points anyway."[5]

The exercise in bad timing was a minor political debacle, but one that should have taught the White House its lesson. It didn't. Less than a week later Bush sallied forth again to talk up the economy during the morning trading session, only to see the market sink lower with every word he spoke. Cable TV newscasters had a field day covering the speech in split screen, juxtaposing Bush on one side trying to assure investors that all would be OK and the tumbling market ticker on the other. Again, as the Dow continued to shed points, the timing of Bush's speech gave the unavoidable impression that he was making things worse.

"I really think the White House should have been more sensitive to the fact that that's precisely the way news editors and many viewers react when the president speaks during market hours," CNN moneyman Lou Dobbs said.[6] He was right. But how could the vaunted White House political operation have made the same stupid mistake not just once—but twice in the span of a single week?

In truth, the Bush-Rove political operation has been caught flat-footed so frequently that it begins to resemble the ham-handed organization employed by his father: the same gang that helped usher the Clintons into power in the first place.

In fact, the missed opportunities for Bush didn't begin with his presidency, but began piling up during the earliest days of the 2000 presidential campaign. The Bush-Rove team's handling of the Elian Gonzalez controversy is a case in point.

Elian Abandoned

The then Texas governor wouldn't have won the state of Florida without Miami's Cuban American voters, who deserted

Al Gore in droves after the Clinton administration ordered the Reno Justice Department to kidnap the six-year-old Cuban boat boy from his mother's family at the point of a machine gun. In Florida's razor-thin race, which ultimately determined the national electoral college vote, the Cuban community made all the difference for the Republican presidential hopeful. But it might have been an even larger factor had Bush played his cards more decisively.

Luckily for Bush, Cuban American animosity toward Clinton-Gore was so intense after the April 22, 2000, raid on the Gonzalez family home in the Little Havana section of Miami that most of the locals hadn't noticed how tepid the GOP hopeful's own support for Elian had been. Florida governor Jeb Bush, for instance, was so silent throughout the imbroglio that he hardly seemed to play any role whatsoever in the biggest national controversy to hit his state until the election fiasco later that year.

Even after shocking photos materialized of a terrified Elian staring into the muzzle of machine-gun–wielding Border Patrol agents, the Bush brothers were still mum. A week later, when then presidential candidate George Bush traveled to New York to attend a talk radio convention, I asked him if he supported an investigation into the paramilitary raid that even left-wing legal experts like Lawrence Tribe and Alan Dershowitz had complained was unconstitutional.

George Bush could have hit the question out of the park by offering support for some sort of legal challenge that might have spared the boy a return to Castro's gulag. Such a gesture might have won him enough Hispanic support nationwide to neutralize Gore's popular-vote advantage at the polls seven months later. But following the Bush-Rove play-it-safe formula, the best response the presidential candidate could muster was, "I just wish they'd solved this in a family court of law. That picture on the front pages of the newspapers in America disturbed me a lot."[7]

Apparently the raid didn't disturb the GOP White House hopeful deeply enough to support calls for a congressional investigation into the probably unconstitutional Elian raid, an idea that was gaining support in Republican circles on Capitol Hill at the time. But two days earlier, then top Bush aide Joe Allbaugh quietly told Senate Republicans to drop the issue because he thought it was "a political loser."[8] Some loser. Without Elian, Bush would likely be back in the Texas governor's mansion today reading directives from President Gore on how best to handle the terrorist threat.

The DUI October Surprise

The play-it-safe strategy nearly cost Bush the election a second time, when he failed to prepare for an October surprise drunk-driving scandal that rocked his campaign and likely clinched the popular vote for Gore. Campaign insiders would later explain that Bush wanted to protect his daughters, and that's why he didn't want to air information about a 1976 drunk-driving incident in Maine earlier in the campaign. But that logic always seemed particularly odd. Entire forests worth of newsprint had already been consumed in media explorations of the battle with the bottle that nearly ended his marriage to Laura—until he gave up alcohol at age forty. A minor one-time only DUI police stop, where Bush was not even arrested, certainly wouldn't have deeply shocked his daughters, given what was already on the public record.

Still, rather than confront the controversy at a time when it could have been easily handled, the silence of the Bush-Rove team allowed a Gore operative in Maine to break the news of the twenty-four-year-old drinking incident during the critical week before the election. On Thursday, November 2—with just five days to go before the polls opened—the DUI story exploded, leaving Bush little time to respond and no time for intervening events to dull the initial shock.

"There's a report out tonight that 24 years ago I was apprehended in Kennebunkport, Maine, for a DUI," Bush told reporters the night the story exploded. "That's an accurate story. I'm not proud of that. I oftentimes said that years ago I made some mistakes. I occasionally drank too much and I did on that night. I was pulled over. I admitted to the policeman that I had been drinking. I paid a fine. And I regret that it happened. But it did. I've learned my lesson."

The candidate may have long ago learned one lesson, but he was about to learn another.

Democrat Dirty Tricks?

Though the Gore campaign denied having anything to do with unearthing Bush's old DUI record, Tom Connolly, a Gore supporter in Maine, admitted to reporters that he had obtained the DUI documents and was trying to distribute them to the press. Connolly also confessed that he tried—unsuccessfully, he insisted—to fax the material to Gore campaign headquarters.[9]

The revelation cast a whole new light on a report from Fox News Channel's Carl Cameron, who had revealed twenty-four hours earlier, "There is something of a mystery that has unfolded since we broke the story. And that is that part of the arrest record and the state of Maine's documentation of George Bush's driving record and arrest record in Maine was faxed to news agencies all over the country after we were on the air with it at 6 o'clock Eastern time."[10]

Even before any Gore connection to the DUI story came to light, former Wyoming senator Alan Simpson proclaimed, "If anybody doesn't believe that this came right out of Gore headquarters, you ought to sprinkle some Peter Pan twinkle dust on them."[11]

Still, none of this was enough to dampen Karl Rove's optimism. Two days after the DUI scandal broke, he told a TV interviewer that Bush was dead even in California and actually up 5 points in Florida. Meanwhile, the devastating DUI revelation was eating away at Bush's support, but the candidate had no way of knowing it. The Bush political team stopped polling that Thursday, the very day the drinking scandal broke—a full six days before the election.

"While Bush aides boasted during the final days of a 5-point victory lead, exit polls on Election Night showed that late undecideds broke 3 to 1 for Al Gore," wrote political and economic analyst Lawrence Kudlow a week later. "This, by itself, is highly unusual, as last-minute deciders usually break against the incumbent who, in this case, was Gore. Why 3 to 1 against Bush? Twenty-five percent decided the DUI arrest was a significant factor."[12]

Like Father, Like Son

It wasn't the first time Team Bush had been cold-cocked on the eve of an election by a Clinton-connected operation, making Rove's failure to anticipate such a stunt doubly disturbing. Going into the closing weekend of the 1992 campaign, Bush Sr. was gaining rapidly on Bill Clinton, with a CNN survey showing him within 1 percentage point of the Arkansas Democrat.[13] Then it happened. Caspar Weinberger, the Reagan administration defense secretary, was indicted on Iran-Contra charges, a story that riveted the press and sucked all the oxygen out of Bush's comeback juggernaut. The Clintonistas seemed so ready to take advantage of the October surprise scandal that suspicion swirled as to whether they had a heads-up on the pending Weinberger indictment. The day of the indictment Clinton himself went on the attack, referring to some of the evidence in the case that he just happened to have ready to go. "Weinberger's note clearly shows . . . Bush has not been telling the truth when he says he was out of the loop," he exhorted crowds along the campaign trail.[14]

"Almost simultaneous with the Oct. 30 announcement of the indictment, the Clinton-Gore campaign issued a release headlined 'New Iran-Contra Evidence Released by Prosecutor Shows Bush Flatly Lied About his Role in Arms-For-Hostages.' That news release was dated Oct. 29—the day before the indictment was disclosed," reported the *Washington Times* after Bush's election loss. A spokeswoman for Mr. Clinton said the date was a mistake, explaining, "We made an error and put the wrong date on a press release." She chalked up the fast footwork to the Clinton-Gore campaign's "quick response team."

It's not clear what role Mrs. Clinton may have played in engineering the campaign's prescient response to the Weinberger indictment, but she certainly wasn't shy about pushing the issue on the campaign trail. With her husband's voice failing, Hillary became his surrogate speaker—speaking to an audience in Mankato, Minnesota, the day the news of the indictment hit. "I think what we learned today is that President Bush was in the loop on trading arms for hostages," she said. "He denied it. He'll say anything to stay in office."[15]

> "I think what we learned today is that President Bush was in the loop on trading arms for hostages. He denied it. He'll say anything to stay in office."
>
> —*Hillary Clinton attacking Bush's father*

Some even suspected that Mrs. Clinton had been involved in the 2000 DUI sandbag effort against Bush Jr., given her past association with Gore's campaign manager, Chris Lehane, who hailed from Kennebunkport, the scene of the 1976 "crime." Before joining the Gore campaign, he had worked inside the Clinton White House as a Whitewater damage controller who helped document Mrs. Clinton's "vast right-wing conspiracy" theory with a 300-page tome entitled, "The Communications Stream of Conspiracy Commerce."

Laying the Groundwork for 2004

Even after losing the 1992 election and nearly losing the 2000 race to what looked like mirror image eleventh-hour dirty-tricks campaigns, the Bush political operation has still given no indication that it has formed a war room of its own to combat the coming Hillary Clinton assault.

Ex-president Clinton's speech to the British Labour Party in October 2002 raised the bar for political audacity to new highs, offering the clearest measure yet of just how far the former first couple are willing to go in their attacks on Bush. It's also worth noting that the over-the-top assault made no political sense whatsoever unless the Clintons were at least contemplating a possible Bush challenge in 2004. This time Mr. Clinton was acting as the surrogate, trying to undermine Bush's support with a crucial ally at a time of war.

Needless to say, the ex-president's attack, though little noted by the U.S. media, also broke the long-standing political taboo that constrains U.S. ex-presidents from criticizing a sitting president from foreign soil. Furthermore, Clinton's comments came when his own country had been engaged in a hot war on terrorism since September 11 and was planning to open a second front against Baghdad.

"I think this whole Iraq issue is made more difficult for some of you because of the differences you have with the conservatives in America over other matters, over the criminal court and the Kyoto Treaty and the comprehensive test ban treaty," he told the Labourites, in a naked attempt to capitalize on growing anti-American sentiment within the British left.

Clinton then proceeded to remind his foreign audience that he also disagreed with the Bush administration "on nearly everything: on budget policy, tax policy, on education policy, on environmental policy, on health care policy." Then he added, "I have a world of disagreements with them."

Turning uglier still, the former U.S. president indicated that he still believed President Bush's 2000 election was illegitimate, complaining sarcastically, "The election was so close in America that they won it fair and square—5 to 4 at the Supreme Court." Then he explained, "We should actually be glad, though, because there were seven Republicans and only two Democrats on the Supreme Court—and two of those Republicans—God bless them, they will be rewarded in heaven—they actually took the decision that we should count votes when the American people vote. And I appreciate that."

Clinton also felt compelled to explain that while he supported "regime change" in Iraq, he disagreed with the White House's support for preemptive military action against Iraq. "If the inspections go forward, I believe we should still work for a regime change in Iraq in non-military ways," he told the Labourites, despite the fact that, that very week, U.S. aircraft patrolling the "no-fly" zone had been fired upon by Iraqi anti-aircraft batteries.

Then, playing right into the hands of Baghdad's propaganda machine, Clinton warned, "A preemptive action today, however well justified, may come back with unwelcome consequences in the future. . . . I do not care how precise your bombs and your weapons are—when you set them off, innocent people will die." But Clinton's most partisan assault came when he told his British audience that the Reagan administration was to blame for giving Saddam Hussein the technology he needed to launch the bioweapons program he later used against the Kurds.

"The West has a lot to answer for in Iraq," he told the Labourites. "When Saddam Hussein gassed the Kurds and the Iranians—there was hardly a peep in the West because he was [fighting] Iran. Evidence has now come to light that in the early 1980s the United States may have even supplied him with the materials necessary to start the bioweapons program. We cannot forget that we are not blameless in the misery under which they suffer."[16]

Bush Team Stays Mum

Despite the ex-president's unprecedented attack, delivered from foreign soil at a time of impending war, the White House stayed mum—not a good sign that Bush-Rove is ready to deal with similar attacks from the Clintons at home when the time is right. In fact, just a few weeks after her husband wowed the Labourites by bashing Bush as an illegitimate president, Mrs. Clinton echoed the theme at a Los Angeles fund-raiser for Senator Jean Carnahan, who lost her race.

Telling the crowd that Bush was "selected" rather than elected, Hillary went on to remind the gathering, "You know, I'm a fan of Clintonomics. And this administration is destroying in months our eight years of economic progress." She then proceeded to complain that the Bush fund-raising operation had raised far more money than the Democrats with the express purpose of trying to "ruin the reputations of our candidates or, if they can't, to depress the turnout" by making campaigns unpalatably nasty. Without a hint of irony Senator Clinton added, "These people are ruthless and they are relentless."[17]

No Plan to Counter Media Bias

But it's not just the unanswered assaults from the Clintons that are liable to render President Bush politically vulnerable in 2004. Consider the spate of media reports after the 2002 holiday shopping season had ended proclaiming that the year's Christmas sales had been horrendous. "Department stores and other traditional retailers are calling this year's holiday shopping season one of the worst in 30 years," announced the *Detroit News* two days after Christmas.

CNN analyst Bill Schneider wasted no time in gauging the political implications of the sagging sales figures: "In November, Americans vote with their ballots, up or down for the president's party. This year they made a strong and clear statement. Up," he reported. "In December, Americans vote with their dollars, up or down for the economy. They've made a pretty clear statement on the economy, too. Down. In fact, it was the worst holiday shopping season in over 30 years. For the third straight year the growth in holiday sales has slowed, cut in half each year."[18]

"You know, I'm a fan of Clintonomics. And this administration is destroying in months our eight years of economic progress."

—*Hillary Clinton*

While news audiences were left wondering how three decades of economic growth could have suddenly been wiped out overnight, leaving the country on the verge of what reporters suggested was possibly the biggest economic calamity since the Great Depression, the actual sales figures reflected nothing of the sort. In fact, retail sales hit their highest total ever during the 2002 Christmas season, with a solid 1.5 percent gain over the previous year's numbers. The rate of growth, however, was indeed the lowest since 1970.[19]

But the real problem here wasn't the almost predictable distortions by the press, which delights in highlighting negative economic news while Republicans are in the White House in hopes of paving the way for a Democrat takeover. It was the Bush White House, which did absolutely nothing to counter the growing perception that the economy's performance during the crucial holiday period had been frighteningly dismal.

Clinton Operatives Now "Newsmen"

To this day, the Clinton administration—now more than two years out of office—still has an effective media team of ex-officials ready to act as spinmeisters at the first sign that damage control might be necessary. Some of them actually play the role of serious journalists. Two members of the 1992 Clinton campaign's war room, George Stephanopoulos and James Carville, now occupy high-profile roles in the television press, with the former now occupying the role once reserved for respected top network newsman David Brinkley. From his perch on ABC's *This Week,* Stephanopoulos has tried to tone down his tendency to play the role of Clinton damage controller—sometimes with little success. In this December 2002 exchange with Secretary of State Colin Powell, Stephanopoulos invoked criticism from a leading Democrat who blamed Bush for abandoning Clinton's policy of appeasement toward North Korea, which, most experts agree, enabled Pyongyang to acquire nuclear weapons.

STEPHANOPOULOS: I want to show something that Senator John Kerry said the other day about the administration's policy. What he said [was]: "What happened in North Korea is predictable and totally anticipated based on [the Bush] administration's complete avoidance of a responsible approach to North Korea in over a year and a half. It is the absence of diplomacy, it is the absence of common sense that has brought this on." How do you respond to Senator Kerry?

POWELL: Well, John Kerry is running for office. And I disagree with the senator as much as I respect him. The fact of the matter is that this [nuclear] program was not started during the Bush administration. It was started during the previous administration. Back in 1998 and 1999, the intelligence shows clearly that North Korea had embarked on a program of enriching uranium. And so, we inherited this problem.[20]

Meanwhile, Stephanopoulos's war-room partner James Carville regularly holds forth as the co-host of CNN's *Crossfire,* alternating appearances with fellow Clinton campaign strategist Paul Begala. While officials from Republican White Houses have occupied the host's chair on *Crossfire* from time to time, no one with Stephanopoulos's partisan pedigree has ever walked into the role of moderator of one of the major Sunday public affairs shows.

Just two years before matriculating to ABC News, the former Clinton communications director was busy trying to keep *This Week* from covering Gary Aldrich's blockbuster White House exposé *Unlimited Access*—unless he appeared immediately afterwards to rebut Aldrich's claims.

"Not since the Nixon administration tried unsuccessfully to block publication of the Pentagon Papers twenty-five years ago has a White House leaned so aggressively on the media to alter a news decision. And the remarkable thing is the heavy-handed pressure may have paid off," reported the *Weekly Standard* a month after Aldrich's book was released.[21] Afterwards the magazine's Fred Barnes noted, "Aldrich became persona non grata in the mainstream media. What happened to the Aldrich menace? 'We killed it,' boasts Stephanopoulos."

"Not since the Nixon administration tried unsuccessfully to block publication of the Pentagon Papers twenty-five years ago has a White House leaned so aggressively on the media to alter a news decision."

—reporter Fred Barnes

Four years before that, the diminutive damage controller was threatening to ruin a witness who said he had evidence suggesting that Clinton had fathered a black love child, an episode chronicled in the 1993 Clinton campaign documentary, "The War Room." And while there's no public record of Carville threatening media sources, his warning to a sitting independent counsel was even more outrageous. In late 1996, he told the *New York Daily News* that Kenneth Starr was, "one mistake away from not having any kneecaps."[22] Noted the *Washington Times* of the Carville warning, "Normally, when a threat like that is made against a federal law enforcement official, the Justice Department and the FBI look into it."

Even beyond the Clintonista A-team, former White House flaks like Ann Lewis and Mark Gearan are still turning up on TV to do battle on behalf of their old boss. While the Bush White House has a few media-savvy types, like Republican strategist Cliff May, who can handle themselves well on TV, the Bush administration has yet to cultivate anything like the phalanx of aggressive and seasoned damage controllers who are still working to burnish the credentials of Bill and Hillary Clinton.

On Defense over Race

The Bush-Rove team's reluctance to assert itself on the media battlefield can have devastating political consequences, as with the December 2002 Trent Lott fiasco.

The former Republican Senate majority leader had made the politically fatal mistake of being caught on camera praising the 1948 Dixiecrat presidential candidacy of then retiring Senator Strom Thurmond at his 100th birthday party. Although Lott's comments made no mention of "segregation," "Dixiecrat," or "Jim Crow" nor any other direct references to racially offensive concepts, the mere fact that he praised the South Carolinian's campaign was interpreted in the press as a racial slur.

While White House insiders like Mary Matalin insisted Bush's orders were to keep hands off the Lott imbroglio, the president's own comments condemning Lott's statements sent the loud and clear signal that he was expendable. The most powerful Republican on Capitol Hill was demoted in short order, joining the ranks of the senators over whom he once reigned just three weeks after his remarks became public.

While the White House garnered well-deserved praise for making clear that segregation had no place in the modern Republican party, Bush failed to signal that the same level of scrutiny would apply to elected Democrats. Trent Lott had been blithely tossed under the bus, but Democrats guilty of far worse escaped any heat whatsoever.

Senator Fritz Hollings, a South Carolina Democrat who had installed the Confederate flag over his state's Capitol building in the 1960s and who once compared African diplomats to cannibals, wasn't challenged by either the GOP or the press, which pummeled Lott relentlessly.[23] And worst of all, Senator Robert Byrd, a former Ku Klux Klansman who repeatedly decried "white niggers" during a 2001 TV interview, got a complete pass from both the Bushies and the reporters.

The GOP's decision not to fight fire with fire was an open invitation to Democrats to play the race card again. The significance of the self-imposed double standard certainly wasn't lost on Senator Clinton, who recognized immediately that this was a battle the White House didn't want to fight. As had become the pattern by the time of Hillary's second year in the Senate, her husband first laid the groundwork for the coming attack.

"How can [Republicans] jump on [Lott] when they're out there repressing, trying to run black voters away from the polls and running under the Confederate flag in Georgia and South Carolina?" Clinton asked CNN after Lott stepped down as majority leader. "I mean, look at their whole record. He just embarrassed them by saying in Washington what they do on the back roads every day."[24]

Hillary Goes for the Jugular

The next day, Mrs. Clinton warned that the Lott demotion wouldn't "cleanse the Republican Party of their constant exploitation of race." Then she added, "I mean, what [Lott] did was state publicly what many of them have stated privately over many years." The comments mirrored her husband's critique almost word for word. Then Mrs. Clinton took aim directly at the White House, leveling an unexpected broadside.

"The campaign for then Governor Bush in South Carolina had a huge outreach effort to say [McCain] adopted a black baby," she complained to reporters. It was a reference to leaflets and phone calls allegedly originating with Bush supporters during the bitterly fought April 2000 primary, where, according to reporters covering the campaign, McCain's adopted dark-skinned daughter was referred to using a racial epithet.

Mrs. Clinton's decision to tar Bush with the Trent Lott fiasco hit pay dirt almost immediately.

"They actually used the word 'nigger,'" Paul Alexander quoted one campaign insider complaining in his McCain biography, *Man of the People*. "The calls said McCain had a 'nigger' baby."[25]

Raising the Bush-McCain South Carolina battle was a clever ploy by Hillary, one that spotlighted a go-for-the-jugular instinct unrivaled by anyone else in modern politics, with the possible exception of her husband. The tactics used against him during the South Carolina primary were a real sore spot for McCain, who continues to be Bush's main rival within Republican ranks.

Mrs. Clinton's decision to tar Bush with the Trent Lott fiasco hit pay dirt almost immediately. A few days later McCain, who had remained publicly silent on the South Carolina controversy, answered questions about the episode for the first time—as posed by radio host Don Imus.

IMUS: Are you happy with the role the White House apparently played to get rid of Trent Lott and selecting Bill Frist?

McCAIN: Oh, I think that they—I think they—it was a dramatic example of Harry Truman's adage, "If you want a friend in Washington, go out and buy a dog." But I think that the president . . .

IMUS: The president never liked him anyway, did he?

McCAIN: I don't know what their relationship was. But I think the president did the right thing by rejecting that kind of language.

IMUS: It would have been nice if he'd have spoken out the same way when they ran that jive up the flagpole on you there in South Carolina, wouldn't it?

McCAIN: Yup. I should have spoken out and . . .

IMUS: Well, no—he should have.

McCAIN: Well, I should have.

IMUS: Well, yeah, you should have, too.

McCAIN: I went down after the campaign and I apologized—that didn't do any good—but I apologized for not taking—I apologized for taking a cowardly stand on that issue after the campaign was over.

IMUS: I guess I have to drop it, don't I, about the president not apologizing to you. It still irritates me but apparently you've got over it. Right? Or maybe you haven't.

McCAIN: Yeah, no, you have to get over these things. You have to move forward and it's in the best interests of the country to do so.[26]

George Bush is far from the only politician who wants to pick his fights carefully, but he has taken the strategy to such extremes that it often seems he and Rove are afraid to engage Bill and Hillary. What began as part of the Republican president's plan to set a "new tone" in order to "move on" from the political bickering over the scandals of the Clinton era had by 2003 become a pattern. It's a pattern not missed by Bill and Hillary Clinton, who would relish a second chance to topple another Bush from his White House perch if they thought there would be a chance of succeeding.

CHAPTER FIVE

Clintonphobia

"If we hadn't passed the big tax cut last spring, that I believe undermined our fiscal responsibility and our ability to deal with this new threat of terrorism, we wouldn't be in the fix we're in today."

—Hillary Clinton to CNN,
November 2001

Much to the chagrin of millions of conservatives who fought tooth and nail to see him elected, President George Bush made it apparent early on in his administration that he would abide by the mainstream media's unwritten rule placing Bill and Hillary Clinton above the law.

When, on the day before his inauguration, Independent Counsel Robert Ray cut a deal with Bill Clinton that allowed him to escape prosecution on an airtight perjury rap that had cost the government $70 million to bring, Bush was uncritical.

After a wave of initial reports that the White House would seek to reverse some of President Clinton's more controversial pardons, including several evidently purchased by the highest bidder, the Bushies backed off. And when reports surfaced that exiting Clintonistas had trashed the White House along with the Old Executive Office Building, Bush press secretary Ari Fleischer told reporters his boss wasn't interested in investigating.

President Bush even personally challenged the authenticity of reports that the former first family had stolen an array of items from Air Force One on their last flight home to Chappaqua. Bush had loaned them the plane for the trip in the first of many goodwill gestures offered to the former first couple.

"All the allegations that they took stuff off Air Force One are simply not true," the president told reporters in early February 2001.[1] Citing an Air Force steward assigned to the presidential jet, *Washington Times* columnist John McCaslin had reported days earlier that the plane was found to have been "stripped bare" when it landed in New York. Missing items reportedly included the entire collection of Air Force One porcelain china, silverware, salt and pepper shakers, blankets and pillowcases—most of which bore the presidential seal.

"What most astonished the military steward was that even a cache of Colgate toothpaste, not stamped with the presidential seal, was snatched from a compartment beneath the presidential plane's sink," McCaslin wrote.[2] Even after Bush's denial, however, the *Times* reporter stood by his report.

"We have reported on the front page of our paper what Bush said," he replied, when questioned about the White House denials. "But in no way am I going to put any kind of a retraction in."[3]

A Clinton-Free Convention

The Republican president's indulgences towards his predecessor didn't begin with his inauguration. In fact, Bush began bending over backwards to accommodate the Clintons' sensitivities as far back as the GOP's 2000 Philadelphia convention, where he sent the clear signal that he had no intention of focusing on Clinton-era corruption in his campaign against Al Gore, let alone prosecuting any of it should he get elected.

The Republican House impeachment managers, many of whom were heroes to the hordes of conservative conventioneers, were kept at arm's length during the four-day Republican lovefest that ended in Bush's nomination. When Philadelphia convention-goers staged an event honoring House Judiciary Chairman Henry Hyde, whose valiant efforts to hold President Clinton accountable to the rule of law had turned him into a conservative icon, it wasn't allowed to happen inside the arena. Instead, *National Review* held a party in his honor far from the Comcast Convention Center.

Even Hillary's opponent Rick Lazio, whose election would have signaled the definitive end of the era of Clintonism, was denied so much as a walk-on role during the convention festivities leading up to Bush's coronation. Instead, the man on whom the GOP had pinned its hopes to win the nation's most important political contest after Bush's own race against Gore was relegated to the media tent, where he answered reporters' questions on the second day of the proceedings for about an hour, then vanished from the scene.

While Democrats remember the Bush campaign as one that focused on the Clinton scandals, in fact, GOP strategists mostly avoided the issue and addressed it only in the vaguest of terms. Everyone knew what Bush meant when he uttered phrases like "returning honor and dignity to the Oval Office," but the candidate and his senior spinmeisters never explicitly referenced Monica Lewinsky, let alone the other branches of the Clinton scandalabra. In August 2000, the Bush media machine tried to make an issue out of Gore's notorious 1996 Buddhist temple fund-raiser. But instead of treating seriously the issue of Asian money illegally funding U.S. elections, the single Bush campaign ad to spotlight a specific Clinton-Gore scandal tried to play the episode for laughs.

In his convention acceptance speech Bush offered only vague references to the scandals of the last eight years. But when conservatives heard him speak the words "To lead this nation to a responsibility era, that president himself must be responsible. . . . I will swear to not only uphold the laws of our land, I will swear to uphold the honor and dignity of the office to which I have been elected, so help me God," they heard the hint of coming Clinton prosecutions.[4]

Chinagate, Pardongate Deep-Sixed

Nothing, it turned out, could have been further from the truth. Almost immediately upon taking office, the Bush Justice Department settled the case against Chinagate moneyman James Riady, the kingpin in what investigators believed was a massive conspiracy to sell American national security secrets to Beijing in exchange for millions of dollars in campaign cash.

With the news that on his last day in office Clinton had pardoned Marc Rich, the worst tax fugitive in U.S. history—this within days of his ex-wife Denise's pledge to donate nearly a half million dollars to Clinton's presidential library—investigators swung into action. Indictments looked almost certain after Mrs. Rich invoked her Fifth Amendment right to remain silent when she was called to testify before the House Government Reform and Oversight Committee in February 2001. That same month witnesses emerged with canceled checks claiming that first brother Roger Clinton had shaken down a Texas family for $235,000 in exchange for a presidential pardon. The Clinton sibling also began stonewalling probers. Newly elected Senator Hillary Clinton suddenly found herself caught up in Pardongate's swirl, as prosecutors began reviewing her husband's grant of clemency for four upstate New York rabbis whose village voted for her by the improbable margin of 1,200 to 14.

Mutual Non-Aggression Pact?

But despite compelling evidence of bribery in the Clinton pardon mess, more than two years of investigation have yielded not a single indictment, with the Bush Justice Department abandoning the case against Mrs. Clinton altogether. Some, like Fox News Channel's Bill O'Reilly, suspected a deal. In fact, the popular cable host told his *Radio Factor* audience in June 2002 that he had evidence Bush had made a backroom deal to keep prosecutors muzzled.

"A very highly placed source—and I mean this guy knows what's going on in the Bush administration—told me about a month ago that when President Bush took office he had meetings with all of the Democratic leadership . . . one-on-one meetings in the Oval Office," O'Reilly said. "The Democratic leadership made it quite clear to Mr. Bush that he would not get any cooperation—zero—on the part of the Democrats in the Senate and in the House if he pursued any kind of a criminal investigation against Bill Clinton.

"Basically, they said look, if you embarrass us—by us we mean the Democratic Party—if you, Bush-Ashcroft, indict Clinton on bribery or go after Hillary or any of this—we're gonna shut you down," O'Reilly explained. "We're not gonna do anything. You're not going to get any [legislation] passed in four years."[5] The Fox News host never indicated who his source might be beyond describing him as "very highly placed."

No Room for Clinton Whistleblowers

Deal or no, President Bush seems to have gone out of his way not to pick a fight with either his predecessor or his senator-wife. Many Republicans, for instance, expected him to do something for the many witnesses who put their careers—and sometimes even lives—on the line in order to get the truth out about Bill and Hillary—people like former travel office chief Billy Dale, whose life was nearly ruined when Mrs. Clinton tried to railroad him with a bogus embezzlement prosecution just so she could give her cronies the jobs Dale and his staff had.

Linda Tripp was smeared by the media on everything from her looks to a youthful shoplifting arrest after she went public with her recordings of Monica Lewinsky admitting an affair with Mr. Clinton. The anti–Linda Tripp press-feeding frenzy shattered her nerves, cost her a government job, and left the Clinton whistleblower near bankruptcy.

Former FBI agent Gary Aldrich resigned from his prestigious White House post to tell the world about the dangerous security lapses and "Animal House" ambience tolerated inside the Clinton administration. When Aldrich's White House partner, fellow agent Dennis Sculimbrene, implicated Hillary's handpicked White House counsel Bernie Nussbaum in the Filegate scandal, Sculimbrene became the target of an FBI probe himself.

Dale, Tripp, Aldrich, and Sculimbrene had all served in the administration of Bush's father before being kept on in the Clinton White House. Their combined efforts to expose Bill and Hillary's corruption probably did more to sour Americans on the Clinton era and pave the way for Al Gore's defeat than anything accomplished by Bush's presidential campaign. Yet nowhere in the second Bush administration could a place be found for Tripp, Dale, and the two FBI heroes. Other whistleblowers whose accounts undermined efforts to vindicate the ex-president by electing his vice president—folks like Chinagate witness Johnny Chung, Sexgate accuser Kathleen Willey, and Whitewater figure David Hale—were likewise

> "[Bush] understands that his role as president is to serve all the people."
>
> —*Rep. Vito Fossella*

left to fend for themselves after being ravaged by the Clinton attack machine. Meanwhile, Bush spared no effort in trying to establish a "new tone" that would put an end to partisan bickering over past scandals and cement his image as "a uniter, not a divider."

An Olive Branch for Hillary

In one of the most vivid signs that he wanted to let bygones be bygones, the new president invited Mrs. Clinton to ride with him on Air Force One to attend John Cardinal O'Connor's funeral in New York in July 2001. In an eyebrow-raising gesture of solidarity between exclusive members of the presidential club, Bush and Clinton sat side by side for the entire flight. "He sat next to her both ways," Representative Vito Fossella, R-N.Y., told WABC Radio.

Fossella also rode the presidential plane for the O'Connor funeral trip and had cosponsored legislation the previous year that honored the much beloved cleric. The magnanimous gesture followed by just a few weeks ex-president Clinton's speech before a Hong Kong audience—full of high officials from Beijing—where he suggested that Bush's China policy was both misguided and possibly dangerous, in contrast to his own more accommodating posture. Still, Fossella didn't sound particularly surprised to see Bush schmoozing Mrs. Clinton as the two sat together for hours.

"Some people joke about his message of compassion, civility and trying to get things done for the good of the country," Fossella told WABC. "But he understands that his role as president is to serve all the people."[6]

Forgiveness Not Mutual

The Clinton camp, however, did not universally appreciate Bush's indulgence. In fact, several veterans of the Clinton-Gore administration began actively pushing for Bush's impeachment in mid-2002 on the Web site Democrats.com, which planned a voter registration drive to win control of Congress and make Bush's impeachment possible. Democrats.com offered headlines like "'Bushgate'—Which Scandal Will Bring About Bush's Impeachment?" and complained, "Bush has run the most scandal-ridden administration since Richard Nixon produced Watergate." The "Bushgate" feature, Democrats.com promised, would "track the progress of ALL of Bush's scandals as they make their way from Internet exposes . . . to columns, books and films . . . to mainstream news stories . . . to Congressional investigations . . . and finally, to IMPEACHMENT."[7]

The anti-Bush Web site might not have attracted any attention except for the identities of the people who put it together: mostly hardened political veterans of the Clinton-Gore administration. Democrats.com co-founder David Lytel was President Clinton's personal Webmaster, who helped to develop and edit the award-winning White House Web site. Former Clinton pollster Stanley Greenberg sits on Democrats.com's advisory board, along with Dick Bell, formerly the head of the Interactive Media Department at the Democratic National Committee.

Jock Gill, another advisory board member, was director of special projects in the Office of Media Affairs in the Clinton White House. He also helped develop the White House's Web site. And Democrats.com advisory board member Greg Simon was the chief domestic policy adviser to Vice President Al Gore.

Shortly after NewsMax.com broke the news of Democrats.com's Bush impeachment drive, the Democratic National Committee quickly moved to distance itself from any formal role in the project. "That's appalling," the DNC's Jennifer Palmieri told WABC Radio. "I am against the criminalization of politics. . . . I watched a president get destroyed and I watched a lot of my friends rack up hundreds of thousands of dollars of legal bills with these crazy investigations."[8] The former first couple, however, declined to comment one way or the other on the Bush impeachment effort.

The Clinton and Bush Dynasties

Part of what makes President Bush's unilateral political disarmament vis à vis the Clintons so disturbing is the seeming inevitability of another face-off between the two political clans. Whether Hillary runs in 2004 or waits till 2008, George W. Bush will likely find himself campaigning against the former first couple in his own name or on behalf of his successor. Only next time it will be far more difficult for the GOP to raise the character issue against Hillary, since Bush or his minions have done nothing in the intervening years about her ethical transgressions.

The New Square and Marc Rich pardons? The Bush Justice Department gave Hillary and Bill a pass. Her probable perjury in Travelgate? When Independent Counsel Robert Ray let her off the hook, the Bushies were silent. How about her husband's role in leaving America vulnerable to the September 11 attacks? Mr. Rove has evidently decreed that the topic is off limits.

Still, whether George W. Bush likes it or not, his family's rivalry with the Clintons is likely to dominate the national scene for years to come. Bill Clinton's stunning 1992 White House win set the stage for one of the most enduring political feuds since the Kennedy-Nixon rivalry, where two leaders and their disciples dominated American politics and shared the reins of executive branch power throughout the 1950s, '60s, and '70s.

As Eisenhower's vice president through eight years of Republican rule in the 1950s, Richard Nixon was on the fast track for the presidency, only to lose the 1960 presidential race by 100,000 votes to then Senator John Kennedy in the closest presidential election of the postwar period—until the Bush-Gore 2000 race. Two years later Nixon looked finished, unable to win even the governor's race in his home state of California. Kennedy's assassination the next year interrupted his dynasty until brother Bobby picked up the torch five years later. And after he was killed in 1968, it was widely presumed that Senator Ted Kennedy would step in to fill the void with his own presidential run in 1972. The plan went over the cliff along with Ted's black Oldsmobile one July night at Chappaquiddick.

But even in death and disgrace, the Kennedys remained a force to be reckoned with in Washington, ultimately toppling Nixon once again through surrogates who ran the Watergate investigation. Special Prosecutor Archibald Cox, after all, was a Kennedy administration alumnus who pursued the family's Republican nemesis with a vengeance. With his demand that the White House turn over the Watergate tapes, Cox set in motion a chain of events that ended Nixon's presidency.

In an ironic accident of history, the next two great presidential dynasties had significant roles within the Nixon and Kennedy camps. Among those sifting through reams of evidence for the House Watergate Committee, listening to the tapes and researching historical precedents for impeachment, was twenty-six-year-old Hillary Diane Rodham. When Nixon finally resigned in August 1974, an event that precipitated that fall's Democratic Party landslide at the polls, the unenviable task of trying to rebuild the party fell to its Republican National Committee chairman, a former Texas congressman by the name of George H. W. Bush. Former President Bush became RNC chairman nine months before Nixon resigned, and he almost didn't take the job for fear the scandal would tarnish his political career. Ultimately Watergate made Bush's task as RNC chair impossible, with the scandal costing the GOP forty-nine seats in the House and four in the Senate in the next election.

Eighteen years later, the Bushes and the Clintons would face off again—this time directly—with the one-time Watergate prober's husband garnering enough votes to deny the former Nixon RNC chief a second term in the White House. Then, after holding executive branch power for eight years, the Clintons were denied the vindication of seeing their legacy continued under Vice President Al Gore by none other than Bush's son.

George W. Bush hadn't even entered politics by the time Bill and Hillary took control of the White House. How galling to be replaced by the son of the man they had defeated eight years earlier—and someone who gave every indication that he meant to unravel the Clinton legislative legacy to boot.

Hillary Fires First Salvos of the 2004 Campaign?

For a politician who has flatly ruled out a presidential run any time before 2008, Senator Clinton has spent an inordinate amount of time, energy, and effort during her first two years in office attacking George Bush, whose White House career will be over by then. Will Hillary Clinton be able to resist a chance to vanquish the Bushes yet again even if it means breaking her vow regarding 2004?

Her decision not to endorse Gore when she had the chance was one clear signal of her intent. But for those who follow the dictum "Trust what they do, not what they say," the handwriting had been on the wall almost from Clinton's earliest days in the Senate.

Right through 2002, reporters continued to insist that Mrs. Clinton had kept a "low profile" as the first of the first ladies to hold elective office, warming instead to the everyday, behind the scene tasks of a first-year senator. This, while she made headlines almost every week, usually for criticizing President Bush on everything from the need for more federal funds to rebuild Ground Zero to the need for more tax revenue to fund the war in Iraq.

The Bush tax cut has long been a subject of particular annoyance for Senator Clinton, so much so that sometimes her criticism of the president's economic plan borders on the hysterical.

Two months after the September 11 attacks, for instance, she actually suggested a causal relationship between the Bush cuts and the attacks.

"If we hadn't passed the big tax cut last spring, that I believe undermined our fiscal responsibility and our ability to deal with this new threat of terrorism, we wouldn't be in the fix we're in today," Clinton told CNN's Jonathan Karl.[9] In addition to undermining the country's ability to deal with terrorist attacks, Clinton said, the Bush tax cuts worsened the economic downturn in the wake of September 11.

"If we hadn't passed the big tax cut last spring, that I believe undermined our fiscal responsibility and our ability to deal with this new threat of terrorism, we wouldn't be in the fix we're in today."

—Hillary Clinton

"We had eight years of prosperity because we paid down our debt and we got rid of our deficit," she complained. "We hit a rough spot, and it was turned into a terrible bump because of the attacks of September 11."

Even more bizarrely, daughter Chelsea Clinton blamed the Bush tax cuts in her first public comments on September 11. Writing her account up for *Talk* magazine, young Clinton claimed she was just blocks away from the Twin Towers when they rumbled to the ground.

Her first thought? "I was worried that with the tax cut we wouldn't have enough money to repair New York and D.C. and to help the families of the thousands I knew must have died," wrote the former first daughter. Chelsea said she was by herself in nearby Union Square and unable to reach her parents by phone as the disaster unfolded before her eyes. "We all thought we were literally going to have fire rain down on us, that we were the next target," she recounted. "I truly thought I was going to die."[10]

More evidence that Hillary seems to have Bush—and not some yet-to-be-imagined 2008 Republican successor—in her gunsights: From day one she's invited comparisons between fiscal records of the Bush and Clinton administrations, regularly complaining that her husband's successor had squandered the so-called budget surpluses built up over the last eight years by giving "tax cuts to the rich."

It's the Economy, Not the Scandals, Stupid!

Of course, unmentioned by Hillary and forgotten by her media cohort is the Clintons' record on the scandal front. While the Bush administration remained free of major scandal going into its third year in office, by a similar point in Bill and Hillary's tenure, an independent counsel had already been appointed to probe the Whitewater and Travelgate scandals—and Mr. Clinton was already enmeshed in the sexual harassment lawsuit that would ultimately lead to his impeachment.

In the rare instances when questions about past corruption cloud her horizons, Senator Clinton has dismissed the issue as something that was resolved to everyone's satisfaction years ago. In fact, both Bill and Hillary have repeatedly cited Independent Counsel Robert Ray's decision not to indict either of them as a complete vindication: confirming their claim that the probe that began with Whitewater and ended with Monicagate was indeed the product of a "vast right-wing conspiracy."

Trashing Tax Cuts

Meanwhile, the former first couple seldom miss a chance to burnish their legacy.

"I believe two terms of the Clinton administration were very good for our country," Mrs. Clinton told reporters in December 2001, adding, "I'm deeply concerned that within a space of a year we seem to have done a U-turn." Bristling at criticism by Republicans that the 1990s economic bubble had burst nearly a year before Bush took office, the senator complained, "Many of us believe the country was in the right condition when President Clinton left us and that we should have built on those successes instead of turning back the clock." The country was "richer and safer and smarter and stronger" when she and her husband were in the White House, she contended. But those achievements had been "eliminated or reversed in the space of a year," she complained.[11]

"Fuck him, Bill. He's Reagan's goddam Vice President!"
—Hillary Clinton, criticizing then Vice President Bush to her husband in the 1980s

Much of Senator Clinton's disdain for the policies of the Bush White House is rooted in objections to the Bush tax cut, an objection she shares with many in her party. But while other Democrats going into the 2002 election stopped short of endorsing actual tax increases, Mrs. Clinton invoked the looming war in Iraq as justification for a politically deadly tax hike during a little-noticed radio interview that September.

"I think if we're in a war and we're thinking about expanding that war to Iraq, you know, the nation and particularly those of us who are in the top 1 to 10 percent of our country's earners, we have to be willing to put our money where our mouths are," she told WABC Radio.[12] Clinton argued that the war on terrorism demanded a new set of budgetary priorities, complaining that the Bush tax cut threatened to put the nation back into "the deficit ditch."

"I didn't support the large tax cut because I thought that it was based on phony arithmetic," she said. "There's no way that you could make the numbers work." Citing the Reagan-era tax cuts, Clinton complained, "We've seen this before. This is what was done in the 1980s and it took about eight years to get out of the deficit ditch and to get a surplus so that we could be prepared for rainy days and even terrible tragedies like what happened to us on 9-11."

Hillary's reference to Reagan is particularly revealing and may explain why, as a once and perhaps future White House occupant herself, she has put presidential etiquette aside to deliver broadside after broadside at the Bush tax cut program. One-time Clinton bodyguard, Arkansas state trooper L. D. Brown recalls a number of episodes in the 1980s where Mrs. Clinton expressed a visceral disdain for the fortieth president. While then governor Clinton admired Reagan and got on well with then vice president Bush, Brown recalls Mrs. Clinton erupting in profanity at the news they'd been invited to attend a clambake at Bush's Kennebunkport estate.

"Hillary flatly refused to go," reported Brown, in his own 1997 memoir *Crossfire: A Witness in the Clinton Investigation.*

"Fuck him, Bill. He's Reagan's goddam Vice President!" Mrs. Clinton allegedly screamed. In another episode, when Brown showed Mrs. Clinton a photo of himself and Nancy Reagan standing together, Arkansas' then first lady was less than impressed. "You ought to burn that thing, L. D.," he recalls her urging. During a 1980s trip to Washington, D.C., Brown remembers taking a taxi with Hillary and daughter Chelsea on the way from the airport.

Passing the Reagan White House, the little girl begged to get a closer look. "Chelsea, we'll take a tour when someone decent lives there!" her mother shot back.[13]

CHAPTER SIX

Hillary's September 11 Scandalmongering

"I am simply here today on the floor of this hallowed chamber to seek answers to the questions being asked by my constituents, questions raised by one of our newspapers in New York with the headline 'Bush Knew.'"

—Hillary Clinton on the floor of the Senate

Those were the words of Senator Hillary Clinton on May 16, 2002, in the most dramatic and telling address she's given since taking office. Less than twenty-four hours earlier, the White House had been rocked by reports that the CIA had briefed President Bush at his Crawford, Texas, ranch, warning that Al Qaeda might turn to airplane hijacking as its next tactic. The date of that briefing, August 6, 2001, was less than five weeks before the terrorist group would kill 3,000 Americans on U.S. soil using the tactic the CIA warned Bush about.

"The president knew what?" Senator Clinton asked in accusatory tones. "My constituents would like to know the answer to that and many other questions, not to blame the president or any other American but just to know, to learn from experience, to do all we can today to ensure that a 9/11 never happens again."

Clinton claimed she wasn't pointing fingers, recalling her days in the crosshairs of investigators who accused the former first lady of masterminding one White House cover-up after another. Nevertheless, she couldn't resist hinting that the crucial news of the pre-September 11 CIA briefing was deliberately kept from Congress, the press, and ultimately, the American people. "Why [do] we know today, May 16, about the warning he received?" she asked her colleagues. "Why did we not know this on April 16 or March 16 or February or January 16 or August 16 of last year?" she complained.[1] Hours later Senator Clinton told reporters, "Clearly the public demands answers immediately. The people of New York deserve those answers more than anyone. I believe that getting the facts out would be the very best response to this troubling news."[2]

Mrs. Clinton's speech hit official Washington like a thunderbolt, ending for all intents and purposes the era of bipartisan cooperation that had characterized the early days of Washington's war on terrorism. The tumult arose not only because the secret Bush-CIA memo suggested that the White House had been less than candid about its advance knowledge of perhaps the darkest day in U.S. history, but also because the first lady of the previous administration was using it to cast aspersions. The White House might have been even more alarmed had it heard the speech delivered by Mrs. Clinton the next night, where she sounded less like a junior senator with no presidential ambitions—and more like a commander in chief in waiting.

Hillary as National Security Expert

Casting aside her usual agenda of health care issues and education concerns, Senator Clinton told a friendly audience gathered at a Long Island high school that, prompted by the September 11 attacks, her top priority had become national security. Her forty-five-minute address constituted, by any measure, a major policy address by the nation's most celebrated elected Democrat. And coming on the heels of her September 11 broadside at the White House, it should have received wide coverage. Yet only News Max.com covered the event—alerted to it by a local newspaper ad placed by the group sponsoring Clinton's visit. The speech was apparently listed nowhere on her public schedule.

"I see three very large challenges. First—national security," she told the Dix Hills, New York, audience. "Make no mistake about it," she explained. "Our adversaries are determined, they're ruthless and they are a continuing threat to us." After giving a synopsis of the United States' military progress in the war on terror thus far, the New York Democrat proclaimed, "We have made an extraordinary success of the initial operations in Afghanistan. And I'm extremely proud of our men and women in uniform."[3]

Clinton continued to dwell on military matters. "The national security challenge is one that is global in scope and encompasses not just the current battlefield in Afghanistan but serious threats throughout the world," she warned. "It is a different kind of war than any ever fought before." Saying she was drawing on her encounters with military personnel who served in her husband's administration, the senator noted, "This is a new kind of military mission. And we have to stay committed, we have to have patience and we have to be aware of the extraordinary dangers that they confront."

At one point Clinton even seemed to be borrowing a page from President Bush's "axis of evil" speech. "Our challenge is much more pervasive than it would be if we were just facing one enemy in one place. [But there's] the Middle East, Iraq, North Korea, Iran. There's a relatively long list that we believe are linked to the al-Qaeda network—in the Philippines, in Indonesia and in Yemen and other places. That makes it very clear that this is a global network."

Homeland security, Clinton told the crowd, was the second of the three challenges that were now a top priority. Omitting the 1993 World Trade Center bombing during her husband's administration, Clinton reminded the audience that Americans hadn't suffered an attack on U.S. soil since the War of 1812. She warned that things have changed. "We have to worry about our nuclear plants, our utilities, our chemical plants. We have to worry about our ports, our railroads, our tunnels, our bridges, our northern border with Canada," she explained. "I've been working very hard on this since 9-11," Clinton told the crowd, before declaring that the third big challenge America faces is everything else that was important before the 9/11 attacks.

Bush Speaks, Hillary Rolls Eyes

Though Republicans were enraged by Mrs. Clinton's attempts to make political hay out of Bush's sudden vulnerability on the war on terror, most bit their tongues. But some recalled Mrs. Clinton's reaction to Bush's watershed September 20 address to Congress, where he rallied a shaken nation and vowed that the deaths of 3,000 Americans would not go unavenged. The Bush speech drew rave reviews from even some of his harshest critics, a few of whom had complained only days before that the president had let the nation down on September 11 by flying to a secure location and staying out of sight. In contrast, New York Mayor Rudy Giuliani had offered updates on the disaster throughout the day in a performance that transformed him into a national hero.

Although many said Bush's September 20 address to Congress more than compensated for any perceived shortcomings early on in the crisis, Hillary Clinton's reaction, captured by TV cameras as she watched the Bush speech from the House chamber, betrayed a visceral level of disdain. As Bush rallied a still-stunned nation, Clinton was apparently unaware that cameras would be trained on her in an effort to gauge her response. As millions of Americans watched in rapt attention, hanging on Bush's every word, New York's junior senator rolled her eyes and looked generally bored by the whole presentation. She even remained seated as her colleagues gave the wartime president one standing ovation after another. It was a scene reminiscent of Vice President Al Gore's exaggerated sighing during his first debate with Bush, which was widely interpreted as a deliberate and thoroughly juvenile attempt to upstage and embarrass his GOP opponent.

Hillary Clinton's reaction, captured by TV cameras as she watched the Bush speech from the House chamber, betrayed a visceral level of disdain.

Though mainstream reporters generally gave Clinton a pass for her own sorry performance, her antics became fodder for talk radio hosts the next morning. "You know why she reacted that way," WABC's Curtis Sliwa told his partner Ron Kuby. "She just saw her hopes to run for president next time around go up in smoke." Nationally syndicated talker Don Imus was even harder on the former first lady. "She was disgraceful," Imus told his partner Charles McCord. "She looked irritable, rolling her eyes and talking." Imus didn't care much for Senator Clinton's post-speech comments either.

"I mean, she was going out of her way to point out how she'd spent the entire week down at Ground Zero, which is not true, by the way. But I think we know what that's all about." Then, with characteristic irreverence, Imus turned his ire toward Mrs. Clinton's husband.

"I just thank God that he's not still the president, that's all, because we didn't have to endure the self-aggrandizing display of lip-biting and head wagging and 'I love you' to some bimbo in the balcony."[4]

One Republican Reacts

While elected Republicans, along with the rest of the nation, were too caught up in the events of the moment to care much about Mrs. Clinton's carrying on, her remarks eight months later had at least one member of the GOP's Senate leadership seeing red.

A few days after her May 16 "Bush Knew" Senate floor speech, Oklahoma Senator Don Nickles, the number two Republican in the Senate, told his home-state newspaper the *Oklahoman* that Clinton's remarks had made him "furious." "If we're going to have an investigation, we should have an investigation of why we didn't respond strongly to previous acts of terror," he added, in what sounded like a warning shot fired across Clinton's bow. "I'm pretty critical of the previous administration," the top Republican explained. "They dropped the ball in the war on terrorism. They never engaged in the war on terrorism."

As he talked, Nickles displayed previously prepared charts listing five terrorist attacks on the United States during the Clinton administration, not counting the Oklahoma City bombing. Juxtaposed with the charts' graphics, the Oklahoma conservative inserted quotes from President Clinton promising a strong and forceful response. But, said Nickles, those promises were never followed by effective action.

"We didn't do anything about it," he complained.[5]

Still, even though a top Senate Republican had threatened to make the Clinton administration the focus of the then upcoming September 11 congressional probe by the House and Senate Intelligence Committees, coverage of Nickles's remarks was confined to his home-state newspaper.

Scandalmongering Old Hat

Of course, those familiar with Mrs. Clinton's style of no-holds-barred political attacks weren't particularly surprised that she was the first to attempt to make political hay over a potential September 11 blunder by Bush. In fact, years of digging up dirt on witnesses against her husband laid the groundwork for some of Mrs. Clinton's most devastating attacks on her New York Senate campaign opponents.

Surprisingly little has been written about what appears to be on its face, one of the Clinton administration's most outrageous abuses of power, one that mirrors Mrs. Clinton's penchant, during her days in Arkansas, for hiring private detectives to silence her husband's sex accusers. However, the relentless use of the Justice Department, the Internal Revenue Service, and other federal investigative agencies by the Clinton White House to go after critics, witnesses, and even election rivals was probably unequaled by any other administration in U.S. history.

Even more startling: the media's virtual silence on this phenomenon through two Clinton terms in office, a trend that continues even as the former first lady has moved to the front of the field of 2004 presidential hopefuls in survey after survey. But with the Clintons mapping out strategy to retake the White House sometime this decade, it's worth reviewing how Senator Clinton used the investigative powers of the executive branch to further her own political interests.

Hillary's Investigators Probe Lazio

Mrs. Clinton's Senate opponent Rick Lazio told me that the probe into his personal investments launched by Securities and Exchange Commissioner Arthur Levitt was "the emotional low point of the campaign for me." The episode began in June, just a month after the Long Island congressman replaced Rudy Giuliani in the race against Clinton. Starting with the *New York Times,* which broke the story, conveniently for Mrs. Clinton, on the day Independent Counsel Robert Ray announced that she had testified falsely in the Travelgate scandal,[6] media reports swirled about Lazio's relatively minor investment in the

Long Island investment house Quick & Reilly. In 1997, the GOP hopeful had purchased $2,300 in Quick & Reilly stock options. A month later the firm was purchased by the Boston-based Fleet Financial Group for $1.6 billion. That same day Lazio cashed in his chips for nearly $16,000, netting a $13,700 profit.[7] Finally Lazio was forced to announce that he was being "informally investigated" by the Clinton SEC. CNN financial expert Lou Dobbs would later note that Levitt's SEC somehow managed to miss the multibillion-dollar accounting scandal that was brewing at the time at Enron, as well as the financial malfeasance of other major corporate giants, while it was busy looking into Lazio's puny profits.[8]

While most of the press smelled a rat in the Lazio probe, few said so out loud. One exception was *Crane's New York Business Weekly,* which noted the Clinton administration's penchant for launching investigations that would help the first lady's Senate bid. "Last week, as quietly as possible, the federal Bureau of Labor Statistics ended its investigation of whether the [New York Governor George] Pataki administration had inflated employment statistics to make it appear that the state's economy was doing better than it actually was. The figures, said the BLS, were in fact correct.

"What is important about this is that the charge had originated with Democrats linked to Hillary Rodham Clinton's campaign. It was leveled just as the status of the upstate economy emerged as an issue in the Senate race between Mrs. Clinton and Rep. Rick Lazio. It's also worth noting that *The New York Times,* which broke the story about the allegedly false data, has yet to report that the charge was found to be utterly baseless."[9]

> "The way supposedly independent agencies of the federal government have been enlisted in the Hillary Clinton campaign . . . says a great deal about Mrs. Clinton."
>
> —Crane's New York Business Weekly

The paper went on to complain that Lazio had also been similarly victimized by the SEC probe into his Quick & Reilly profits before noting: "The way supposedly independent agencies of the federal government have been enlisted in the Hillary Clinton campaign, all on the basis of false and misleading reports aired in *The New York Times,* says a great deal about Mrs. Clinton. It also gives great credence to the trust issue that Mr. Lazio has justly made the centerpiece of his campaign."

By August the SEC had determined that Lazio had done nothing wrong. But the damage was done. The Republican candidate had been forced to spend weeks on defense, diverting precious campaign resources to respond to the Clinton campaign's efforts to create a completely bogus scandal. Predictably, after Lazio's exoneration, there were no *New York Times* editorials decrying the outrageous and obvious attempt to discredit and intimidate someone who was not merely a political rival—but also a player in the most widely watched political race other than the presidency in the year 2000.

Perhaps more frightening still, the GOP Congress, weary from eight years of nonstop Clinton investigations, said and did nothing. In the House, Speaker Dennis Hastert and his Senate counterpart Trent Lott had basically decided that after the impeachment of Bill Clinton, efforts to check executive branch abuses of power via Congress's constitutionally mandated oversight authority were pretty much a waste of time.

Probing Giuliani

Even before the Lazio and Pataki episodes, Mrs. Clinton had signaled she was willing to bring the full authority of the executive branch down hard on her opponents. In early 1999, only weeks after the shooting by New York City police officers of unarmed African immigrant Amadou Diallo, President Clinton decided to make police brutality the subject of his weekly radio address.

"I have been deeply disturbed by recent allegations of serious police misconduct and continued reports of racial profiling that have shaken some communities' faith in the police," Clinton noted. "While each specific allegation will have to be dealt with on its own merits, it is clear that we need a renewed determination as a nation to restore those bonds of trust."[10]

The president's comments came as Mrs. Clinton was gearing up for her "listening tour," a march across New York that would determine, she said, whether she would enter the Senate race against Rudy Giuliani. In his address, Mr. Clinton outlined a federal program to combat racial profiling and to increase police recruitment of minorities. The next day the *New York Post* covered his remarks under the headline, "Prez: I'll restore your faith in cops."[11] A few days later, Dick Morris wrote in his *Post* column that the new Clinton program amounted to "an $87 million contribution to Hillary's campaign."[12]

Pressure on Giuliani over the Diallo case grew throughout the spring and summer of 1999, with daily protests at NYPD headquarters led by Al Sharpton and his allies. In March 2000, when an Albany jury acquitted the four officers involved in the shooting of manslaughter charges, the Diallo family requested that the Justice Department review the case.

Then, in mid-March 2000, Patrick Dorismond, an unarmed black man who worked in Manhattan as a security guard, was approached outside a midtown bar by undercover cops who suspected he was a drug dealer. Angered by the presumption, Dorismond got into a struggle and was shot to death. Anxious to defend the police against another Diallo-like feeding frenzy, Giuliani released Dorismond's sealed juvenile arrest record, which showed that the dead man was, in the mayor's words, "no altar boy."

The Clinton campaign wasted no time making hay over Giuliani's attempts to defend the police. As the city's tabloids blared headlines about the case on a daily basis, Mrs. Clinton traveled to Harlem to fire a particularly toxic salvo. "I do not believe bad relations with the police are necessary to keep our streets safe," the Senate candidate told a crowd of 1,100 that had gathered at the Bethel AME church. "The Mayor has hunkered down, taken sides and further divided the city and growing, mistrust makes it harder to keep all of us safe."

Clinton continued, "We need someone who will work for reconciliation, not retribution. We need someone who will lift up, not put down. . . . There are many police officers in this city who want badly to work with the community, but they are caught up within the Mayor's policies." Clinton concluded, "We must all bridge the chasm of mistrust. We all know it, except the Mayor of New York."

"I haven't seen anything like this since the Civil Rights Movement. . . . Rosa Parks may not be here today, but we have someone who can now drive us [to] freedom."

—Rep. Charles Rangel praising Hillary Clinton

Among the dignitaries in the audience was Harlem congressman Charlie Rangel, who told reporters afterward, "I haven't seen anything like this since the Civil Rights Movement. . . . Rosa Parks may not be here today, but we have someone who can now drive us [to] freedom."[13]

Within days Rangel was off to Washington, along with fellow congressman Jerrold Nadler to meet with Attorney General Janet Reno's top deputy Eric Holder. Echoing the Diallo family's request for a federal review of NYPD shooting and brutality cases, Rangel and Nadler wanted something else: They wanted Giuliani and his then police commissioner Howard Safir to be investigated as well. The Democratic duo told reporters after the meeting that Holder had assured them that Giuliani's decision to release Dorismond's records would be part of the federal probe.[14] In the meantime, Reverend Sharpton was calling for a full federal takeover of the NYPD.

Giuliani reacted angrily to calls for federal intervention. "I didn't see the Justice Department in 1993, when there were 212 intentional shootings, investigating the NYPD during an election year for David Dinkins. Or giving me and Police Commissioner Howard Safir and the police a commendation for having reduced that horrendous intentional shooting record by 77 percent. The NYPD has a better record for restraint than they do for crime reduction. . . . The Justice Department should be giving them an award," concluded the mayor, "not an investigation."[15]

Trashing Giuliani's Success

The heavy-handed calls for Clinton administration intervention were particularly audacious in light of the mayor's astonishingly successful record of reducing the city's skyrocketing crime rate. In fact, Giuliani's war on crime was not only the greatest success of his two terms in office, leading the way to a New York City renaissance and reversing decades of middle-class flight, but it was also the crown jewel in what members of the Clinton administration regularly boasted was one of their most significant achievements.

Mr. Clinton, had, after all, run for president as a tough-on-crime New Democrat. So when FBI statistics showed the crime rate plummeting nationwide, the Clintonistas naturally claimed full credit. But the crime drop in New York was far and away the deepest of any major city in the country, and made the national statistics look substantially better than they would have without the mayor's success. The city's murder rate, for instance, dropped by two-thirds under Giuliani, from a peak of nearly 2,100 murders in the early 1990s to just over 600 by 2000. Meanwhile, nationwide, the rate dropped from 41 per 100,000 to 32 per 100,000, a 28 percent decline. Reporters who fell for the Clintons' line that the Diallo and Dorismond cases showed somehow that Giuliani was out of control might have pondered the murder rate in Arkansas with the Clintons at the helm. From 1983 to 1992, the state murder rate had exploded by nearly 50 percent.[16]

For a press corps weaned on Watergate, the politicization of the federal government's powers of investigation should have set off smoke alarms. But while every twist and turn of the Lazio and Giuliani "scandals" was dutifully covered in the press, reporters never made much of an effort to explain the bigger picture. The sense that Mrs. Clinton was using her husband's executive branch authority to dirty-up her opponents was lost in the daily hustle and bustle of the campaign.

Compounding the problem, Lazio and Giuliani did what Republicans usually do when targeted by Clinton investigators. They complained once or twice—but quickly moved on to "issues of substance" when the press didn't go after the story on its own.

The entire episode recalled former Senate majority leader Bob Dole's complaint: As the Clinton scandals piled up during his own 1996 White House bid, Dole complained bitterly to audiences, "Where's the outrage?" But Dole never explained exactly what Americans should be outraged about. Later, while facing off with Mr. Clinton during one presidential debate, Dole boasted proudly that he'd made no attempt to make an issue out of the Paula Jones case, never realizing, of course, that he was taking a pass on the scandal that would later lead to Clinton's impeachment. Handlers for Lazio and Giuliani learned little from the Dole debacle, staying firmly on the defensive rather than demanding an investigation into how and why the full force of the federal government was suddenly being arrayed against them.

CHAPTER SEVEN

Hillary's Temper

"When you show up in the Senate, you can't hire, fire, and insult your colleagues if you don't get along with them."
—Hillary Clinton complaining about
Rudy Giuliani during her 1999 listening tour

It was more than a little odd that Hillary Clinton's earliest Senate campaign attacks on New York City Mayor Rudy Giuliani centered on his temperament. He was too abrasive, she said. He didn't work well with others. His bull-in-the-china-shop style wouldn't fit into the refined and respectful atmosphere of the Senate, where protocol, deference, and senatorial courtesy supposedly reined.

"He gets angry quite often," Mrs. Clinton said in December 1999, referring to her then Senate opponent's sharp reaction to the decision by the Clinton housing department to co-opt $60 million in city funding for the homeless. "I can't be responding every time the Mayor gets angry about something because that's all I would do."[1] While candidate Hillary pounded away at the notion that Giuliani was too hot-tempered to effectively represent New York in the Senate, the establishment press dutifully reported her every word—without, of course, noting her own track record in the temper department.

"She is angry. Not all of the time. But most of the time," wrote a usually sympathetic Gail Sheehy in her Clinton biography, *Hillary's Choice,* which was released just a few months before the first lady began zeroing in on Giuliani's temper.[2] The reference was to Sheehy's first impression of Mrs. Clinton, after spending time with her right after the first couple's triumphant 1992 appearance on *60 Minutes*.

Longtime Hillary aide Carolyn Huber, who saved Mrs. Clinton's buns in 1996 with a convenient cover story about how her mysterious Rose Law Firm billing records magically appeared in the White House book room, described the former first lady's fits of rage to Sheehy as nearly lethal. "The person on the receiving end never gets over it," Huber remembered, reportedly shivering as she spoke those words.[3] Another former Clinton adviser revealed anonymously that Mrs. Clinton "is in a perpetual state of suspended anger because of all that she has absorbed."

Others have also noted Mrs. Clinton's rages, though the New York press declined to revisit their accounts during her Senate race. During her husband's 1992 campaign, Mrs. Clinton once got so mad she threw a briefing book at her husband while the first couple was being chauffeured to church, according to retired Secret Service agent William Bell, who revealed the incident to investigative reporter Ron Kessler in his 1995 best-seller *Inside the White House.* According to Bell she missed, hitting their Secret Service driver instead.[4]

Angry Profanity

The rages continued even after Mrs. Clinton took up residence in the White House, where she blew up at a Secret Service agent for declining to carry her bags. When the agent explained that he needed to keep his hands free in order to protect her, she replied, "If you want to remain on this detail, get your fucking ass over here and grab those bags."[5]

According to investigative reporter Richard Gooding, who broke the story of Dick Morris's fling with a hooker in 1996 for the supermarket tabloid *Star,* Mrs. Clinton became so abusive during her husband's impeachment that Secret Service agents strongly considered filing a formal complaint. "*Star* has learned that on nearly a dozen occasions in the last three months, Hillary has viciously lashed out at numerous Secret Service agents for getting in her way—or for simply doing their jobs. . . . A young Secret Service officer stationed at the South Portico says he did nothing more than smile and say, 'Good morning, Mrs. Clinton.' Mrs. Clinton brushed by him, actually shoving him out of her way, an informed source tells *Star.* As she did, she snapped at him and cursed, 'Get f——d!'"

"That officer made a report of Mrs. Clinton's behavior to his superiors and *Star* has learned that about 10 other similarly ugly incidents have also been reported in recent months. In other cases she is reported to have said such things as: 'Get the f—— out of my way!' Or, 'Get out of my face!'"[6]

The late Barbara Olson offered perhaps the most intriguing report of Hillary's volatile temper, one that showed no deference to rank or age. "It was she whose obsession with secrecy was so intense," revealed Olson in her 1999 book *Hell to Pay,* "that when White House counsel and former judge Abner Mikva finally bowed to the law and delivered subpoenaed documents, she and her White House scandal team lashed at him with such a vicious streak of profanity that he resigned."[7]

Clinton Press Secretary Confirms Temper Tantrums

Even ostensible allies, like former Clinton press secretary Dee Dee Myers, confirm Hillary Clinton's penchant for scorching tirades, in an equally revealing account that showed that even Mr. Clinton's top aides weren't spared from her explosive attacks. Gathering her recollections for a PBS documentary marking the end of the Clinton administration, Myers recalled the internal administration debate in 1994 over how to handle the then burgeoning Whitewater inquiry.

Myers, George Stephanopoulos, and several others in the meeting favored turning all documents from the Clintons' controversial land deal over to the *Washington Post.* But when Hillary entered the room and demanded to know what was going on, everybody "clammed up." "Mrs. Clinton wanted to know what was going on and she looked at George," Myers said. "And George began to make the argument that we'd all been making and nobody backed him up. Nobody backed him up. Everyone just sat there and let George take the beating, you know."

"And Mrs. Clinton got really angry," remembered Myers. "She attacked George, which everyone knew was coming, which is why I guess nobody was willing to ride in there to the rescue. . . . Here were 12 people in the room who all basically agreed and only one of them was willing to stand up and tell her what she had asked. And that took a lot of courage."[8]

"The president didn't really attack people personally, Mrs. Clinton sometimes did."
—*former Clinton press secretary Dee Dee Myers*

Myers told PBS that Hillary's penchant for personal attacks could be devastating for anyone on the receiving end. "Anybody that stood up and tried to say this was a bad idea was, you know, smashed down and belittled, very personally," the Clinton loyalist revealed. "And I mean where I said the president didn't really attack people personally, Mrs. Clinton sometimes did. . . . not only would she sort of humiliate you in front of your colleagues or whoever happened to be around," Myers said, "Hillary tended to kind of campaign against people behind their back, and that was certainly my experience."

Hillary Screams at Senate Colleague

Throughout her 2000 Senate campaign the press kept Hillary's secret for her, never delving into past accounts of her abusive treatment of both peers and underlings. And even when she exploded at a fellow senator, no one in the media saw it as part of a pattern. In a July 2002 incident, Clinton blew a gasket during a closed-door Senate meeting, shouting at campaign-finance–reform crusader Senator Russ Feingold, D-Wis., in an embarrassing scene that broke all rules of Senate collegiality and decorum. The former first lady unleashed her notorious temper after Democratic Party campaign lawyer Bob Bauer warned senators that the kind of fund-raising tactics Democrats had relied on in past elections could send them to jail under the recently passed McCain-Feingold campaign finance law.

When Feingold rose to address the issue, he made the mistake of dismissing the warning, prompting Clinton to "scream," according to the *New York Daily News,* "Russ, live in the real world! . . . They will be all over you like a June bug."

Feingold shot back, "I also live in the real world, Senator, and I function quite well in it."[9]

Because it involved another senator in a debate about an important policy issue, this time the press decided to lift the veil on Clinton's outburst. A day later she privately offered her apologies to the Wisconsin Democrat.

"Fucking Jew Bastard"

Only once during her Senate campaign did Hillary's notoriously nasty temper ever draw significant media attention. But when it did, the Clinton campaign went immediately to DEFCON3 damage-control status.

The controversy over whether Hillary Clinton had ever called a campaign aide a "fucking Jew bastard" is revealing on a number of levels, not the least of which was the desperate efforts by news editors to see that the story never reached a mass audience. In fact, months before the news exploded at the height of her Senate campaign, the accusers, Paul Fray and his wife Mary Lee, had revealed the toxic tidbit to at least two mainstream reporters. But they promptly deep-sixed the news. A third source who made similar claims about the first lady to NewsMax nearly a year earlier was completely ignored by the mainstream press.

The claim that a sitting first lady had used the vile ethnic slur was buried deep inside the pages of *State of a Union: Inside the Complex Marriage of Bill and Hillary Clinton,* by veteran author and one-time *National Enquirer* reporter Jerry Oppenheimer. In contrast to other much-ballyhooed Clinton books, this one got almost no advance publicity. But *Union* turned out to have perhaps the biggest political impact of any book of its genre.

"BOOK CHARGES: HILLARY CALLED AIDE 'JEW BASTARD,'" blared the "Drudge Report" headline on July 14, 2000. "In one particularly shocking passage in the book, Oppenheimer quotes a campaign official who describes an angry attack by Hillary in which she screams at him, 'You fucking Jew bastard!' Two sourced eyewitnesses confirmed to Oppenheimer that they heard the verbal assault."

In the ensuing days, three more witnesses to the ethnic slur—or other incidents like it—came forward with damning accounts. It was, far and away, the most intense moment of the campaign and the only one that offered Republican Senate hopeful Rick Lazio a chance to defeat Hillary. A week after the charge surfaced, Lazio was leading Clinton by 7 points, according to a *New York Post* poll—the only time he held a lead greater than a poll's margin of error during the entire campaign.

The now legendary confrontation with Clinton campaign manager Paul Fray took place in 1974 on election night. With the election returns showing that the future president was going to lose his first bid for office against Representative John Paul Hammerschmidt, the mood at Clinton campaign headquarters had deteriorated into recriminations. Hillary had not yet married Bill, but she had ended her stint on the Senate Watergate committee just three months earlier to work with him in Arkansas. Defeating Hammerschmidt would mean she'd get an early reprieve from having to take up residence in Arkansas, a place she despised. But as the final returns trickled in, it became clear that Hillary wouldn't be living the glamorous life of a congressman's wife in Washington anytime soon.

"By three A.M. it was all over," Oppenheimer reported. "Clinton had lost by a mere six thousand votes. He, Hillary and Fray went back to Fayetteville in their cars. . . . The minute Paul walked into the back room at the Fayetteville headquarters that night, Hillary hit him between the eyes. She was angrier than Paul had ever seen her. 'You fucking Jew bastard!' she screamed."[10]

> "Hillary hit him between the eyes. She was angrier than Paul had ever seen her. 'You fucking Jew bastard!' she screamed."
>
> *—author Jerry Oppenheimer quoting campaign aide Paul Fray*

The accusation would have been easy enough to deflect if it had been merely Hillary's word against Fray's. But this time there were at least two other witnesses who heard the outburst and two more from the Clintons' past who remembered similar outbursts. It mattered not that Mr. Fray was not Jewish. His father was Jewish and the younger Fray was very proud of his roots.

Witnesses Attacked

Still, within days, the Democratic Party and its media handmaidens began circling the wagons around Mrs. Clinton. At a dramatic press conference on the front lawn of her Chappaqua mansion, Hillary vehemently denied the charge. Taking their cue from Clinton spinmeisters, the press joined in the effort to discredit three of the five witnesses against her.

Fray, the Clinton's crack dirt-diggers immediately learned, had been disbarred for altering court records and suffered from memory loss due to a brain hemorrhage. And Neil McDonald, who told Oppenheimer that he'd heard the slur while listening outside the door, was smeared by President Clinton personally as a business failure who had to move to Dallas to work for his brother because "no one else would hire him."

"I was there and [Hillary] never said it," Clinton insisted in a call to the *New York Daily News.* It was a risky strategy. Up till now, only the New York tabloids had covered the story, while the so-called respectable press, not wanting to give credence to yet another set of whistleblowers from the Clintons backwoods past, stuck their heads in the sand and hoped the storm would pass. But Clinton's personal testimonial on his wife's behalf forced even the *New York Times* to report the incident, though *Times*' editors declined to print the slur verbatim. "In 29 years, my wife has never, ever uttered an ethnic or racial slur against anybody, ever," the president protested. "She's so straight on this, she squeaks."[11]

However, Mr. Clinton did concede that Fray might have got part of the epithet right. "She might have called him a bastard," he explained to the *News.* "I wouldn't rule that out. She's never claimed that she was pure on profanity. But I've never heard her tell a joke with an ethnic connotation. She's so fanatic about it. She can't tell an ethnic joke. It's not in her."

While the first family succeeded in raising questions about Mr. Fray's credibility, his wife, Mary Lee, who also claimed to have witnessed Hillary's outburst, remained a problem. "[She] went after him for losing," Mrs. Fray told the *News.* "Paul was not an Ivy League person. She could've called him a redneck or any putdown. She chose that, and it was unfortunate." And there was more.

Not the Only Ethnic Slur

Even before the Frays' account appeared in print, Arkansas state trooper Larry Patterson, a thirty-two-year law enforcement veteran who helped guard the Clintons from 1986 until they left for the White House, had told a similar story.

"It was fairly common for both [Clintons] to tell ethnic jokes and use ethnic slurs about Jews," Patterson told NewsMax.com in 1999. When asked for the exact words, the trooper responded, "Jew Motherf—— r, Jew Bastard." Patterson later told WABC Radio in New York, "If she disagreed with Bill Clinton or she disagreed with some of the Jewish community in Little Rock—or some of the ethnic community—she would often make these statements."[12] And Dick Morris, the Clinton insider whom Hillary had summoned time and again to rescue her husband's career, offered another revealing anecdote.

"I'm Jewish," he told Fox News Channel's "Hannity & Colmes" in November 1999. "And I would often go to the governor's mansion and I would often have dinner with them. And it was kind of a joke. Every time before dinner, Hillary would take me aside and say, 'Dick, I'm sorry. We're having pork. I just wasn't thinking about it.' And I would say, 'It's OK, Hillary, I don't mind pork.' And the third and the fourth time, I finally said, 'You've asked me this four times. I eat pork. I like pork.' So we joked about it, we kidded about it."[13]

Morris continued: "Then about a year later, I was having a meeting in the breakfast room in the governor's mansion with Betsey [Wright, Clinton's then chief of staff], Hillary, Bill and me. And Bill and I were fighting about my fee. I was pushing for more money. . . . And Hillary was upset because of the limited income they had to live with and that I was making so much money from their campaign. And she was getting really annoyed at me for the battle. And she exploded in anger and I'll just quote her.

"She said, 'That's all you people care about is money!' And I backed up. And I said, 'Hillary, I assume by "you people," you mean political consultants.' And she said, 'Yeah, yeah, that's what I meant, political consultants.'"

> "She said, 'That's all you people care about is money!' And I backed up. And I said, 'Hillary, I assume by "you people," you mean political consultants.'"
>
> —*Dick Morris*

Perhaps as important as Morris's story was his revelation that he'd shared the anecdote with Hillary biographer Gail Sheehy for her then upcoming biography, *Hillary's Choice*. But when the Sheehy book came out, the Morris "you people" story about Mrs. Clinton's money complaint was nowhere to be found.

Previous FJB Reports Quashed

Three days after Fray's allegation exploded, NBC White House correspondent Andrea Mitchell admitted that the old Arkansas political hand had recounted the incident, including the dynamite charge about Hillary's anti-Semitic slur, during a 1999 interview for the network's *Dateline NBC* program. But NBC News editors decided to kill the bombshell report because they doubted Fray's credibility, Mitchell claimed.[14] Still, since Fray's wife Mary Lee was also a witness to Mrs. Clinton's outburst, it doesn't appear that Mitchell or her colleagues tried very hard to confirm the story.

Mary Lee Fray shared the blockbuster allegation with Sheehy for her Hillary book. But the author, who has enjoyed special access to Mrs. Clinton over the years, decided not to report the toxic charge. She told *Newsday* that since Mr. Fray hadn't volunteered his account of the incident during her own conversation with him, the charge was suspect. Evidently the author decided it wasn't worth a second call to Fray to see if his wife's story checked out—even though Morris's "you people" anecdote would have had any good reporter's antenna up for just such a corroborating tidbit.

The media's obliging indulgence in covering up even the most well corroborated allegations has been the key ingredient in the Clintons' rise to power and will be indispensable when Hillary makes her bid to reclaim the White House.

CHAPTER EIGHT

Hillary and the Jews, the Arabs, and Osama

"I don't believe she said it,
and if she said it 26 years ago, so what?"
—Ed Koch, former mayor of New York City,
reacting to reports that Hillary Clinton had
once called a campaign aide a "fucking Jew bastard"

As a general rule of thumb in New York politics, no Democratic candidate can win statewide office without at least 65 percent of the Jewish vote. So it's a measure of Clinton's damage control instincts, honed through twenty years of scandal management in Arkansas and Washington, that she managed to win her Senate seat by a landslide that included a mere 53 percent of the Jewish vote.[1]

Multiple allegations that Mrs. Clinton had used an ugly anti-Semitic epithet shook her Senate campaign to its core and might have forced a lesser candidate to withdraw from the race. But within days of the allegations exploding onto the media's radar screen, a number of prominent Jewish Democrats announced that, in essence, it didn't matter. Even if they didn't believe her denials, it didn't mean she was an anti-Semite. "I don't believe she said it, and if she said it 26 years ago, so what?" former New York City Mayor Ed Koch told the *New York Post*.[2] While Koch counts his own Jewishness as one of the things about which he's most proud, he saw no incongruity in defending Mrs. Clinton, even assuming she was guilty as charged. "Did she say it yesterday?" he complained. "There must be a statute of limitations."

Anti-Defamation League head Abe Foxman, who can usually be counted on to react with outrage at the slightest hint of anti-Semitism, also decided to cut Mrs. Clinton a country mile worth of slack. "If in fact she said it, that does not make her an anti-Semite, because there is a public record of Hillary Rodham Clinton of the past 26 years which has no iota of anti-Semitism," he told reporters.[3]

Even Clinton's opponent Rick Lazio, who suddenly found himself with a 7-point lead over Clinton after two weeks of the controversy, declined to overtly capitalize on what turned out to be his last chance to beat the then first lady. After initially telling reporters he didn't know whether to believe the story or not, Lazio even declined to attribute his breakout in the polls to the brewing brouhaha. "I can't really say. I don't know," he explained to NewsMax, when asked why Mrs. Clinton's Jewish support had suddenly taken a disastrous 12-point decline to less than 50 percent. "All I know is that we had two good appearances this weekend in front of synagogues, one Reform, one sort of eclectic, out on the east end of Long Island. And our reception at both was very, very good." Rather than credit Mrs. Clinton's alleged epithet, Lazio attributed his abrupt success to his reputation for moderation, saying, "I think people respond to a mainstream record."[4]

The rising GOP star, who had built something of a reputation as a giant-slayer with his surprise 1994 win over Long

Island Democrat Tom Downey, had adopted the tried-and-true political strategy: Never interfere with an opponent in the process of self-destructing. But like too many Republicans, Lazio's advisers failed to appreciate that the tactic works only for Democrats, who can count on the press to keep ginning up new angles on even the most tepid and stale revelation.

What's more, despite Clinton's reputation as a ruthless political street fighter, Lazio hadn't anticipated the lengths to which the Hillary 2000 campaign was willing to go to tarnish his image. "We certainly tried to run a high road campaign," Lazio told NewsMax two years after he went up against the Clintons. "And they had a campaign that was reflective of the guy who was really developing their field operation, Harold Ickes. That was not the kind of person who reflected our kind of values in the campaign. So, they were capable of doing a whole litany of things that we wouldn't even imagine—and then deny, by the way."[5]

Hillary's Hardball Players

In fact, the mere presence of Ickes should have been a major public relations liability for the Clinton campaign. Denied an appointment as President Clinton's chief of staff because his past associations with suspect union activities rendered him unlikely to survive Senate confirmation, Ickes performed all manner of political dirty work for the White House.[6]

Fresh from a Senate Whitewater Committee criminal referral that recommended he be probed by the Justice Department for possible perjury in his own testimony, Ickes almost immediately cropped up as a central figure in Clinton's campaign finance scandal.

But perhaps the episode that tells the most about the son of a top aide to President Franklin Roosevelt had nothing to do with the Clintons. There is, for instance, the often alluded to—but seldom detailed—incident where a young Ickes is said to have actually bitten another political operative during a particularly nasty disagreement. James Vlasto, now a New York City public relations executive, remembered the attack of more than a quarter century ago vividly, in an account to the Associated Press offered during the height of Senator Clinton's campaign. "I was working with him on a 1973 New York mayoral campaign when he got into a knockdown fight with the campaign manager," Vlasto said in June 1999.[7] "I tried to break it up and that's when he bit me. It wasn't a soft bite either." Vlasto said he disinfected the wound by pouring vodka on it. Tellingly, though the Associated Press found Ickes' Mike Tyson–like behavior newsworthy enough to report, not a single New York City daily decided to pick up the story.

The kind of hardball tactics practiced by Mrs. Clinton's campaign became apparent when the Securities and Exchange Commission in her husband's administration announced that it was launching an investigation into Lazio's investments. More than two years later, the former New York congressman believes the probe was entirely political. "Absolutely," he told NewsMax. "[New York State Comptroller and Hillary ally] Carl McCall wrote, among all the other letters he wrote for jobs for his family, this was a letter that he wrote [to the SEC] that they were clearly behind. . . . There was absolutely no basis for [the SEC probe]. None."

Lazio explained that the Clinton SEC "did a thorough review and they found that there was no basis to believe that there was anything but a proper investment." He added, "We're talking about all of, whatever it was, less than $10,000, I think. That's, again, reflective of the [Hillary-Ickes team's] personal hardball tactics."[8] Obviously still stung by Mrs. Clinton's scorched earth campaign style, Lazio complained, "The thing that's disturbing about it is that there's just no limit. There's no sense of conscience about what kind of impact it has on decent people and their families and the people that are close to them. And so they're capable [of] doing just about anything to win."

That same commitment to win at all costs had allowed President Clinton to survive a yearlong sex scandal that exposed him as a perjurer and sexual predator—and it would see his wife through the revelation of her anti-Semitic slur.

"Fucking Jew Bastard" Damage Control

A week after Paul Fray's allegations hit the press, Adam Dickter, a reporter for the *Jewish Forward,* exposed one of the Clinton campaign's more heavy-handed attempts at damage control. Dickter got his hands on a copy of a memo sent to Clinton's "Jewish Advisory Committee" by campaign aide Karen Adler, which included talking points on how to trash Fray; his wife, Mary Lee; and Neil McDonald—the three witnesses to Hillary's 1974 anti-Semitic epithet.

While there was nothing particularly unusual about the talking points, distributed to Jewish friends and acquaintances of Mrs. Clinton with instructions to contact the media on her behalf, this particular memo came with a troubling disclaimer. "It is important that you do not say you are calling because the campaign asked you to, but because you are outraged with what was said about her. . . . The most important thing is to let them know that you know Hillary and you know that she would never make these kinds of anti-Semitic or racist comments." Mrs. Clinton, in other words, was asking her Jewish supporters to cover up on her behalf in order to help tamp down the burgeoning scandal.

"I received seven or eight phone calls from people saying that they wanted to go on the record on this subject," Dickter told WABC Radio. He said he found the rapid succession of the messages left on his answering machine . . . "suspicious."[9] "They were all within a few minutes. And mostly from people I don't usually hear from." One of those people was Senator Charles Schumer, whose office confirmed to NY1 News that Hillary's campaign called to warn Schumer that Dickter was working on a story about Mrs. Clinton's outburst. "I've known Hillary Clinton now for eight years," Schumer told reporters after he got the memo—but before it was exposed. "She does not have an anti-Semitic thought or an anti-Semitic bone in her body." Schumer was one of eight Jewish Democratic lawmakers who held a news conference at the Democratic National Committee to support Mrs. Clinton that afternoon.

Of the Clinton strategy to deceive reporters, Dickter said, "It probably wasn't a smart move. . . . The picture that comes out of it is that of being very, very concerned about the impression being left by the alleged slur, and frankly, the appearance of not having confidence that people would take [Hillary's denials] at face value."

> "It is important that you do not say you are calling because the campaign asked you to, but because you are outraged with what was said about her."
>
> *—an unidentified Hillary 2000 campaign aide*

Despite intriguing developments like Dickter's exposé, the story began to fade as media outrage subsided and Republicans failed to complain. Trooper Patterson, for instance, who estimated he'd heard Hillary use anti-Semitic slurs on up to twenty different occasions, was ignored by both the national and state Republican Party. And though his earlier accounts of Bill Clinton's womanizing had been confirmed in spades with the tidal wave of revelations that accompanied the Paula Jones and Monica Lewinsky scandals, even the conservative press declined to cover his story of racial slurs. Patterson did get wide exposure on talk radio and on the Fox News Channel, but in those venues he was largely preaching to the converted, audiences that were already predisposed to vote against Mrs. Clinton.

Dick Morris, who had been the object of much media fascination when he emerged from the shadows in early 1996 as Bill Clinton's top political adviser, was likewise ignored by the major media when he came forward with his own revelation suggesting Mrs. Clinton might have betrayed her anti-Semitism when she complained about his request for a raise with the retort, "That's all you people care about is money!"

In the end, most in the media decided to apply the same standards to the anti-Semitic allegations that they had to all other Clinton scandals. Without DNA evidence or videotape, Mr. Clinton had always been let off the hook before. "Why should the standard be any different for his wife?" the reasoning went. Besides, Senator Schumer, who is Jewish himself, had already given Hillary a kind of backhanded inoculation against suspicions that she was less-than-friendly toward the Jews. Two weeks before the anti-Semitic allegations broke, Schumer addressed a Woodmere, New York, audience rampant with worries that Hillary couldn't be trusted to vote the right way on Israel. Schumer observed, "I believe that Hillary Rodham Clinton will vote whatever her feelings are and I think that will be better than you think. But my guess is she will vote exactly as I do on Jewish issues. She will look to me to see how to vote."[10]

If Schumer had indeed secured Hillary's word on the "vote as I do" pledge, it constituted quite an abdication. One of the first lady's staunchest supporters had just admitted that Jews couldn't trust her judgment when it came to representing the state with more Jews than any other in the nation.

Hillary and the Arabs

"She leans very closely towards the Arabs, and that is very dangerous." Those were the words of former Israeli prime minister Yitzhak Shamir, as quoted by the *Jewish Press* in early July 2000, even before news of the anti-Semitic allegations broke. "I view Hillary Clinton as a great danger to Jews if she is elected," Shamir had also added, in remarks that went virtually unreported by the mainstream press, even though, according to the *New York Daily News,* they were "circulating widely in the state's heavily populated Jewish communities."[11] Shamir's warning against Clinton was particularly unusual, since foreign leaders—even former ones—are usually loath to meddle in U.S. elections. In fact, what made Paul Fray's charges that Hillary was no stranger to anti-Semitic epithets particularly toxic to her senatorial prospects—as well as any hopes she had of ever seeing the inside of the White House again as anything but a visitor—was the fact that they emerged against the same backdrop that Shamir perceived when he noted the "danger" of her being elected.

But the facts support Shamir's concerns, as well as the fears of other Clinton critics worried about her Middle East loyalties. Indeed, by numerous accounts, the senator-to-be had a long history of flirting with enemies of Israel. Writing in the *Jewish World Review* during Mrs. Clinton's Senate campaign, Beth Gilinsky, head of the Jewish Action Alliance, detailed the then first lady's long record as a friend to terrorist-sympathizers.

Ties to Terrorists

"Mrs. Clinton herself hosted a reception at the White House with leaders of the American Muslim Council, the Council on American-Islamic Relations (CAIR), and other apologists for Hamas terror," Gilinsky noted. "The affair's coordinators were a Mr. Salam al-Marayati, Director of the Muslim Public Affairs Council (MPAC), and his wife, who headed an entity calling itself the Muslim Women's League."[12] Salam al-Marayati had praised Hezbollah, the JAA spokeswoman said, noting that the group's so-called freedom fighters have perfected the art of car bombing, the technique they used in the 1983 bombing of the U.S. Marine barracks in Lebanon that killed 242 G.I.s.

Ibrahim Hooper, spokesman for the Council on American-Islamic Relations (CAIR), was another member of the group that attended the White House reception organized by Hillary, and he personally handed her a copy of the Koran. Noted

Gilinsky, "According to former FBI chief of counter terrorism, Steve Pomerantz, CAIR is but one of a new generation of new groups in the United States that hide under a veneer of 'civil rights' or 'academic' status but in fact are tethered to a platform that support[s] terrorism." (In November 2002 Hooper told WABC Radio that Osama bin Laden was no worse than Reverend Jerry Falwell and Christian Broadcasting Network chief Pat Robertson, both of whom, he claimed, would kill Muslims with September 11–like fervor if given the chance.)[13]

> "I view Hillary Clinton as a great danger to Jews if she is elected."
>
> —*former Israeli Prime Minister Yitzhak Shamir*

In a measure of the Clintons' affinity for folks usually considered enemies to both the United States and Israel, Palestinian Liberation Organization head Yasser Arafat was invited to the Clinton White House more than any other head of state. Some were unsurprised by Arafat's frequent visitor status, given Mrs. Clinton's past history with friends of the PLO such as Grassroots International, a group she helped funnel cash to when she chaired the New World Foundation in the 1970s.[14]

When Mrs. Clinton broke with her husband's administration in May 1998 and announced her support for a Palestinian state, it sent shock waves around the world and had White House spinmeisters scrambling to explain her bombshell remarks. Speaking to a group of Arab and Israeli teenagers in Switzerland, Hillary had announced, "I think that it will be in the long term interests of the Middle East for Palestine to be a state, and for it to be a state that is responsible for its citizens' well-being, a state that has responsibility for providing education and health care and economic opportunity to its citizens, a state that has to accept the responsibility of governing. . . . I think that is very important for the Palestinian people, but I also think it is very important for the broader goal of peace in the Middle East."

"That view expressed personally by the First Lady is not the view of the President," explained White House press secretary Mike McCurry. Even Mrs. Clinton's press officers sought to disavow any connection between U.S. policy and their boss's sudden outburst, echoing McCurry's "personal view" line.[15] Some suspected it was a little too personal and that Hillary was using her own clout as first lady to complicate matters for her husband as payback for humiliating her with the Monica Lewinsky scandal. But the former first lady's long history of sympathy with the Palestinian cause, while never widely reported during her Senate campaign, was always a pool of gasoline waiting to ignite. And ignite it did when Hillary traveled to the Middle East a little more than a year after the Palestinian state endorsement and attended a speech delivered by Arafat's wife, Suha.

Sealed with a Kiss

Standing at Mrs. Arafat's side next to the podium, the Senate hopeful listened to the speech, delivered in Arabic with a translation piped through headphones. In the middle of an otherwise unremarkable address about the plight of her people, Mrs. Arafat rolled a verbal hand grenade down the aisle, complaining about the "intensive daily use of poison gas by the Israeli forces in the past years which has led to an increase of cancer cases among Palestinian women and children."[16] The first lady of the United States listened politely to the rest of the speech and then gave the wife of the Palestinian terrorist leader—who had just accused a key U.S. ally of war crimes—a kiss on the cheek.

News of Mrs. Clinton's apparent endorsement of the Palestinian first lady's poisonous charge traveled back to the states at the speed of light. By midday, conservative talk radio shows based in New York City were having a field day over the Hillary-Suha episode, a situation made worse by the absence of so much as a clarification from Clinton's campaign as the day progressed. It would be a full day before Hillary 2000 caught up with the explosion—too late to temper the front pages of U.S. newspapers the next day, which featured prominent reports on the incident. The campaign had failed to heed a cardinal lesson of Clinton public relations strategy: When an allegation surfaces, respond to it immediately and forcefully. Delays only tend to compound the error, as the former first lady's team was about to find out.

"I do not believe any kind of inflammatory rhetoric or baseless charges are good for the peace process," Mrs. Clinton finally offered the next day, but she never convincingly explained why it took her so long to clarify her actions.[17] Her aides first blamed a bad translation, then suggested that Hillary didn't object to Suha's comments sooner because she didn't want to cause an international incident. While the campaign had been able to keep Mrs. Clinton's past affiliations with Arab groups that had blatant ties to terror off the public's radar screen, her Suha Arafat moment came to epitomize, at least until the anti-Semitic slur story broke, the New York Jewish community's worst fears about sending her to the Senate.

In New York especially, Suha plus Fray would spell political oblivion for just about any other candidate—Democrat or Republican. And as Clinton's reputation as someone hostile to Israel grew, she had her share of rough moments. In June 2000, when she marched in the Israeli Day parade, the then first lady was booed for block after block. In the months that followed, with the election fast approaching, animosity over Hillary's pro-Palestinian image still hadn't subsided, as a crowd at a "Solidarity for Israel" rally outside the Israeli consulate in Manhattan made clear.

"We are here today to say to the world that we stand firmly behind Israel," Mrs. Clinton began, struggling to be heard over a crowd that had suddenly erupted into loud jeers.[18] Only hours earlier, news of the deaths of two Israeli soldiers had reached the United States. The soldiers had been captured earlier that day and were being held in a Palestinian jail. At that point an angry mob stormed the police station and beat them to death. Their bodies were dragged through the streets of the West Bank town of Ramallah. Furious over the latest development, people in the crowd were apparently taking their frustrations out on the first lady.

"There was a spontaneous uprising of anger and boos from the crowd," Jewish Action Alliance spokeswoman Beth Gilinsky told WOR Radio's Bob Grant. "And we sustained [the boos] for quite a while to the point where she finally just walked off the stage."[19] New York City Council member Noach Dear told WABC Radio's Sean Hannity that "it was unbelievable": "She gets up there and she starts to speak and they don't let her speak. She's trying to say something but they don't let her."[20] The Senate candidate who was counting on up to 70 percent of New York's Jewish vote had just been booed off the stage at a rally in support of the Jewish state.

It could have been worse. At the outset of Hillary's Senate campaign listening tour, predictions abounded that members of the New York press corps would more than live up to their reputation as pit bulls ready to attack at every possible hint of scandal—past, present, and maybe even future. But it didn't happen.

Secret Palestinian Fund-Raisers

Some of the most intriguing news about Hillary's pro-Arab sympathies emerged in the *Jewish Forward*—only to be ignored by the big media despite an obvious relevance to her Senate bid. In May 2000, Hillary attended a controversial off-the-record fundraiser hosted by Hani Masri, a Yasser Arafat crony with business interests pending before the Clinton administration. Federal Election Commission records show, in fact, that Masri and his family had funneled $134,000 to the Democratic Party in the month of May alone. For her part, Mrs. Clinton collected a cool $50,000 at the May 12 event, which was held at Masri's Washington, D.C., mansion. The Masri fund-raiser was, according to the *Forward*, closed to the press and, in fact, wasn't even listed on the Senate candidate's daily public schedule.[21]

The reason for all the secrecy became clear with the revelation that Masri's company, Capital Investment Management Corporation, had been awaiting approval from the Clinton administration for a $60 million loan guaranteed by U.S. taxpayers through the Overseas Private Investment Corp (OPIC). Masri told the *Forward* that he was asked by Mrs. Clinton's campaign to stage the secret fund-raiser.

Hillary attended a controversial off-the-record fund-raiser hosted by Hani Masri, a Yasser Arafat crony with business interests pending before the Clinton administration.

The trail of the first lady's mysterious Muslim-based fund-raisers grew longer just a few days before Election Day, when the *New York Daily News* discovered that she had accepted another $50,000 from the Boston chapter of the American Muslim Alliance. At first Clinton claimed she had no idea that the June 2000 event was sponsored by the American Muslim Alliance, a group that advocates the use of force against Israel. But evidence soon emerged suggesting the then first lady had been less than truthful. A letter written on White House stationery that specifically thanked the AMA's Massachusetts chapter for staging the event rocked Clinton's campaign and sent the vaunted White House spin machine into overdrive. The letter had Mrs. Clinton's signature on it and was dated almost three months before she claimed to have ever heard of the group.

"Dear Friends," the Senate candidate wrote to the group she claimed never to have heard of. "It was a pleasure to be part of the Massachusetts Chapter meeting of the American Muslim Alliance. The plaque is a wonderful reminder of my visit. Please extend my appreciation and thanks to the entire membership. With best wishes, I am—Sincerely yours, [signed] Hillary Rodham Clinton."[22] Caught red-handed, Mrs. Clinton made her first attempt to deflect criticism before a local Jewish group, saying, "This is a typical thank-you letter that people get as a matter of course." She said a White House clerk had undoubtedly authored the note "based on whatever they were told."

And her signature? Autopen, of course, insisted the first lady.

As evidence mounted that she was lying, Mrs. Clinton stuck to her guns. Photographs on the AMA's Web site showed a smiling Hillary holding the plaque she had just accepted from the group. The engraved words "American Muslim Alliance" were clearly visible. "I get thousands of plaques," Hillary protested, contending that she couldn't be expected to read every one. But suddenly she seemed to recall details about the episode, saying she now remembered immediately giving the AMA's plaque to a White House aide and never seeing it again.

It's unlikely, however, that there was ever any doubt in the first lady's mind as to whom she was speaking. Her speech, quoted on the Muslim group's Web site for months afterward, began, "On behalf of the American Muslim Alliance and the Muslim community . . ."[23] At the same time it emerged that Clinton had accepted a $1,000 donation from Abdurahman Alamoudi, an official with the offshoot group the American Muslim Council. It didn't take long for the press to uncover damaging quotations from Alamoudi, including one where he bragged that he had earlier been invited to the Clinton White House and defended the notorious terrorist group Hamas. Mr. Alamoudi had also donated $1,000 to the Bush campaign. But without the myriad of details that made Clinton's association with admitted terrorist sympathizer seem like part of a pattern, the then Texas governor was able to escape with minimal criticism. (Both campaigns returned the tainted donations.)

The American "Museum" Council

Another aspect, uncovered by NewsMax.com, made the Alamoudi donation to Clinton's campaign look even more suspicious. Apparently campaign aides had tried to camouflage the donation in their report to the Federal Election Commission, which listed the American Muslim Council money as coming from "The American Museum Council."[24] A typo, Clinton's aides blithely explained. "That's the real story," Clinton's opponent Rick Lazio told reporters a day later, reacting to news of his opponent's effort to disguise the fact that Clinton had taken cash from a terrorist sympathizer who supported driving Israel into the sea.

In their third and final debate, which followed the bombing of the USS *Cole* by two and a half weeks and preceded the September 11 attacks by a little more than ten months, Lazio warned New Yorkers, "I think it's important for people to know that when you cavort with terrorists, you give them credibility, you embolden them."[25] In a move that Democrats widely criticized as an act of Republican desperation, telephone calls went out across that state linking the *Cole* tragedy and the cash Clinton had accepted. Mrs. Clinton complained to reporters after the debate that she was "outraged" over Republican claims that her donor "supported a terrorist group, the same kind of terrorism that killed many on the USS *Cole*."

"It is an act of despicable desperation for Mr. [Rick] Lazio to use a secret smear campaign to politicize the deaths of our sailors," Clinton said while campaigning in upstate New York a week before the election. "No one should exploit this tragedy for political gain. Today Congressman Lazio owes an apology to the families of the 17 men and women who were murdered on the USS *Cole*."[26]

Though the attack on Clinton's terrorist ties was entirely legitimate, the pre–September 11 mentality still reigned. The first lady's allies in the press helped her sell the notion that it was unfair to tie the *Cole* attack to Mr. Clinton's inaction in the war on terrorism at the same time that Mrs. Clinton was pocketing hundreds of thousands of dollars from terrorist sympathizers. Lazio and other Republicans associated with the *Cole* phone call campaign took a beating in the media, forcing them to abandon the effort.

Still, as yet another Clinton scandal unfolded—complete with Hillary's requisite dissembling—the momentum seemed to have shifted. In fact, Lazio's prospects looked good for the first time since the anti-Semitic slur stories had sent the first lady's poll numbers plummeting in late July. But reporters never challenged Mrs. Clinton directly on the issue of whether her husband's decision to go soft on terrorism had anything to do with the Muslim money she collected. And the GOP's timidity on the *Cole* issue—mounting what seemed like a sneaky whispering campaign rather than hitting Clinton broadside with unabashed TV spots pointing out her ties to people who had just killed seventeen U.S. sailors—left most voters completely in the dark over the controversy.

New York's Jews, who might have been expected to desert Mrs. Clinton in droves over her terrorist-friendly record, remained almost completely unmoved. A Zogby poll released just days before the election showed 69 percent still backed her. And while the actual numbers on Election Day showed some significant slippage for Hillary, the woman whom a former Israeli prime minister had called "dangerous" to Jews still carried the state with 53 percent of their votes.

Hillary Pardons Encouraged Bin Laden

Tragically, just as she was finishing her work on *The Final Days,* Barbara Olson found herself aboard American Airlines

Flight 77 on September 11, 2001. The unparalleled Clinton investigator died never knowing how prescient one of her insights would turn out to be. Olson warned that Bill Clinton's bid to garner Hispanic support for his wife's Senate bid by pardoning several of the FALN bombers who had targeted New York City buildings would "send a signal" that the United States wasn't serious about fighting terrorism. As part of the warning the investigative author even invoked the name of her own killer. "In the mind of Bill Clinton, political considerations outweigh even life-and-death matters of great concern to his own law enforcement officials, not to mention the nation," Olson wrote. "As many in his own cabinet had repeatedly stated, terrorism, both foreign and domestic, was the nation's primary security anxiety. Since the end of the Cold War, Soviet aggression had been replaced by a number of particularly venomous threats, from Timothy McVeigh to Osama bin Laden."[27]

> "Hillary Clinton was on the phone from North Africa forcefully expressing a different view to the President: 'I urged him to bomb,' she told Lucinda Franks, a reporter on the trip."
>
> *—Hillary biographer Gail Sheehy*

When Hillary runs for president, will the national press do what the New York press didn't in 2000—call Senator Clinton to account for the FALN pardons—not to mention her long record of cozying up to terrorist sympathizers? Will reporters ask whether, as co-president, she played any role in the Clinton administration's decision not to respond forcefully after the 1993 World Trade Center attack, the 1996 Khobar Towers bombing, the 1998 African embassy attacks, and the near sinking of the USS *Cole*?

The record suggests that Mrs. Clinton, in addition to wielding ultimate authority over the White House Counsel's office and the Justice Department—as well as the Clinton administration's premier legislative initiative, health care reform—played a central role in certain national security decisions, including the debate over whether to unleash U.S. air power over Bosnia in 1999. "Both Defense Secretary William Cohen and Army General Hugh Shelton, chairman of the Joint Chiefs of Staff, were blunt in giving their negative assessments on an airborne bombing campaign: 'You can't control a territory with airplanes,'" they maintained, according to Gail Sheehy in her biography *Hillary's Choice*. "[But] on March 21, Hillary Clinton was on the phone from North Africa forcefully expressing a different view to the President: 'I urged him to bomb,' she told Lucinda Franks, a reporter on the trip."[28] Four days later the U.S. bombing campaign over Kosovo commenced, as Mrs. Clinton's advice superseded that of the defense secretary and chairman of the Joint Chiefs.

Hillary's Role in Bin Laden's Escape

It turns out Mrs. Clinton may have played a similar role in sensitive negotiations for the extradition of Osama bin Laden to the United States in 1996. Or at least she claims to have known enough about what transpired to contradict her husband's account of the episode seven years later. In remarks reported exclusively by NewsMax.com, on February 15, 2002, former president Clinton told the Long Island Association's annual luncheon that he had a chance to have bin Laden taken into custody but decided not to do so: "Mr. bin Laden used to live in Sudan. He was expelled from Saudi Arabia in 1991, then he went to Sudan. And we'd been hearing that the Sudanese wanted America to start dealing with them again. They released him. At the time, 1996, he had committed no crime against America so I did not bring him here because we had no basis on which to hold him, though we knew he wanted to commit crimes against America. So I pleaded with the Saudis to take him, 'cause they could have. But they thought it was a hot potato and they didn't and that's how he wound up in Afghanistan."[29]

Mr. Clinton has not been asked to elaborate on his startling admission since he offered it, but his decision not to take bin Laden into custody certainly looks like one of the greatest blunders ever in the war on terrorism, given the destruction visited on the United States by the terrorist mastermind just five years later.

Up until recently, Hillary Clinton had never been confronted with her husband's confession either, although she was quizzed about a secondhand report where Mr. Clinton reportedly acknowledged the mistake. In September 2002, NBC's *Meet the Press* host Tim Russert put the question to the New York senator like this: "There are at least three instances—Sudan, Saudi Arabia are two—where they offered to help bring Osama bin Laden to justice. It never happened. The London *Times* says President Clinton now says it was one of the biggest mistakes of his presidency, not entering into one of those arrangements. Why didn't the president spend more time on terrorism and Osama bin Laden?" Hillary replied, "Oh, Tim, I think the record is clear that he spent an enormous amount of time and, you know, I don't think that a lot of what is being said and written about now actually is accurate. There's quite an extensive record of the Clinton administration's efforts against terrorism."[30]

But what Russert didn't do was quiz Mrs. Clinton using her husband's own words to the Long Island business group instead of citing a British newspaper report that contained no quotes; an account she easily dismissed by implying the story wasn't accurate. Astonishingly, no reporter tried to follow up on Senator Clinton's quasi denial, just as few news organizations had bothered to cover Mr. Clinton's original bombshell admission that he turned down the bin Laden extradition deal. But in January 2003 that changed, during an encounter I had with Senator Clinton on WLIE radio's Mike Siegel Show.

NEWSMAX: Senator Clinton, in February of last year your husband addressed the Long Island Association here, well in Woodbury. And he said that he had an offer from the government of Sudan in 1996 to take bin Laden into custody. His exact words: "At the time, 1996, bin Laden had committed no crime against America, so I did not bring him here because we had no basis on which to hold him, though we knew he wanted to commit crimes against America."

What's your reaction to ex-President Clinton's admission that he had a chance to take bin Laden into custody but declined the offer?

CLINTON: Well that is, you know, first of all, that's not my understanding of the facts. But, as I understand the facts, there was never a full and thorough offer. But remember, when we were looking to try to deal with bin Laden, there wasn't any, at that point, any absolute linkage, as there later became, with both the bombings in Africa and the U.S.S. *Cole*. And it was also the fact, that I think it's hard for us now to remember, that the United States, at that point in time, as well as our allies, had a very different mindset about the best way to deal with these potential problems around the world. We didn't have the support of many of the country's intelligence agencies that we were able to obtain after 9/11.[31]

Which Clinton Is Lying?

This time Senator Clinton didn't try to deny the accuracy of the report on her husband's remarks—but instead suggested his memory of what transpired was faulty, explaining "that's not my understanding of the facts." The question of which Clinton's version of events is more truthful should perhaps be a focal point of the 9/11 Commission's review of the events leading up to September 11. Did Mr. Clinton have a chance to take bin Laden off the table, as he clearly claimed last year? Or is Mrs. Clinton correct when she says that no real offer from Sudan was ever proffered? And why can't the former first couple get their stories straight on what may turn out to be one of the most significant blunders in the history of America's war on terrorism?

> "When we were looking to try to deal with bin Laden, there wasn't any, at that point, any absolute linkage, as there later became, with both the bombings in Africa and the U.S.S. *Cole*."
>
> —*Hillary Clinton*

Interestingly enough, former Clinton administration National Security Advisor Sandy Berger, along with a whole swarm of former Clinton administration officials, backs Hillary's version of events. In September 2002, Berger testified before a joint House-Senate Committee probing the September 11 attacks. "There was never such an offer,"[32] he insisted.

Perhaps the best indication of where the truth may lie came moments later in Mrs. Clinton's WLIE interview, when she expressly blamed the Bush administration for ignoring clear warnings from her husband's aides about the Al Qaeda threat: "I know that during the transition between the Clinton and Bush administrations that the outgoing administration told the incoming one that they would spend more time on terrorism and bin Laden than anything else because that had just exploded on the international scene," she recalled. "And that wasn't their priority. Their priorities were different. And obviously that all changed on September 11."[33] No matter what the truth of the bin Laden extradition deal, in Hillary's mind the September 11 attacks were the fault of the Bush administration because they ignored the prescience of their predecessor's warning. Accurate or not, the anecdote provides both Clintons the cover they may one day need should further questions about the bin Laden extradition offer materialize.

But it's worth noting also that Hillary doesn't merely claim to "understand" what happened during the bin Laden negotiations, instead preferring the construct, "I know," suggesting her knowledge is firsthand. Truthful or not, it's a cover story designed to minimize what is likely to be a sore point for a presidential candidate who hopes to win the White House by running on the record of her husband's administration.

Damage control about September 11 never seems to be far from Senator Clinton's mind—at least that's the explanation some offer for her virtual obsession with the topic. But by 2003 the top Democrat was branching out, making sure that other Clinton administration blunders, such as the 1994 deal with North Korea that provided Pyongyang with two light-water nuclear reactors that were quickly put to work enriching uranium for nuclear bombs, didn't cause further damage to the already hobbled Clinton legacy.

Hillary: Bush "Mishandled North Korea"

In another fascinating insight into the thinking of the person most likely to be the first of her sex to occupy the Oval Office, Mrs. Clinton chose the same January 2003 radio interview to engage in some classic blame-shifting over North Korea. "The way [the Bush administration has] mishandled North Korea," she told radio host Mike Siegel, "I mean—we don't think that Iraq yet has nuclear weapons, or Iran. We know darn well that North Korea is trying to commit nuclear blackmail on us and we have to be more vigilant there." And in the next breath the former first lady was finger-pointing again, this time alleging that the Bush administration tried to cover up the testimony of FBI September 11 whistleblower Coleen Rowley. "If you remember when Coleen Rowley was going to testify, that was the very day that the administration announced all of a sudden that they were in favor of a Homeland Security Department after having opposed it for months," she told radio host Siegel. "And many of us believe that it was an intentional effort to divert attention from her testimony because she raised a lot of unanswered questions."[34]

Plainly Senator Clinton is concerned about a major weak spot in her presidential portfolio, the role she and her husband played in leaving America vulnerable to the worst attack on U.S. soil in American history. Luckily for her, the media doesn't share her worry.

CHAPTER NINE

Hillary and the Police

"I wanted to let you know how personally offended I was to hear of the treatment of your officers by [a] handful of people at the New York State Democratic Convention."
—Hillary Clinton apologizing after her supporters spit on a police honor guard carrying the American flag

The boos from New York City cops and firemen gathered at Madison Square Garden just thirty-nine days after the September 11 attacks reportedly reduced Senator Clinton to tears behind the scenes. For a politician with bigger plans, someone who had vowed to make servicing her constituents a hallmark of her Senate tenure, expressions of scorn from the heroes who symbolized the nation's patriotic defiance in the wake of its searing violation not only stung, but also clouded her political future.

When Hillary's husband sought the presidency in 1992, his campaign courted and won the endorsement of the National

Association of Police Officers. Although the 135,000-member organization had not endorsed a presidential candidate in 1988,[1] the unexpected law enforcement backing was enough to neutralize the first President Bush's endorsement from the Little Rock Chapter of the Fraternal Order of Police the next month.[2] It was all part of the Clintons' "New Democrat" strategy designed to dispel suspicions that he was soft on crime. To prove he was pro–death penalty earlier in the campaign, Bill Clinton had traveled home to Arkansas in the midst of the New Hampshire primary campaign to preside over the execution of brain-damaged black convict Rickey Ray Rector.

But Mrs. Clinton took a different tack for her New York campaign, openly courting critics who blamed Mayor Rudy Giuliani for setting a tone that encouraged police brutality in New York City. The image of Hillary as cop-hater quickly took root among NYPD's rank and file. It worked like a charm while she was playing the race card against Giuliani, who, for all his success in lowering the city's murder rate by two-thirds, would get steamrollered on the issue. But three days after the September 11 attacks the ploy came back to haunt her, when the heroes of Ground Zero refused to shake her hand.

Courting the Cop-Haters

Ever since Paul McCartney's October 20, 2001, concert for the city's fallen heroes, where Senator Clinton struggled to be heard above the jeers, then cut short her remarks and withdrew, she has redoubled her efforts to win over members of the city's uniformed services. By 2003, hardly a week would go by without the New York tabloids reporting that Clinton was pressing Washington to provide more relief for firefighters who suffered from Ground Zero respiratory distress or complaining that nearby nuclear power plants continue to render the city's residents vulnerable—or even lobbying for increased funding for the first responders who had treated her so derisively in the wake of the attacks. But when she was campaigning against Giuliani, it was a different story entirely. Playing the race card worked, not just with the state's African American voters, but also with the city's press corps. They began to openly question whether Giuliani's biggest success, a reduction in the city's murder rate from 2,100 to under 700 per year, an accomplishment that had saved literally thousands of mostly minority lives, was worth the occasional accidental shooting.

By the time the New York mayor was forced to withdraw from the race a year later, prompted by a newly diagnosed case of prostate cancer and a very public marital breakup, Hillary Clinton had surged ahead in the polls. The lead was slight but it was consistent over a period of months. And she did it, in part, by painting Giuliani as a racially divisive dictator whose success in reducing the city's crime was tainted by racial insensitivity. It's hard to remember now, but the man who *Time* would dub "America's Mayor" after September 11 was routinely derided as "Adolf Giuliani" by critics who echoed Hillary's line that Giuliani was deliberately divisive.

Meanwhile, Mrs. Clinton pulled out all the stops, traveling in January 2000 to Harlem and the headquarters of Reverend Al Sharpton's National Action Network; there she referred to the "murder" of Amadou Diallo, the case that had become the rallying point for the city's anti-Giuliani elements. (The West Indian immigrant had been gunned down as he refused to yield to police orders to drop what they thought was a gun, though it later turned out to be a wallet.)

"Senator Schumer, I know, who was here earlier, gave a speech after the tragic murder of Mr. Diallo in which he said that what every community, but particularly the African community—African American community—wants is to be respected and protected," Clinton said, invoking a term that implied the Diallo cops were guilty, not of an accidental shooting, but of premeditation. In the next breath the then Senate candidate used her clout as wife of the man who ran the federal government to threaten Justice Department intervention.

"The process has already started to bring this matter to the attention of the federal authorities," she told Sharpton's crowd. "And certainly, I think all of us will want to be sure that justice is done. And if there is a role for the federal government, I will certainly encourage and urge that that occur."[3]

The Diallo cops were eventually tried and acquitted, and Hillary later apologized for alluding to his death as a "murder." But the NYPD rank and file never forgot.

In March 2000, with the wounds of the Diallo case still festering, city cops got into a scuffle with another unarmed African American, Patrick Dorismond, who became violent when undercover cops asked him for drugs. In the midst of the struggle Dorismond was shot dead. In a bungled attempt at damage control, Giuliani had Dorismond's juvenile arrest record unsealed, saying it showed a "propensity towards violence."[4] Civil libertarians and minorities were livid. The New York press had a field day. And the more contentious the city's racial climate got, the better Mrs. Clinton did in the polls.

Hillary's Cop-Spitters

Against that backdrop, New York Democrats gathered in Albany to officially name the first lady as their Senate candidate. It was May 16, three days before Rudy Giuliani would stun the country by announcing his withdrawal from the race. But without a clue of what was to come, anti-Giuliani passions had reached a fevered pitch among convention-goers, especially those bused up from the city to attend the event. The result was one of the ugliest incidents in U.S. political history, an episode so repulsive that New York City's big media couldn't bring itself to cover the story. It was left to the *Albany Times-Union* to break the story the next day:

"Members of an Albany Police Department Honor Guard were harassed and spit on by a few people as they carried flags into Tuesday's Democratic state convention at Pepsi Arena, officials said. The five-member honor guard, which is made up of Albany police officers, told authorities that some people in the crowd of 11,500 Democratic supporters called them 'Nazis' and members of Giuliani's 'Third Reich.'

Making matters worse, the Albany police honor guard were in full dress uniform and carrying the American flag. Detective Thomas McGraw, president of the Albany Police Officers Union, told the paper, "We are very upset. The honor guard were asked to act as ambassadors to the city of Albany. They were invited guests and they were volunteering their time." Though it was impossible to know exactly who the perpetrators were, the spitting seemed to come from the floor of the arena, an area that was off-limits to everyone not carrying a delegate pass.[5]

"The process has already started to bring this matter to the attention of the federal authorities."

—*Hillary Clinton, promising to investigate police brutality under Mayor Giuliani*

The attack on the flag-carrying Honor Guard was outrageous by anyone's standards. Still, with the exception of a lone editorial in the *New York Post,* the city papers held the story. Meanwhile, leery of attracting media attention to the tawdry episode, state Democratic Party Chairman Judith Hope worked quietly behind the scenes to make amends. When she penned a letter to Albany police officials apologizing for the incident and promising to track the perpetrators down, mainstream reporters obliged by ignoring it. After more than a week, with controversy over the cop-spitting incident raging on talk radio and the Internet, the Senate candidate herself felt compelled to write a letter of apology to Albany Police Chief John Neilsen.

"I wanted to let you know how personally offended I was to hear of the treatment of your officers by [a] handful of people at the New York State Democratic Convention," Clinton wrote nine days after the incident. "These attacks were completely contrary to the spirit of the event, and to the values we hold. I have condemned them sharply. I know the debt of gratitude we all owe to police officers who risk their lives every day to keep us safe, and I have said so often."[6]

A signed copy of the first lady's apology for the repugnant episode was faxed to major New York City media outlets by NewsMax, which first reported the letter. News editors decided the unprecedented apology from a sitting first lady wasn't particularly newsworthy and declined to cover it. Of course, had mainstream reporters picked up the story at that late date, they would have had to explain to their readers how the entire cop-spitting scandal transpired under their noses with nary a peep from the press. So rather than play catch-up on yet another Clinton scandal, they didn't want to inflict on an impressionable New York electorate, the press pretended it wasn't newsworthy.

Giuliani Speaks Out

NewsMax was the only news outlet that attempted to get a reaction from Mayor Giuliani, long a champion of law enforcement, about Mrs. Clinton's cop-spitters.

"I mean, spitting is an assault. I think it is," the New York mayor said, when I questioned him about the cop-spitting outrage by Hillary's delegates on his weekly WABC radio show. "I remember my criminal law pretty well and tort law pretty well. If you spit at somebody and make contact with them, I think it's at least a misdemeanor of some kind."

Giuliani continued, "It should have resulted technically and equitably in an arrest and at least some form of a fine or ticket. And if the persons can be identified on tape, there's no reason why it can't happen right now." Then the mayor, who had dropped out of the Senate race a week earlier, publicly called on Mrs. Clinton to apologize. "It seems to me that [whether it's a] Republican, Democrat, Liberal, Conservative convention, whatever—you spit on somebody in a situation like that, where you're seeking to disgrace them or I don't know what the heck they were seeking to do, there should be consequences for that. And there's no question that the Democratic Party and Mrs. Clinton should apologize for that."[7]

The mayor of the city where most of Hillary's political base resided had issued a public demand for a sitting first lady's apology because her supporters had spit on a police honor guard carrying the American flag—into a convention hall where she was about to be nominated, no less. And yet the *New York Post*, the *New York Daily News*, *Newsday*, and the *Wall Street Journal* declined to report Giuliani's comments. The next day, the *New York Times*, prompted by a fax of NewsMax's report on the mayor's call for an apology, covered the episode—but buried the story in its Metro Section. When New York voters went to the polls six months later, the overwhelming majority were completely unaware that the spitting attacks had even taken place.

Why Cops, Firefighters Booed Hillary

But the police and the firefighters knew. And so, when Mrs. Clinton tried to portray herself as an advocate for the rescue workers who died at Ground Zero during the televised McCartney concert, the reaction was swift. Three days later, firefighter Mike Moran, who lost a brother on September 11 and who thrilled the Madison Square Garden crowd with his dare to Osama bin Laden to "Kiss My Royal Irish Ass," explained the sentiments that provoked the harsh reaction.

"I think when times are good and things are going well, people will sit there and listen to the kind of claptrap that comes out of her mouth," Moran told the nation's number one radio host, Rush Limbaugh. "When things are going like this, when it's serious times and serious men who actually suffered losses and she wants to get up and spew her nonsense—she doesn't believe a thing she says. She says whatever she thinks will fit the moment." Moran told the radio host that he and most of his brethren saw through Mrs. Clinton's phoniness. "I think it comes through. And in serious times, people don't want to stand for it." The hero firefighter then detailed the sacrifices of Manhattan's Ladder Company Number 3, twelve of whom, including Moran's brother, perished while trying to rescue burn victims from the fortieth floor of World Trade Center Tower One.

"The captain, Paddy Brown, gave a report from the North Tower that they had 30 to 40 severely burned people that they were trying to get down the stairs," the fireman told Limbaugh. "A few minutes later, he gave the most urgent kind of message a fireman could give—a mayday that the building was coming down around him." Moran said the building didn't fully collapse for another ten minutes, more than enough time for his colleagues to escape certain death. But "they wouldn't leave those people."[8]

> "I think when times are good and things are going well, people will sit there and listen to the kind of claptrap that comes out of her mouth."
>
> *—9/11 hero firefighter Mike Moran*

The efforts to expunge the record of Mrs. Clinton's McCartney concert humiliation took on a particularly extreme form, though it's not clear whether she, her husband, or some unknown third party instigated the cover-up. The concert had been telecast live on VH1, and millions of people nationwide saw firefighters and cops boo her off the stage. But when the cable channel rebroadcast the McCartney concert, the booing and jeers for Mrs. Clinton had vanished. "The boos were . . . replaced with general crowd noise," reported the late New

York gossip maven Neal Travis, adding, "the cable channel evidently wants to keep on Hillary's good side."[9] VH1, it turns out, is owned by Viacom, the parent company of Simon & Schuster, the book publisher that had showered Mrs. Clinton with an $8 million book advance a year before.

No September 11 Funerals for Hillary

Hillary was hit by another controversy related to September 11 when Fox News Channel host Bill O'Reilly noticed she never appeared at any of the victims' funerals, which, with over 2,800 dead, stretched well into 2002. "We sent both Senator Clinton and Senator Chuck Schumer letters asking them which services they attended and which families they visited," O'Reilly announced nearly three months after the attacks. Senator Clinton's office ignored FNC's letter and repeated phone calls, he reported, "most likely because the only events we know she attended were three highly publicized memorial services." Senator Schumer's office, on the other hand, was far more cooperative, informing O'Reilly's producers that he had attended ten services and promising to provide a list of each one. New York Mayor Rudy Giuliani and Governor George Pataki, of course, had attended hundreds of funerals for WTC victims.

Three high-profile events Mrs. Clinton attended were a memorial service at Yankee Stadium a week after the attacks, a similar event at Ground Zero in early October, and the funeral for New York City Fire Department Chaplain Father Mychal Judge, where she delivered the eulogy. All three services were televised.

Associated Press reporter Beth Harpaz defended Mrs. Clinton, telling O'Reilly that "her core supporters and the main victim groups of 9/11 are pretty much two distinct groups." The AP scribe noted that among the victim pool, "we have a lot of male-dominated professions here, firefighters, cops, Wall Street, a lot of suburbanites, a lot of political conservatives"—apparently not

Mrs. Clinton's cup of tea. Harpaz also suggested that Mrs. Clinton couldn't attend many funerals because "she's been busy in Washington" and she also feared being booed again, as she was at the McCartney concert. Visibly angered, O'Reilly shot back:

"If I were the senator of New York, I would have tried to attend as many of those funerals and memorial services as I could. And if they booed me, they booed me. I'd get down on my knees and say a prayer for that dead person and then I would go and leave."[10]

Hillary and the Black Panthers

The history of Mrs. Clinton's animosity toward police goes back, apparently, to her college days at Yale Law School in the early 1970s, when she became a supporter of the Black Panthers. Several Panthers, including the notorious Bobby Seale, were then on trial in New Haven for the torture death of one of their own members, Alex Rackley. Members of the local chapter of the thuggish radical revolutionary group suspected Rackley was a police informant, the kiss of death for that crowd.

But Rackley wouldn't be even that lucky. Before he died, his Panther brethren had clubbed him, burned him with cigarettes, scalded him with boiling water, stabbed him with an ice pick, and finally shot him twice. Police found his mutilated body floating in the Coginchaug River, twenty-five miles north of New Haven.[11]

"Hillary formed a close association with [Panther lawyer Charles] Garry and manifested no misgivings about the violent rhetoric of his clients, who called for police assassinations and said, 'If Bobby dies, Yale fries,'" revealed the late Barbara Olson in her stinging Hillary biography *Hell to Pay.* Hooking up with Mr. Garry would prove particularly fortuitous for Mrs. Clinton in later years, since Garry employed Jack Palladino—the private detective Mrs. Clinton would later hire to help suppress "bimbo eruptions,"—to do investigations for the Panther case.[12]

Hillary threw herself into the Panther case with apparent relish, attending the Rackley murder trial and helping to organize other like-minded students to monitor courtroom proceedings and report any alleged "civil rights abuses."[13] Around the same time she co-edited *The Yale Review of Law and Social Action,* a pro-Panther publication that featured in one edition a cartoon depicting a police officer as a bullet-riddled pig with its head cut off. The caption: "Seize the Time!"—the Panthers' revolutionary battle cry.[14]

According to David Horowitz, a former radical leftist who cut his teeth working with the Black Panther Party and editing that bible of the 1960s New Left, *Ramparts,* it was a young Hillary Rodham, along with the Clintons' future head of the Justice Department's Civil Rights Division, Bill Lann Lee, who organized demonstrations on behalf of the Panthers.

She co-edited *The Yale Review of Law and Social Action,* a pro-Panther publication that featured in one edition a cartoon depicting a police officer as a bullet-riddled pig.

"What they did was shut down Yale University to try to stop the trial of six Panther leaders who were accused of torturing a black man named Alex Rackley," Horowitz said in a 1999 radio interview. "The fact is that the Panthers were torturers and murderers of black people," he recalled. "And Hillary Clinton and Bill Lann Lee organized those demonstrations to get them off."[15]

Predictably, none of the news about Mrs. Clinton's Panther past made it into the mainstream press while she was running for Senate, and many who have heard snippets of the story on talk radio or elsewhere suspect it is a myth.

Hillary Mows Cop Down

Like the cop-spitting incident and Hillary's Panther past, the case of Westchester, New York, police officer Ernest Dymond received the same silent treatment from the press. It was October 14, 2001, a little more than a month after the World Trade Center attacks. Dymond was assigned to the Westchester County Airport near the Clintons' home in Chappaqua that Sunday, manning a key security checkpoint, when Senator Clinton's full-sized Ford conversion van, complete with Secret Service driver behind the wheel, came barreling toward him at 35 mph. The van blew through the mandatory checkpoint without so much as slowing down. Having no idea of the van's "precious cargo," Dymond sprung into action.

Dymond grabbed the side of Clinton's car and began yelling and pounding away. "I didn't know if we had a terrorist," he told the *Washington Times.*

Fearing another attack like that of September 11, Dymond grabbed the side of Clinton's car and began yelling and pounding away. "I didn't know if we had a terrorist," he told the *Washington Times* two days after the incident.

"What the hell are you doing?" Dymond reportedly shouted at Clinton's driver as he clung to the black van. Only after Westchester cop threw his shoulder into the vehicle and began banging on its side did Clinton's car come to a halt, about 100 yards beyond the checkpoint, the *Times* said. He described Senator Clinton's driver as "quite agitated" when he was stopped and ordered to produce identification. After the hero cop cleared Clinton's car, he was taken to Saint Agnes hospital in White Plains for treatment of his injuries, which a hospital spokesman described as a sprained elbow.

Yet two weeks later Dymond was still unable to return to work, suggesting the encounter with Clinton's van left him in much worse shape than the hospital had let on. That's when a shroud of secrecy descended upon the case.

Silenced

Asked by NewsMax.com to describe the extent of his injuries or predict when he thought he might be able to return to work, the nineteen-year police veteran would only say, "I wish I could. Our department has a policy that all information go through the public information officer."[16] Still, repeated calls to the public information officer inquiring about Dymond's case went unreturned. Dymond did note, however, that neither Clinton nor her staff had contacted him to inquire about his condition or apologize for the accident in any way.

The shroud of silence surrounding the case was still intact nearly two months later, when NewsMax reached officer Dymond at his home once again. He declined to comment at all this time. It was 1 o'clock in the afternoon, indicating that he was still sidelined by the injuries he sustained from his encounter with Mrs. Clinton's van. A few days later the *National Enquirer* managed to get the policeman's wife on the phone. Asked to comment on what had happened to her husband, she replied, "Not that he wouldn't like to talk. But none of us are allowed to."

The silencing of Officer Dymond seemed particularly unusual compared to a case that happened at almost the same time involving one of the most powerful Republicans in Congress. Two weeks before Dymond was injured, leading House Republican J. C. Watts was involved in an altercation with airport security at Oklahoma's Will Rogers Airport after Watts saw police Sergeant Edward Stupka ticketing his car while he took a minute to help his wife Not only *wasn't* Stupka silenced, but after Watts apologized verbally, the offended officer also demanded that the powerful GOP congressman put it in writing. Unlike the Dymond-Hillary altercation, Stupka's close encounter with Congressman Watts garnered print coverage from coast to coast.

However, when America's voters render a judgment on Mrs. Clinton's fitness to occupy the Oval Office, the overwhelming majority will likely do so without hearing a word about the day Officer Dymond was injured by Hillary Clinton's van.

CHAPTER TEN

Arkansas Omerta

"I would not cross these people for fear of my life."
—Monica Lewinsky on tape to Linda Tripp

There's simply no question that Bill and Hillary Clinton could have never gone as far and as fast as they did in politics without their astonishingly successful damage control operation. And Senator Clinton will need every bit of that operation up and running if she is to succeed in her drive to recapture the White House. She may have the political wind at her back, the best presidential poll rating in her party, unparalleled fund-raising ability compared with any other elected Democrat, and a level of enthusiasm among her supporters that's completely unequaled. But those advantages by themselves would not be enough to transport Senator Clinton back into the White House. For that, as in the past, the ability to keep the press away from damaging stories will be essential.

But even those who know the Clintons' unscrupulous ways well may be shocked to learn how even relatively influential people have been made to pay the price for threatening the first former first couple's grip on power.

Daytime TV talk star Richard Bey, for instance, is so well remembered seven years after his hit talk show vanished from the airwaves in late 1996 that he says people still recognize him on the street. But while many recall Bey as the inventor of the genre currently practiced best by Jerry Springer, few know how his television career ended, or even why.

It wasn't ratings. The day before he was fired his show drew the largest audience of the season to that point. And he had just signed a seven-figure contract with his syndicator that certified his unorthodox stardom.

Bey, now a talk radio host on WABC in New York, isn't exactly sure why he got the axe. But this much is beyond dispute. He was the king of daytime TV talk up until the day he put Clinton sex accuser Gennifer Flowers on the air.

"I kept reading in the trade papers about Gennifer Flowers being booked on one show or another—and then when she shows up they tell her they don't need her," Bey said in his first public statement on the episode three years later. "Every time I book her somewhere, it gets mysteriously deep-sixed," Flowers's publicist explained, according to Bey.

A Democrat who had never voted for Clinton, Bey decided it wouldn't happen with his show. The decision ended his career overnight. On the October 8, 1996, broadcast, Flowers claimed that then governor Clinton had put her in a family way back in 1979, then paid her $200 in cash with the understanding that she would abort his child. She also recounted how her home had been broken into three times, saying she suspected Bill Clinton was responsible for the break-ins.

"The show got the highest ratings of the book," Bey told NewsMax. "And I had just started a new contract for a lot of money. But the day after it airs, I'm called into the office and told that we're going out of production." As the TV host tells it, he asked directly, "Is this because of the Gennifer Flowers show?" Too ashamed to reply, the unnamed network executive simply stared at his shoes.

"But I have a contract," Bey protested.

"You'll be paid off," came the response.

Bey said he was paid a "tremendous amount of money" every week for the next year—after his mega-hit talk show was abruptly yanked from the air. The ex-TV talker said the experience left him completely stunned. He thought about going public at the time with the behind-the-scenes story of his dismissal, but worried that he'd be trashed in the press.

"You know, the press is so controlled. If I started to yell at that time, I imagined they'd write something like, 'There's Richard Bey, they canceled his stupid show and now he's trying to blame it on Clinton.' But those are the facts," Bey insisted to NewsMax. "The day after the show aired, we go out of production. And they paid me big money for doing nothing for the next 11 months."[1]

Bey is far from the only person to cross the Clintons and subsequently have a career suffer. Flowers herself had a lawsuit against Hillary Clinton and former White House advisers James Carville and George Stephanopoulos reinstated in fall 2002 based in part on her claims that efforts have been made to discourage prospective employers from hiring her as a nightclub singer. In 2000 she opened her own nightclub in New Orleans.

Some might wonder, Is this type of thing possible in modern-day America? Can someone in the White House, with a few phone calls, torpedo careers and put employment in jeopardy?

Another Talk Host Runs Afoul of Hillary

When Mrs. Clinton launched her Senate campaign in 1999, no other candidate in modern political history had been at the center of so much scandal—with so many disgruntled witnesses willing to talk—without having had any of it become the focus of media attention while the candidate made a first bid for office.

Stephanopoulos, communications director in the first Clinton administration, had good reason to worry about Mrs. Clinton's decision to throw her hat into the ring, having warned her in March 1999 that she'd face an onslaught of scrutiny about her role in Travelgate, Whitewater, Filegate—and about her attempts to discredit and intimidate women who had accused her husband of sexual improprieties. But even he didn't anticipate the lengths to which the supposedly hard-nosed New York media would go into the tank for Hillary.

The toughest questioning faced by candidate Clinton didn't come from investigative reporters who had spent a decade tracking her checkered career—neither their editors nor Mrs. Clinton's handlers allowed them to get anywhere near her. The single episode where Mrs. Clinton was grilled, as any other male candidate would be while seeking high office, took place on a Buffalo talk radio show, where she appeared in January 2000.

The would-be senator might have sensed what was coming when WGR-AM's Tom Bauerle began his interview by reminding her, "I'm no Matt Lauer," a reference to the *Today* show host's solicitous interview with the then first lady just days after the Monica Lewinsky scandal broke. It was there that Lauer had allowed her to debut, unchallenged, her wacky "vast right-wing conspiracy" theory.

As if to prove his point, Bauerle broke the mainstream media's taboo against pressing Clinton on her personal life, specifically on the numerous stories—some just rumors, others backed by eyewitnesses claiming compelling evidence—that she, like her husband, had broken her marital vows.

"Mrs. Clinton, you're going to hate me," Bauerle began. "You were on television last night talking about your relationship with the president, Bill Clinton. Have you ever been sexually unfaithful to him, and specifically, the stories about you and Vince Foster—any truth in them?"

It was a political Kodak moment—a confrontation that any normal candidate carrying the same baggage would have expected to happen. The press had no problem asking her then Senate opponent, Rudy Giuliani, about rumored indiscretions in his own marriage. Mrs. Clinton herself, after being humiliated in 1992 by Gennifer Flowers's claims of a twelve-year affair with her husband, had even urged reporters to look into specious claims that then President Bush was involved with a State Department aide.

> "Mrs. Clinton, you're going to hate me. You were on television last night talking about your relationship with the president, Bill Clinton. Have you ever been sexually unfaithful to him?"
>
> *—radio host Tom Bauerle*

"Why does the press shy away from investigating rumors about George Bush's extramarital life?" Hillary asked *Vanity Fair* writer Gail Sheehy at the time. One reason might have been that, unlike Flowers, "Bush's Jennifer," as Jennifer Fitzgerald became known inside the Clinton camp, had denied the story. Still, under similar questioning from the Buffalo radio host, Mrs. Clinton cried foul.

"Well, you know, Tom, I do hate you for that. Because, you know, those questions—I think—are really out of bounds. And everybody who knows me knows the answers to those questions. You know, I just . . ."

Bauerle pressed ahead. "Is the answer no?

"Well, yes. Of course it's no," candidate Clinton shot back. "But it's an inappropriate question. And, you know, at some point, people should start focusing on their own families and their own needs and desires to keep families together."

Undeterred by Clinton's remonstration, Bauerle pressed ahead on another front, this time questioning her on whether she'd ever used drugs, as claimed by ex-boyfriend David Rupert when interviewed by Sheehy for her Clinton biography, *Hillary's Choice.*

"In light of this country's war on drugs, this seems like a fair question. Have you ever used pot or cocaine?" Bauerle asked.

"Tom, what did you have for breakfast this morning?" the first lady bristled.

"Same thing I always have. Breakfast of champions, Diet Pepsi," Bauerle replied, before reiterating the question. "Did you ever use pot or cocaine?"

"Well, no wonder you're so wired," Mrs. Clinton dodged, in hopes of evading the question altogether. But Bauerle persevered.

"I'm completely relaxed. Have you ever use pot or cocaine?" he repeated.

Finally the then first lady relented. "No," she said in a miffed tone. "And, you know, again, I think, you know, this is the kind of stuff that—I think that we ought to be talking about what we're going to do to bring good jobs to western New York."[2]

Hillary's Griller Comes under Attack

Bauerle's confrontation with Clinton had immediate repercussions, most of them not good for his career. The story hit the wires by mid-morning, and by that afternoon, requests for interviews were pouring in from across the country. But less than twenty-four hours after his encounter with America's most celebrated Senate candidate, the radio host had vanished from his perch on WGR's *Breakfast with Bauerle* broadcast.

"I can't say anything," a nervous-sounding station executive explained at the time. "The only person who can talk about this is Tom Bauerle, according to our corporate office. So I can't say anything and frankly, Tom isn't going to say anything either. He's done talking."[3]

The next day Bauerle returned to the microphone, explaining that he had merely been exhausted. And for the next two weeks he made good on the bulk of his interview commitments, even appearing with the *Today* show's Mr. Lauer. But instead of winning praise for asking Mrs. Clinton the questions that nobody else dared to, questions that other candidates are routinely asked and that she herself had urged other candidates to address, the Buffalo radio talker found that the proverbial roof had caved in.

Typical of the mainstream press reaction were comments from the *Washington Post*'s Howard Kurtz and Mary McGrory, offered on CNN's *Reliable Sources* four days after the Hillary brouhaha, along with remarks by co-panelists Bruce Morton and Bernard Kalb.

"Mary McGrory, those radio questions about infidelity, [are they] merely obnoxious or down in the gutter?" Kurtz asked.

"Yes," McGrory replied. "And this, to me, even Hillary Clinton, even in New York, I think that New Yorkers will think well, we may be a little brusque and to the point, but we're not oafs. And to me this was oafish and I agree with Hillary Clinton, it was out of bounds."

"I vote the straight McGrory ticket on this one," Morton chimed in. "I think yes, I think that's out of bounds. I, you know, I don't know if she confessed infidelity, half the country might have cheered and said good for you. But I just don't think that you need to know about your possible senator [doing] those kinds of things."

Sources panelist Kalb offered the harshest assessment of Bauerle, telling his colleagues, "Clearly the interviewer of Hillary Clinton was prophetic, she was going to hate him, and I think we all have, share that feeling. . . . Even for Hillary Clinton, even for anyone, there is such a thing as a ridiculous, monstrous invasion of privacy."

Only veteran newscribe Jack Germond begged to differ—and then only slightly.

"I'll make one point here, one small point. Hillary Clinton and her husband are the ones who brought this into the business when they went on the '60 Minutes' show eight years ago and talked about their marriage. And she is running first and foremost as his wife. It is her major credential. So if she's not going to talk about it, she shouldn't talk about it at all and she did right before. I don't think the guy had a right to ask that question, but she is asking for this. I don't know why she even bothered to answer it, but she did."[4]

Eleven days after the Buffalo radio host dared to ask the questions no one else would, WGR executives pulled the plug on *Breakfast with Bauerle,* transferring the show's namesake to an all-sports-talk morning broadcast. Station executives said the change had been planned even before Mrs. Clinton's interview.

Goon Squads

While those in the media who dared to challenge the Clintons rarely escaped without paying a price, critics with less clout were subject to cruder methods of damage control. Thanks to a complacent media who still desperately want Mrs. Clinton to succeed, most Americans have no idea about the startling revelation offered by one longtime campaign insider just last year—the kind of confession that would certainly prompt a deluge of negative press were it about a lesser political figure. Any thoughts of a White House bid by the official in question would be dashed. In fact, that candidate would likely be criticized as a threat to America's First Amendment freedoms and probably be unable to continue in public life without delivering an abject prime-time TV apology.

But as it was, when longtime Hillary Clinton advance man Patrick Halley revealed in his 2002 book *On the Road with Hillary* that he recruited "goon squads" to rough up demonstrators, the press pretended not to notice. Halley was no Clinton hater, a fact that should have made the revelation doubly hard to dismiss. In fact, the Boston-based political operative's 2002 account of his nine years organizing events for the Clintons is chockfull of praise for both Hillary and Bill. Describing his first meeting with the future first lady as she prepared for a major 1992 campaign event, for instance, the political pro said he instantly perceived her as political star material.

"That late in any national campaign, the presidential and vice presidential candidates and their wives are like rock stars," observed Halley, adding that "Some people have trouble living under that kind of pressure." But not Mrs. Clinton.

"I could sense that Hillary was a natural for the role," the advance man recalled. "She exuded strength and confidence, clarity and purpose, yet somehow they were all tempered by a palpable sense of humanity. Her smile that day was unforced, warm and sincere. It conveyed both friendship and appreciation. . . . This woman was the real thing."

"Hillary Clinton and her husband are the ones who brought this into the business when they went on the *60 Minutes* show eight years ago and talked about their marriage."

—reporter Jack Germond

But when it came to handling protesters, Halley left nothing to chance—Mrs. Clinton, her "strength and confidence" and "palpable sense of humanity" notwithstanding.

"Less genteel souls sometimes referred to them as goon squads," wrote Halley about the enforcers he'd hire to quash anti-Hillary demonstrations. "But I objected to that term. I was proud of the fact that not one of them had ever been arrested."

In a stunning burst of candor, the Democratic operative revealed that he preferred to use the term "etiquette squad" to describe the tough guys he'd recruit to stake out campaign stops and political events where the first lady was likely to encounter static. Without blinking an eye, Halley confessed that his etiquette enforcers "could certainly be intimidating if the occasion called for it."

"The make-up of the etiquette squad differed from event to event, and I always found it best to use folks who were indigenous," he explained. "After all, you wouldn't want to send a team of broad-shouldered teamsters into an event at a women's college." Halley revealed that whenever an anti-Hillary protest looked likely, he'd "sprinkle" the Clinton goons throughout the crowd "so there was always someone able to respond quickly."

The Clinton campaign "never advocated physical confrontation and always insisted that the etiquette squad stay within the boundaries of the law," he claimed. But in the next breath Halley confessed, "Sadly, but inevitably, things sometimes got a little frisky, but my recruits knew how to handle themselves."[5] The Clinton operative recalled that one of his goon squad gangs "had come from the longshoreman's union," adding "I had heard rumors that they had been very adamant about defending themselves when set upon by protesters."

In fact, among reporters who covered Mrs. Clinton out on the political hustings, it was an open secret that her campaign had resorted to brown-shirt tactics more appropriate to Hitler's Third Reich than to any democracy that prides itself on freedom of speech and the right of assembly. But most reporters kept obediently silent, fearing that reporting the news would prompt Mrs. Clinton to exact punishment by cutting off access altogether, putting the offending news organization at a competitive disadvantage.

Reporter Complains about Hillary's Goons

One reporter who declined to keep silent, at least in interviews with fellow journalists, was *New York Post* Albany bureau chief Fred Dicker. In June 2000 MSNBC's Chris Matthews asked Dicker why reporters never seemed to ask Hillary Clinton tough questions.

"We try and the Secret Service stops us," the *Post* bureau chief complained. "I mean, she'll show up at a local event and you'll go up to her like you would any candidate, and say, 'Mrs. Clinton, can I ask you . . .' and she runs off and the Secret Service blocks us. She's done that time after time after time. You can't get to her."[6]

Dicker had no idea that the tough guys he ran into were probably not Secret Service, but more likely the rough customers hired by Halley. He complained to Matthews, "She's using the resources of the federal government to prevent us from just having the kind of access you would take for granted with any other politician." A few days later, however. Dicker was even more candid about the Clinton campaign's tactic in a New York radio interview.

> "I tried to get close to her. There were some legitimate questions to ask her. And these guys, they were like goons."
>
> —New York Post *reporter Fred Dicker*

"I tried to get close to her. There were some legitimate questions to ask her. And these guys, they were like goons," he told WABC. "They don't offer you a rational explanation of why they're doing it. They just block you. And you say, 'Can I try to get over there?' Either they won't answer you. Or they just say no." He criticized the tight security as "not legitimate in a real political campaign."[7]

The *Post* reporter said he was dismayed to learn that more people didn't know about the heavy-handed tactics employed by the then first lady to keep reporters at bay. "I was surprised at the response my comments got," Dicker said of his earlier remarks on MSNBC. "Because I've been hearing this from my colleagues for months. I mean, this is not a mystery." Still, even his own newspaper, the *New York Post,* declined to report the astonishing news that in America in 2000, the most celebrated politician in the nation was using "goon squads" to subvert the First Amendment's protections.

The St. Patrick's Day Media Massacre

Rumors of Clinton operatives roughing up both reporters and protesters during Hillary's 2000 Senate campaign continued to swirl—even as the mainstream press declined to cover the assaults. One such altercation was practically broadcast live as Mrs. Clinton marched in New York's St. Patrick's Day parade that year. Recounting what had happened only moments before, Metro Network News reporter Glenn Schuck assumed that rogue Secret Service agents assigned to Mrs. Clinton had been responsible for the thuglike tactics:

"Secret Service agents literally are pushing press to the ground. They just lost their minds, in my opinion," Schuck told WABC Radio's Sean Hannity. "I mean they just started pushing and shoving; female camera people five feet tall were getting thrown to the ground, cameras flying. Myself, I was grabbed by the shoulder, I was thrown back over. I think somebody from Channel 11 landed on my back. From that point it really didn't get any better."[8]

A few days after Schuck's report, a caller to WOR Radio's *Bob Grant Show* reported that she and her family had also been accosted by the Clinton goons along the parade route. Caller "Maureen" reported that her family had been booing Mrs. Clinton as she marched down Fifth Avenue when "they were surrounded by men in trench coats with radios." She quoted the men as saying her family "did not have the right" to heckle and ordering, "We think you should stop this now."[9]

"Teamsters for Clinton"

The goon squad tactics Halley described were apparently also practiced by Mr. Clinton's advance team. During an October

1998 protest of the then president's visit to Philadelphia, demonstrators were set upon by goons wearing T-shirts bearing the message "Teamsters for Clinton." Philadelphia native Don Adams was beaten severely during the confrontation and later filed suit against city officials. Though covered live on the Fox News Channel, the altercation didn't make news till the *Wall Street Journal* editorial page complained about the incident weeks later. By October 2000, five teamsters involved in the altercation had pled guilty to various charges in the case, including assault and conspiracy.[10]

Before the revelation in Halley's book, no one previously associated with the Clinton White House had ever acknowledged using goon squads to stifle the right of protest and assembly.

Private Detectives

In fact, the darkest side of the Clinton sex scandals involved not Bill but attempts at damage control by Hillary, who was able to silence most of her husband's accusers using tactics more appropriate to the mob than a presidential campaign. Even at the height of her husband's impeachment drama, with reporters poring over six-year-old transcripts of Gennifer Flowers's tapes for any hint that might have foreshadowed the Monica Lewinsky scandal, almost no one paid attention to Mrs. Clinton's role in directing the 1992 Clinton war room's bimbo-eruption SWAT team, including the hiring of private detectives.

"I am somebody you call in when the house is on fire, not when there's smoke in the kitchen," bragged West Coast private detective Jack Palladino in a 1999 interview with the *San Francisco Examiner.*[11] "You ask me to deal with that fire, to save you, to do whatever has to be done to the fire. . . . People call me when they are in a great deal of trouble, and sometimes a great deal of pain." Hillary knew of Palladino, reports biographer Gail Sheehy, from her days defending the Black Panthers. The pricey PI had done investigations for attorney

Charles Garry, who defended some of the bigger names in the Panther pantheon like Bobby Seale, Huey Newton, and Eldridge Cleaver.

Federal Election Commission records reveal that the Clinton campaign disbursed $100,000 to Palladino, listed as "legal fees." Meanwhile, the tough-guy PI roamed the country chasing down women suspected of having affairs with the future president—and met with much success. He convinced reporters that there was no truth to nasty rumors, for instance, about an affair between Clinton and a young student he taught as a law professor at the University of Arkansas. The woman was married, became pregnant, and then committed suicide.

Gennifer Flowers has told reporters that Palladino intimidated her mother and inquired of her roommate, "Is Gennifer the kind of person who would commit suicide?" When the California arm-twister ran into resistance, he would glean damaging material on prospective Clinton sex accusers by visiting relatives and ex-boyfriends. Confronted with embarrassing tidbits from their own pasts, most decided silence was golden. According to Sheehy, the San Francisco tough guy eventually reached out and touched six of the Jane Doe witnesses who were later named in the Paula Jones case.

"Bimbo" Eruptions Hit the Bush Radar Screen

Mary Matalin, who helped manage then President Bush's 1992 reelection campaign, was stunned to learn how important Palladino's work had become to the Clinton political operation.

"I controlled the money in the [1992 Bush] campaign," Matalin said in 1997, during a stint as a talk radio host in between Bush presidencies. "And Betsey Wright announced that she was putting $28,000 on the 'bimbo' patrol and on Jack Palladino and Pellicano, the other guy."

The phrase "bimbo eruptions," oddly enough, came not from any GOP spinmeister, but instead from Wright, who had during the 1980s become Clinton's de facto guardian angel in charge of keeping the lid on his private life. In hopes of getting ahead of the "eruptions," Wright circulated a list of nineteen women whom the campaign warned might claim affairs with the Arkansas governor. But instead of discrediting prospective sex accusers, Wright's list of "bimbo eruptions" only heightened the Bush campaign's curiosity about Clinton's private life.

"Twenty-eight thousand dollars, to me, the political director," said Matalin, "was four states in the Rocky Mountains. You had a limited budget. I said, how could they spend this much money? How could they basically give up four states to track down 'bimbos'? That's why it was kind of shocking to me that it must have been a bigger priority than putting money into states for the purpose of winning and that's why I flagged it at the time. I don't even remember how many or what kind of women."

> "I got the letters from Pellicano to these women intimidating them. I had tapes of conversations from Pellicano to the women. I got handwritten letters from the women."
>
> —*White House aide Mary Matalin*

The top GOP strategist and senior adviser to both President Bush and Vice President Cheney before she left the White House to work from home in December 2002 said she had hard evidence of the kind of hardball tactics that Hillary's enforcers were willing to use in order to camouflage the candidate's inconvenient past—evidence documenting the activities of Palladino's Los Angeles counterpart, Anthony Pellicano.

"I got the letters from Pellicano to these women intimidating them. I had tapes of conversations from Pellicano to the women. I got handwritten letters from the women." Matalin continued, "I got one letter from [the father of] one of the women . . . saying, 'This is so horrible. Here's what they're going to do to us,' you know, essentially. It's not like they said, 'We're going to go out there and bust your kneecaps. [It was more like] we're going to say this, that and the other.'"[12]

Bush Sr. Takes a Pass

Matalin said that even though she had smoking-gun proof of the Clinton campaign's heavy-handed attempts to silence the future president's ex-girlfriends, then President Bush refused to use the damaging material to save his reelection bid.

"When I went to my boss in the campaign with this information and then they went to Bush, Bush himself called me up and said, 'I don't want to hear it. Don't even tell me what you have. Throw it all out,'" she told her radio audience.

It would have been bad enough if Mr. Clinton had masterminded the bimbo-eruption strategy. But instead, different accounts over the years suggest it was Mrs. Clinton, who—while playing the wounded spouse in public—went on the attack behind the scenes, deploying professional silencers to seal loose lips. Years before Palladino and Pellicano, the future first lady hired Ivan Duda, a former FBI agent turned private detective, to probe her husband's nocturnal wanderings. It was 1982, and the Clintons were preparing to reclaim the governor's mansion after Bill's humiliating defeat two years before.

"It was damage control, pure and simple," Duda told Clinton biographer Christopher Andersen about his bimbo-patrol efforts. "[Hillary's] purpose in having me find out about those women was not so she could confront Bill with the hurt attitude of, 'How could you do this to me?'" Instead, his investigation, he said, "enabled Hillary to go to Bill and work out arrangements for keeping those women quiet—by offering them jobs, promotions, contracts to better positions or whatever it took to keep everything hush-hush."[13]

Hillary Advises "Clinton Love Child" Aunt

Corroboration of Mrs. Clinton's reliance on private detectives came from another unlikely source, Lucille Bolton, sister of Bobbie Ann Williams, the black Little Rock prostitute who claimed that Bill had fathered her son Danny in 1984. A comparison of incomplete DNA samples in 1999 suggested her paternity claim was baseless. But in 1987, when the family was convinced of a blood tie, Bolton contacted the Little Rock governor's mansion and claims to have gotten Hillary herself on the line. In the conversation, which Bolton said lasted two or three minutes, Hillary asked, "Is it true that he has this illegitimate child?" When she got an affirmative response, Mrs. Clinton supplied Bolton with the phone number of a security agency that would help her "get the publicity to stop."[14]

Oddly enough, Hillary's PI Pellicano popped back into the headlines in November 2002, after FBI agents raided his Sunset Boulevard offices and discovered a small arsenal in plastic explosives, hand grenades, detonating cord, and blasting caps. Pellicano's stash of explosives was powerful enough "to bring down a plane or blow up a car," an FBI agent told reporters.[15] As luck would have it, the explosive find was a complete surprise to investigators, who wanted to search Pellicano's offices instead because an informant had implicated him in a witness-intimidation scheme. The victim, *Los Angeles Times* reporter Anita Busch, eventually resigned from the paper after her car was vandalized, leaving her with a smashed windshield and a dead fish on the front seat—a single red rose in its mouth.

Media reports on the case noted Pellicano's ties to other big name clients like O. J. Simpson and over-the-hill pop star Michael Jackson. The Clinton name, however, was conveniently omitted from the coverage.

CHAPTER ELEVEN

Hillary's Sexgate Minefield

"I'm not going to comment on any specific allegation, because I've learned we need to put all of this into context, and it will be put into context."
—Hillary Clinton on *Today,* addressing allegations that her husband had been involved with Monica Lewinsky, January 27, 1998

For Mrs. Clinton it's the ultimate paradox. Her supporters believe she's the smartest, most independent woman in the world. Yet she continues to cling to a dysfunctional marriage precisely because it's always been her springboard to power. When her husband won election as Arkansas' attorney general, Hillary became one of the first female lawyers accepted into Little Rock's Rose Law Firm. When Bill became governor, she was made a partner. When he won the White House, Mrs. Clinton became co-president with control over health care reform and the Justice Department. And his Sexgate impeachment resulted in so much spillover sympathy for her that it turned Hillary into the first of the first ladies to win elective office in her own right.

Several insiders who have witnessed the Clintons' marriage up close have noticed a distressing pattern: Time and again through more than two decades of married life, Bill Clinton has made up for his private failings by awarding Hillary with public power. Veteran presidential advisor David Gergen, who was brought into the White House in May 1993 to combat the chaos that permeated those early days, recalled the effect on public policy of allegations from four of Mr. Clinton's former Arkansas state trooper bodyguards that he used them to procure sex partners.

"What happened was that that Troopergate story put that see-saw up so that she went way up and he went way down," Gergen told PBS's *Frontline* for a retrospective look at the Clinton era. "And I never saw him challenge her on health care in the weeks that followed—on the politics of what was going on, on sort of how to get it presented to the Congress properly, how to get it through the Congress."

The one-time senior Clinton adviser said that after Troopergate, it was clear that Mrs. Clinton was in charge of every aspect of the administration's most important legislative initiative. "I really think that it sealed her position. It put her firmly in charge of how to get health care done."[1]

Gergen even perceived an element of marital blackmail in the way Hillary extracted concessions from her husband after the troopers went public with their allegations. "Watching him in that time, it was very much like watching a golden retriever that has pooped on the rug and just curls up and keeps his head down. And it put him in a situation where he was in her doghouse. And I think it put him in a situation where on health care he never challenged it in a way he ordinarily would have, had he been under a different psychological situation."

No Divorce

In the public's mind, the Clinton's broken marriage is their most enduring legacy—the aspect of their time in the national spotlight that has most perplexed supporters, infuriated critics, and fascinated most observers. Democratic Party apparatchiks can tout the official accomplishments of their time in office—a booming economy, a sky-high stock market, inflation under control, and eight years of relative peace—till they're blue in the face. But whatever the achievements, real or imagined, that can be credited to Bill and Hillary, it was his 1998 impeachment on Sexgate charges—a disgrace visited on no other *elected* president in U.S. history—that provided her with a platform to run for the Senate.

As Mrs. Clinton builds her own political machine along with an independent legislative track record, she may no longer need to play the victim to win her party's nomination for president. But Bill Clinton will remain her essential credential for higher office. No matter how stellar Hillary's Senate career may eventually turn out to be, when she runs for the White House she'll do it by comparing her husband's record with that of her opponent, something she's been doing since late 2001 with President Bush. And so Bill must inexorably remain in the picture as Hillary's ally and biggest asset. Speculation in dozens of tabloid reports to the contrary, Senator Clinton can't divorce her husband, because it would compromise her ability to tout their joint record of success as superior to Bush's.

Senator Clinton can't divorce her husband, because it would compromise her ability to tout their joint record of success as superior to Bush's.

A marital split is out of the question for a number of other reasons as well, not the least of which is the impact it would have on Hillary's ability to finance a presidential run. Divorce would be taken as Mrs. Clinton's admission that her husband's impeachers were correct, that his behavior had been intolerable and that her efforts to suggest otherwise had been a lie. The Democratic Party's—indeed the country's—decision in 1999 not to throw Mr. Clinton out of office had been based almost entirely on the proposition, often stated outright by Clinton defenders at the time, that Sexgate was a private matter between Bill and Hillary. If Hillary could live with it, the argument went, then the country should be able to as well.

The Democratic Party's big-bucks donors like Ron Burkle, Denise Rich, and Walter Shorenstein rallied round the White House's Monicagate rationalizations by donating the maximum to the Clintons' Legal Defense Fund. *Power Rangers* and *Teenage Mutant Ninja Turtles* cartoon mogul Haim Saban, for instance, ponied up $10,000 for the Clintons' legal kitty, the legal allowable limit. He's also pledged between $5 and $10 million to the Clinton's Little Rock Library, to help repair the damage to their legacy.[2]

But Saban isn't merely a high-rolling Clinton donor. He has also given the party $9 million in the last two years, making him the largest soft-money donor to either party.[3] And if that weren't enough, the children's TV tycoon offered to foot the bill for the DNC's new Washington, D.C., headquarters, a pledge Saban acknowledged last year would cost "no more than $10 million."[4]

Big-money players like Saban and the others, who are indispensable to the Democratic Party's hopes to reclaim the White House, had their trust severely tested—most would say abused—in the crucible of Monicagate. They were forced to suspend disbelief almost immediately, with Hillary Clinton's decision to appear on *Today* on January 27, 1998, six days after the scandal had exploded in the *Washington Post*.

Hillary's Monicagate Non-Denial

Few recall the actual details of Mrs. Clinton's comments to *Today* host Matt Lauer, beyond her claim that her husband was being persecuted by a "vast right-wing conspiracy." But, in fact, she repeatedly declined to expressly deny her husband's affair with the White House intern:

LAUER: But he has described to the American people what this relationship was not . . .

CLINTON: That's right.

LAUER: . . . in his words.

CLINTON: That's right.

LAUER: Has he described to you what it was?

CLINTON: Yes. And we'll—and we'll find that out as time goes by, Matt. But I think the important thing now is to stand as firmly as I can and say that, you know, that the president has denied these allegations on all counts, unequivocally, and we'll—we'll see how this plays out.[5]

Later she told Lauer, "I'm not going to comment on any specific allegation, because I've learned we need to put all of this into context, and it will be put into context." The closest Hillary came to any outright denial was when she said of the Lewinsky allegations, "Well, I think—if all that were proven true, I think that would be a very serious offense." She then predicted, "That is not going to be proven true." But she never said point-blank that allegations her husband had been involved with a twenty-one-year-old intern were untrue.

Mrs. Clinton's guarded responses to Lauer's questions should have set off smoke alarms among her husband's supporters, since they left plenty of wiggle room for an eventual clarification. And in fact, she was forced to abandon any similar ambiguousness under tougher questioning the next day by ABC's *Good Morning America* host Lisa McRee.

McREE: We have to ask the Monica Lewinsky questions. You've said that you heard of the allegations as the story hit the press last week, as most of the nation did. Did you privately ask your husband if it was true?

CLINTON: I have talked to my husband about everything. But I don't, you know, ever talk about my conversations with my husband. But I can state unequivocally that, as my husband has said, these are false allegations.

McREE: Do you believe he's told you the whole story?

CLINTON: I know he has. And I know that the American people will eventually know the story.[6]

Hillary was likely speaking the truth in at least one regard. By the time the Lewinsky allegations exploded, she had known, as McRee put it, "the whole story."

And that story went well beyond Gennifer Flowers's allegations in 1991, when Bill Clinton, with his wife looking on, flatly denied to *60 Minutes* Flowers's claims while simultaneously acknowledging that he had "caused pain in [his] marriage."

Tales of Monicas Past

By at least one account, that pain started right from the very start, even before their wedding day had ended. In 1999 an old friend of the Clintons confided what she saw at their wedding reception to biographer Christopher Anderson. "One woman—a member of the Fayetteville contingent who would remain a friend of the Clintons for decades—pushed open the bathroom door and was 'totally floored' by what she saw: Bill 'passionately kissing a young woman. He was fondling her breasts. I was so shocked I just closed the door quickly and quietly.'"[7]

And if Mrs. Clinton hadn't been privy to what transpired just hours after she took her wedding vows, she certainly found out about other wanderings indulged in by her husband. Biographer Sheehy describes a "Come-to-Jesus" meeting insisted upon by Hillary in 1990, after she discovered Bill was serious about one of his conquests.

"[Hillary] was shattered by learning that her husband had actually fallen in love with another woman," the author told NBC's Stone Phillips.[8] "And this affair, which has never been described before, almost drove a stake through their marriage." Hillary reportedly gave Bill an ultimatum: Either get his ravenous libido under control or their marriage—and his hopes for the White House—would be over. Clinton promised to try, but Arkansas state trooper Danny Ferguson—who as a codefendant along with Clinton in the Paula Jones case was ostensibly on his side—testified that his boss's affair with the woman known as Jane Doe 1 continued right up to the last possible minute.

"[Ferguson] said he escorted a woman past the Secret Service for a 5:15 A.M. Little Rock rendezvous with Clinton in January 1993—just days before he was sworn in as president. The woman reportedly slipped past security at the Arkansas governor's mansion clad in a long trench coat and a baseball cap. . . . Ferguson said in a sworn deposition that he escorted the woman to Clinton four times late at night."[9]

Hundreds of Sex Partners

And, of course, there were others, "hundreds," in fact, according to Clinton himself in separate comments to trooper-bodyguard L. D. Brown and Monica Lewinsky. In his book, *Crossfire: Witness in the Clinton Investigation,* Brown describes one encounter suggesting that Hillary and Bill's unorthodox marriage was so open, it verged on partner swapping.

"The 'significant other' for [Bill] Clinton was Beth Coulson . . . described as a 'Kewpie doll with brains,' being diminutive with sky-blue eyes while an intellectual lawyer as well. Beth was always there for Bill and was indeed his soul mate," writes Brown. The Clinton bodyguard described numerous Clinton rendezvous with Coulson, then a married Little Rock attorney, including one that took place in front of her husband, Mike—as well as Hillary. They had all gathered at Little Rock's Fu Lin restaurant, owned by Charlie Trie, who would eventually become infamous for his illegal donations to the Clintons. Vince Foster—who, according to numerous sources in Little Rock, was involved with Hillary—along with his wife Lisa, was also on hand.

"Hillary was kissing Vince like I've never seen her kiss Bill," Brown claimed. "And the same sort of thing was going on with Bill and Beth. Mike and Lisa's oblivion to the escalation of amorous activity left me bewildered. No one seemed to notice me except for Vince, who would give me the occasional furtive glance, sometimes accentuated by a wink."[10]

Against this backdrop, it's extremely unlikely that Hillary Clinton didn't at least suspect the Lewinsky story was true when she told ABC's *Good Morning America,* "I can state unequivocally that, as my husband has said, these are false allegations."

Harassment, Assault, and Rape

"We must never again shy away from raising our voices against sexual harassment," said Hillary Clinton on August 9, 1992, presenting the American Bar Association's annual achievement award to Anita Hill, the woman who accused Clarence Thomas of sexual harassment.

Fifteen months after Mrs. Clinton spoke those words, her husband cornered White House volunteer Kathleen Willey in the study off the Oval Office and tried to coax her into having sex, physically assaulting her in the process. Unlike Juanita Broaddrick's later rape accusation, which the press was able to dismiss because Clinton's impeachment trial had ended by the time she emerged, Willey's release of her story couldn't have been more timely.

"Hillary was kissing Vince like I've never seen her kiss Bill."
—*former Clinton bodyguard L.D. Brown*

It was January 1998. The Monica Lewinsky case had just exploded when Willey finally decided to cooperate with Paula Jones's lawyers, who had been trying to obtain her testimony since the previous summer. She had been in intermittent contact with *Newsweek*'s Michael Isikoff for most of the previous year but had been hesitant to talk about what had happened to her in any detail, reluctant to get caught up in the swirl of the Paula Jones case.

But with Lewinsky's story of her affair with Clinton spilling forth in transcripts of taped conversations with Linda Tripp—and Tripp already on the record about Willey confiding in her about her own encounter—she had no choice. Willey would become the most explosive cooperating witness in the independent counsel's investigation of Clinton's attempts to obstruct the Paula Jones case.

Willey's story had been the subject of much speculation before she let all the details be known. Isikoff had detailed the circumstances surrounding the Oval Office attack in a report the previous August, but at the time Willey was still trying to fight off subpoenas from the Jones legal team. The full dimensions of her account would not be known until March 15, 1998, when CBS's *60 Minutes* broadcast her interview with Ed Bradley. That night, an America that had been skeptical of Paula Jones's claim that Clinton was a sexual harasser was jarred to a new reality by another witness who not only sounded more credible, but whose story also meant that Clinton continued to accost women even after he'd reached the White House.

Spoken in halting tones, Willey's revelations to Bradley would, for the first time, begin to unravel Clinton's support with that all-important Democratic Party demographic—women:

WILLEY: I pushed back away from him and he—he—he—he—he's a big man. And he—he had his arms—they were tight around me, and he—he—he—he touched me.

BRADLEY: Touched you how?

WILLEY: Well, he—he—he touched my breast with his hand, and I—I—I—I was—I—I was just startled. I was—I—I w—j—was just . . .

BRADLEY: Thi—this wasn't an accidental, grazing touch?

WILLEY: No, no. And—and then he—he whispered—he—he w—he said in—in my ear, he said, "I've—I've wanted to do this ever since I laid eyes on you." And—and I remember—I remember saying to him, "Aren't you afraid that somebody's gonna walk in here?" The—and he said—he said, "No. No, I'm—no, I'm not." And—and then—and—and then he took my hand and he—and he put it on him. And that's when I pushed away from him and—and decided it was time to get out of there.

BRADLEY: When you say he took your hand . . .

WILLEY: Right.

BRADLEY: . . . and put it on him . . .

WILLEY: Mm-hmm.

BRADLEY: Where on him?

WILLEY: On—on his genitals.

BRADLEY: Was he aroused?

WILLEY: Mm-hmm.

BRADLEY: He was.

WILLEY: Mm-hmm.[11]

As Willey's story exploded on the front page of nearly every newspaper across the land the next day, no reporter dared question the nation's leading feminist figurehead, Hillary Clinton, who only six years earlier had warned, "We must never again shy away from raising our voices against sexual harassment." In fact, the woman whom she had praised for stepping forward with her own harassment claim against Supreme Court justice Clarence Thomas took to the op-ed pages of the *New York Times* to justify Clinton's Oval Office sex attack.

"We must never again shy away from raising our voices against sexual harassment."

—*Hillary Clinton, in praise of Anita Hill in 1992*

Anita Hill Defends Bill

"As was true in my situation with Clarence Thomas," Hill wrote, "Ms. Willey has not brought a sexual harassment claim against Mr. Clinton. Moreover, Ms. Willey has not alleged that the one incident she described was so severe and pervasive as to become a condition of her employment, which is what the law on sexual harassment requires."[12]

Not a condition of employment? Professor Hill's screed never quite got around to explaining how Clinton's accosting Willey moments after she had asked for a paying White House job didn't strongly imply that her sexual receptiveness would be "a condition of employment." Hill's essay, along with a companion piece defending Clinton in the same space, defined what became known as "the one free grope" policy.

With the Kathleen Willey, Paula Jones, and Juanita Broaddrick stories, there were now three compelling accounts suggesting that Bill Clinton's sexual proclivities weren't always confined to the realm of the consensual. Author Roger Morris's "young woman lawyer in Little Rock" would make four. The woman who told Arkansas Republican gubernatorial candidate Sheffield Nelson that she was raped while drunk would be number five. And in 1998, former Miss America Liz Ward Gracen finally acknowledged a sexual encounter with Clinton sixteen years earlier after a friend told Jones's lawyers that she remembered Gracen saying the sex was forced.

In his 1999 book on the Jones-Lewinsky case, *Uncovering Clinton,* Isikoff noted: "According to Gracen's later account . . . it was rough sex. Clinton got so carried away that he bit her lip."[13] Although in her final version the beauty queen turned actress insisted the episode was consensual, both Broaddrick and the "young woman lawyer in Little Rock" had also described biting during forced encounters.

Another Oval Office Attack

A seventh woman had privately alleged yet another Oval Office sexual attack in a story remarkably similar to Willey's. She contacted Isikoff after his first report on Willey in August 1997, but has declined to go public to this day. The Oval Office mystery victim told the *Newsweek* reporter that she had met Clinton at various political events the two had attended over the years. After he became president, she was invited to stop by the White House whenever she was in town on business. In early 1996 she did, and when she entered the Oval Office, Clinton immediately ushered her into his hideaway annex—the same place he took Lewinsky for their romps together.

The two old friends chatted at first. But then, "Clinton started getting physical, trying to kiss her, touching her breasts," Isikoff said. "She was stunned. She had no idea how to respond. 'I've never had a man take advantage of me like that,'" she confided. As the president of the United States continued to paw her, she began to resist, pushing him away. Finally he gave up and turned away. "What happened next?" Isikoff asked. "I think he finished the job himself," the unidentified victim recalled, unwittingly describing the Clinton M.O. that would become familiar a year later with the release of the Starr report.[14]

There was another incident, she revealed, confided by a female "administration official" who "had told her about Clinton slipping his hands up her leg." She, too, refused to go public with details of the assault. "It was just too awful," Isikoff's mystery tipster told him.

Rape!

Ironically enough, as Mrs. Clinton weighed her political options in the early days of January 1999, another woman was pondering an equally momentous decision. Having been beseeched for nearly a year by NBC investigative reporter Lisa Myers, Arkansas businesswoman Juanita Broaddrick was finally ready to step into the public square and tell her story—a story Mrs. Clinton has yet to be asked about.

Exactly two years to the day before the end of the Clinton administration, on January 20, 1999, Broaddrick sat down with Myers to give her account of a brutal rape by Bill Clinton twenty years earlier. The network had already thoroughly vetted her story, hiring private investigators to comb through every aspect of her life. NBC producers had managed to turn up four witnesses who corroborated different aspects of her allegations, including a friend, Norma Rogers Kelsay, who discovered Broaddrick bruised and bleeding moments after the attack. The Clinton rape accuser sat for NBC for eight hours, five of which, she was told, yielded usable videotape, where she went through every conceivable detail of her life that could have been remotely relevant to the attack.

The political stakes couldn't have been higher. Clinton's impeachment trial was just getting underway, with the president accused of trying to rig Paula Jones's sexual harassment case by covering up the truth about Monica Lewinsky. The story had the potential to turn the Lewinsky scandal thermonuclear, transforming conduct that Democrat spinmeisters had successfully defended as "lying about sex" to an entirely different level. Broaddrick's story also had the potential to transform Mrs. Clinton's image from that of a stoic victim whose feminist credentials transcended her marital humiliations to that of a victimizer who actually enabled her husband's predations.

NBC Drags Its Feet

NBC clearly recognized how explosive its Broaddrick exclusive was, deciding to delay its broadcast past the end of Clinton's Senate trial in the apparent fear that the revelation could tip what looked like a sure acquittal into a guilty verdict that would remove a president from office. A month earlier MSNBC's Chris Matthews had revealed that it was a rape allegation, documented amidst other secret impeachment evidence stored in Washington, D.C.'s Ford Building, that had persuaded up to forty wavering House Republicans to vote for Clinton's impeachment. In a very real sense, it was Broaddrick's account, and not the Lewinsky scandal, that catalyzed the first impeachment of an elected president in U.S. history.

Meanwhile, NBC's delays were making Broaddrick nervous. Word was out on the Drudge Report that she had sat down with Myers. As the most damaging of all Sexgate whistleblowers, she feared retaliation without the protection of having the American people know her story. On January 26, 1999, six days after her session with Myers, NBC told Broaddrick her story would be broadcast on the network's prestigious *Dateline NBC* newsmagazine within three days. In her first comments to any media outlet since her sit-down with Myers, Broaddrick told NewsMax.com that day she was concerned about the network's foot-dragging, especially after Myers passed along the comments of network higher-ups. "The good news is, you're credible," Myers told the Clinton rape whistleblower. "The bad news is, you're very, very credible."[15]

Growing suspicious, Broaddrick worried aloud, "I think there probably are some Clinton people [at NBC] who probably do not want this aired." She complained that the decision to come forward had been emotionally wrenching and that she had made it only after NBC had chased her for months—and now she had a bull's-eye painted on her back without the public at large knowing her story. She feared she might have to go through it all again with another network if her story was ever to come out. "It's terrible, the most terrible thing I've had to go through in my life," she said. "To bring my husband and my family into this and to finally submit after nine months of them harping and harping on this—telling me how important it is, and then to have them sit on it like this, I'm getting very disheartened."

> "The good news is, you're credible. The bad news is, you're very, very credible."
>
> —*NBC reporter Lisa Myers to Clinton rape accuser Juanita Broaddrick*

In the same January 26 conversation, the presidential rape accuser confirmed that she had considered coming forward seven years earlier in 1992, while Clinton was campaigning for the White House. Had she done so at the time, in the aftermath of the Gennifer Flowers revelations, for which reporters had given Clinton a pass on the basis that it was a one-of-a-kind consensual affair, the co-presidency of Bill and Hillary Clinton would almost certainly never have happened.

Other Rapes?

In a meeting Broaddrick had with Sheffield Nelson, Clinton's gubernatorial opponent in the 1990 race, Nelson told her that she was not alone. "A friend of his and his wife's was raped by Clinton but she couldn't come forward because she was drunk at the time," she remembered the state's top Republican as saying.

Broaddrick told NewsMax she wasn't sure whether the other rape victim was the same woman who talked to Clinton biographer Roger Morris, who detailed an attack for his 1996 book about Bill and Hillary's political rise, *Partners in Power:* "A young woman lawyer in Little Rock," reported Morris, "claimed that she was accosted by Clinton while he was attorney general and that when she recoiled he forced himself on her, biting and bruising her. Deeply affected by the assault, the woman decided to keep it all quiet for the sake of her own hard-won career and that of her husband. When the husband later saw Clinton at the 1980 Democratic Convention, he delivered a warning. 'If you ever approach her,' he told the governor, 'I'll kill you.' Not even seeing fit to deny the incident, Bill Clinton sheepishly apologized and duly promised never to bother her again."[16]

While many familiar with both Broaddrick's story and the Morris account believed they were different versions of the same episode—both attacks took place in 1978, both involved biting and bruising—in fact, they were not. Broaddrick said she had never talked to Morris, who in turn told me in 1997 that he had interviewed both the unnamed rape victim and her husband multiple times in late 1993 and early 1994.

NBC Sacrifices Mega-Exclusive to Protect Clinton

Broaddrick herself was indeed forced to turn to another mainstream outlet before NBC would broadcast her account. After

NewsMax.com tipped the *Wall Street Journal* to her frustration over the network's delays, the Journal sent its Pulitzer Prize–winning reporter Dorothy Rabinowitz to Arkansas in a bid to win Broaddrick's trust. Finally, on February 19, the story exploded on the *Journal*'s editorial page under the headline "Juanita Broaddrick Meets the Press," a none too subtle slap at NBC's premier Sunday news broadcast, headed up by Tim Russert. The show's host was caught between his bosses' apparent desire to protect Clinton and his own reporter's bombshell scoop—the biggest exclusive NBC ever had—which he had to throw away.

The *Journal* recounted the basics of the ugly encounter; how Clinton first put his arms around her, startling her. Broaddrick recalled, "He told me, 'We're both married people,'" whereupon she responded that she was deeply involved with another man. The "argument failed to persuade Mr. Clinton, who, she says, got her onto the bed, held her down forcibly and bit her lips."

"The sexual entry itself was not without some pain because of her stiffness and resistance," Rabinowitz recounted on the basis of Broaddrick's comments. "When it was over, she says, he looked down at her and said not to worry, he was sterile—he had had mumps when he was a child."

"I felt paralyzed and was starting to cry," Broaddrick said. Clinton turned before leaving, she recalled. "This is the part that always stays in my mind—the way he put on his sunglasses. Then he looked at me and said, 'You better put some ice on that.' And then he left." Minutes later her friend Norma Rogers Kelsay, "a nurse who had accompanied her on the trip," came into the room and found her still on the bed. Broaddrick was, Kelsay told the *Journal,* "in a state of shock—lips swollen to double their size, mouth discolored from the biting, her pantyhose torn in the crotch. She just stayed on the bed and kept repeating, 'I can't believe what happened.'"

Broaddrick Aired

Five days later, its big scoop preempted, NBC finally relented and broadcast its Broaddrick report to little fanfare. *NBC Nightly News* anchor Tom Brokaw refused to cover Myers's bombshell on his own newscast. The network, meanwhile, promoted other *Dateline* segments that night instead of the explosive rape account. Still, Broaddrick's video presentation was significant. Even without any promotion, 24 million people tuned in to hear her level an accusation never before made against any sitting president:

MYERS: Is there any way at all that Bill Clinton could have thought this was consensual?

BROADDRICK: No, not with what I told him and with how I tried to push him away. It was not consensual.

MYERS: You're saying that Bill Clinton sexually assaulted you, that he raped you?

BROADDRICK: Yes.

MYERS: And you have no—there's no doubt in your mind that that's what happened?

BROADDRICK: No doubt whatsoever.[17]

Within days polls suggested that those who watched the *Dateline* broadcast believed Juanita, with 54 percent telling a Fox News Dynamics/*New York Post* survey that they found her charges credible. Just 23 percent disagreed. In an unscientific online poll taken by MSNBC.com immediately after the broadcast, 83 percent said they believed the president of the United States was a rapist.

Several of Clinton's leading female defenders in the media were rocked by Broaddrick's account, including Cynthia Alksne, a former federal sex crimes prosecutor who had become a rising star on MSNBC by arguing Clinton's case during impeachment.

Defenders Desert Clinton

"Here, in a nutshell, is the problem," Alksne argued in the *Wall Street Journal* two weeks after the rape accuser's account appeared. "One woman's word is enough to prosecute a rapist. Rape cases are routinely won or lost when a victim takes the stand to accuse the defendant of the crime. Indeed, the law explicitly permits a jury to convict a rapist on the word of the victim alone if her testimony is deemed credible. And anyone who watched Juanita Broaddrick's NBC News interview with Lisa Myers would have to conclude that, at a minimum, Ms. Broaddrick was a credible accuser."

Turning on Clinton with a vengeance, Alksne complained, "When I was a sex-crimes prosecutor, rapists often got at least eight years of public housing—in jail, not the White House. If these allegations are true, jail is where Mr. Clinton belongs."[18] A month after Alksne's *Journal* column, MSNBC canned her as co-host of *Equal Time*.

In its own backhanded way, the press had acknowledged that the Broaddrick story was the one Clinton scandal that might have prematurely ended his presidency. And the Broaddrick episode remains political poison to Hillary's own political aspirations, including any plans to retake the White House. The rape bombshell exploded the same month rumblings began to emerge that Mrs. Clinton was weighing a Senate run. Still, no reporter dared ask whether the first lady of the United States believed that her husband might be a rapist. Had she ever gotten wind of such an allegation during her days in Arkansas? After all, if Clinton knew about her husband's propensity for Lewinsky-like dalliances, then how could Mr. Duda and other private detectives she hired over the years have failed to come across these other, more distressing stories? Broaddrick herself suspects Hillary knew, recalling what she remembers as a direct effort to keep her from going public with the rape accusation against Bill as his political career was just getting off the ground.

Hillary Silenced Rape Accuser?

"Hillary sought me out," Broaddrick told author Christopher Andersen. "And when somebody told her where I was, she came straight for me and cornered me and grabbed my hand very forcefully." The bizarre encounter between Hillary and her husband's victim took place just three weeks after the attack, at a fund-raiser for Mr. Clinton's first gubernatorial bid. "I can't explain why I went," Broaddrick said. "I was still sort of in a state of denial, a state of shock. I didn't know what to think, what to do."

Broaddrick recalled Mrs. Clinton's words verbatim, as well as her demeanor: "I want you to know how grateful we all are for all you've done for Bill," Hillary said, eyes glaring as if to underline another message. "We are so grateful for all you've done for Bill, and all you'll keep doing." Broaddrick remembered that Hillary's grasp lingered before she let go.

"She was looking at me straight in the eye and I understood perfectly what she was saying. I knew exactly what she meant, that I was to keep my mouth shut," the Arkansas businesswoman said. "That meant she knew [what had happened] almost from the beginning. . . . But apparently it was something she was willing to overlook." Clinton's rape accuser said she was so shaken by the encounter that she exited the gathering because she felt "sick to [her] stomach."[19]

Rape? Something she was willing to overlook? Perhaps that's why the media never make mention of a biographical detail that might otherwise be considered one of Mrs. Clinton's proudest accomplishments—her role in establishing Arkansas' first rape-crisis hotline during her early days as the attorney general's wife.

Hillary as Anti-Rape Crusader

"Hillary began making impressive achievements that soon commanded wide media attention," reported the late George Carpozi in his 1994 comprehensive tell-all, *Clinton Confidential.* "She had broadened her legal service work into efforts to have state legislators pass a law requiring judges to rule from the bench whether evidence of a rape victim's prior sexual behavior was admissible before being presented to a jury. Although the bill didn't make it out of committee, Hillary Rodham stuck to her guns on this sensitive issue involving women's rights. She also single-handedly campaigned, with success, for the establishment of a rape crisis center, the first in Fayetteville. Furthermore, she instituted a program of education for women on sexual violence, a subject that had commanded little attention in the area until then."[20]

"Ann Henry and Hillary had bonded over their activist role in raising a cutting-edge issue for feminists: rape. Together they set up the first rape crisis phone line in Arkansas."

—*author Gail Sheehy*

Hillary biographer Gail Sheehy confirmed Mrs. Clinton's role as an anti-rape crusader for her own book, *Hillary's Choice:* "Ann Henry and Hillary had bonded over their activist role in raising a cutting-edge issue for feminists: rape. Together they set up the first rape crisis phone line in Arkansas."[21]

Andersen uncovered the same ironic detail for his own Clinton tome: "One afternoon, Hillary called a meeting of like-minded feminists at the Henry home to hammer out plans for the state's first hotline serving victims of rape and domestic abuse. She was also a vocal advocate of state legislation barring testimony concerning a rape victim's sexual history. . . . Her first legal case involved a rape victim who did not want her own sexual history used against her by the defense."[22]

So confident is Mrs. Clinton that the press won't challenge her to reconcile her credentials as anti-rape crusader with her silence on a myriad of sexual assault allegations against her husband that, in 2002, she actually took up the cause again. "We've had a steep increase in the number of reported rapes here in New York City," the senator complained to the *New York Times*.[23] "It is now apparent that unless we process [the backlog of rape kit DNA] information and start putting it to use, we are likely to see people who are serial rapists continue their crimes when we could have apprehended them before they could strike again."

Even the usually pro-Clinton *Times* seemed to cringe a bit at the thought of Hillary crusading against sexual assault. Rather than report her remarks as hard news, editors buried them in a Bob Herbert column headlined "Weapon Against Rape." Briefed on Mrs. Clinton's new rape campaign, Juanita Broaddrick told NewsMax, "If Hillary can accept what Bill did to me, then she shouldn't even be involved in anything like that. . . . You just wonder if she shouldn't start at home with this crusade."[24]

Gore Gored by Broaddrick Query

But it was Al Gore, and not Mrs. Clinton, who became the only high-level candidate forced to address the sexual assault allegation against the president. And it wasn't even a reporter who raised the incendiary issue, which hit the presidential hopeful like a shovel in the face.

In what was easily the most dramatic confrontation of the entire 2000 campaign, Katherine Prudhomme, a twenty-nine-year-old home-schooler and supporter of John McCain, rose from the audience at the Derry, New Hampshire, town hall meeting and, in a steady voice, challenged the American vice president about his boss's possible sex crime:

PRUDHOMME: When Juanita Broaddrick made the claim, which I found to be quite credible, that she was raped by Bill Clinton, did it change your opinion about him being one of the best presidents in history? And do you believe Juanita Broaddrick's claim? And what did you tell your son about this?

GORE: Well, I didn't know what to make of her claim because I don't know how to evaluate that story. I really don't.

PRUDHOMME: Did you see the interview? Did you see the interview?

GORE: No, I didn't see the interview. No.

PRUDHOMME: I'm very surprised that you didn't watch the interview.

GORE: Well, what show was it on?

PRUDHOMME: ABC [sic] I believe.

GORE: Yeah, I didn't see it. There have been so many personal allegations and such a non-stop series of attacks. I guess I'm like a lot of people in that I think that enough is enough. I do not know how to evaluate each one of these individual stories. I just don't know. I would never violate the privacy of my communication with one of my children or a member of my family, as for that part of your question.

PRUDHOMME: Do you disbelieve Juanita Broaddrick's claim?

GORE: No, I didn't say that. I just—I said I don't know how to evaluate it. And I didn't see the interview. But I want to say something else to you about this. Why don't you stand back up, and I'd like to be able to look you in the eye. You know, I think that—I think that whatever mistakes he made in his personal life are, in the minds of most Americans, balanced against what he has done in his public life as president.

> My philosophy, since you asked about my religious faith, I'm taught in my religious tradition to hate the sin and love the sinner. I'm taught that all of us are heir to the mistakes—are prone to the mistakes that flesh is heir to. And I think that in judging his performance as a president, I think that most people are anxious to stop talking about all the personal attacks against him and trying to sort out all of the allegations and want to instead move on and focus on the future. That's what's important to me.
>
> Secondly, I felt the same disappointment and anger at him during the period when all this was going on that most people did. You may have felt a different kind of emotion. I don't know. I sense that maybe you did. I certainly felt what most Americans did. Third, I have been involved in a lot of battles where he and I have fought together on behalf of the American people. And I think we've made a good, positive difference for this country. Number four, I'm running for president on my own. I want to take my own . . .
>
> PRUDHOMME: You're supporting him.
>
> GORE: . . . I want to take my own values of faith and family to the presidency. And I want you to evaluate me on the basis of who I am and what you believe I can do for this country as president.[25]

Luckily for Mr. Gore—and even more luckily for then senatorial wannabe Hillary Clinton—the big media decided that the confrontation over presidential rape charges that had been broadcast live by New Hampshire's WNDS-TV just wasn't newsworthy. Beyond viewers of the Fox News Channel and MSNBC, listeners to talk radio, and those who turned to the Internet for their news, the vast majority of Americans had no idea that the vice president of the United States had refused to rule out the possibility that his boss was a rapist.

Hillary's Faustian Bargain

Faced with this much evidence, a woman with half the intellect of Hillary Clinton would understand that she's married to a ravenous sexual predator at best—a brutal serial rapist at worst. And she would have done something about it. For someone with Mrs. Clinton's means and background—even during the early days in Arkansas, her six-figure salary at Rose Law meant that she was financially dependent upon no one—the options were limitless.

She could have forced Bill into counseling and therapy under pain of divorce. She could have withheld her public support—as did Lee Hart in 1988, when her husband Gary was accused of merely indulging in a consensual fling, let alone a pattern of sexual assault. As the woman who set up Arkansas' first rape-crisis hotline, the very least she could have done was to see that her husband's victims were somehow taken care of.

But there was a problem. Any measure of honesty in this regard—even the slightest hint that Mr. Clinton had acknowledged to a therapist that he was a sexual predator —would sink any chance the Clintons had of ever reaching the White House. Rather than sacrifice her personal ambition, Hillary Clinton chose to sell out every one of her feminist principles—and along with them, the interests of every woman in the world who looks to her as a fighter for sexual equality and justice.

Hillary's War on Women

But instead of fighting for the Paula Joneses, Kathleen Willeys, and Juanita Broaddricks of the world, Hillary Clinton made war on them. One of the more intriguing attempts to discredit Willey's account came from Harolyn Cardozo, who befriended Willey when the two were volunteers in the White House social office together.[26]

Cardozo was especially close to Webb Hubbell and his wife Suzy. Along with Vince Foster, Hillary and Hubbell had worked together for years at Little Rock's Rose Law Firm. Mrs. Clinton had brought Hubbell and Foster to Washington to form a critical conduit between the White House, where Foster served as deputy White House counsel, and the Justice Department, where Hubbell served as Assistant Attorney General, acting as Mrs. Clinton's eyes and ears. Harolyn's husband Michael ran the Clinton Legal Defense Fund for a time, a project that was generally under Mrs. Clinton's jurisdiction.

Instead of fighting for the Paula Joneses, Kathleen Willeys, and Juanita Broaddricks of the world, Hillary Clinton made war on them.

But Mrs. Cardozo was also considered a part of Hillary's White House family. In July 1994, for instance, Mrs. Clinton invited both Michael and Harolyn for an intimate gathering of Arkansans at the White House to greet Lisa Foster, who had come back from Little Rock to testify about her husband's suicide the year before. Foster's sister Sheila and her husband would be there, along with Hubbell and his wife, trusted Hillary aide Marsha Scott, and Kaki Hockersmith, Mrs. Clinton's personal decorator from Little Rock. The Cardozos were the only non-Arkansans present.[27]

It's impossible to say whether Harolyn's status as a member of Hillary's inner circle had anything to do with the way she trashed Kathleen Willey while testifying at the 1999 trial of Willey accuser Julie Hiatt Steele that the Clinton sex attack victim had actually sought a relationship with the president. "If I play my cards right, I could be the next Judith Exner," Cardozo claimed Willey had boasted, in a reference to one of John F. Kennedy's White House lovers. She continued with her over-the-top account, claiming that Willey schemed half-jokingly, "We've got to get Hillary out of town!"[28]

The allegedly envious Exner reference was particularly odd, since the 1960s Kennedy gal-pal was shared with Chicago mobster Sam Giancana and led a very troubled life after both men had died. Cardozo's quote made about as much sense as having Willey say she was looking forward to becoming the next Mary Jo Kopechne.

Harolyn was also the daughter of Nate Landow, the Maryland real estate developer who was investigated for allegedly trying to discourage Willey from testifying in the Paula Jones case. In February 1999 ABC News reported that Landow hired Jared Stern, a private investigator, to intimidate Willey after she became a key witness in both the Jones case and the Monica Lewinsky probe then being conducted by Independent Counsel Kenneth Starr. Stern says he was asked to pull Willey's phone records, look for dirt in her medical files, and try to scare her off by conducting a "noisy" investigation that would "let Willey know she was being watched."[29]

Better-known attempts to intimidate Willey include the notorious episode where she was approached by a still-unidentified man while out jogging one morning just before she testified in the Paula Jones case in January 1999. The stranger asked about her missing cat, mentioned her children by name, and asked about her recently vandalized car, a trademark intimidation tactic of the Clinton bimbo-eruptions team. "Don't you get the message?" he warned.

Though no evidence ties the Stern and jogging episodes to Mrs. Clinton, the use of private detectives to intimidate inconvenient females was something she specialized in over the years. Recalling Hillary's reaction after Gennifer Flowers nearly sunk the Clintons' 1992 White House bid, biographer Gail Sheehy noted that the first lady, together with Clinton damage-controller Betsey Wright "mounted a sub-rosa black arts campaign against women." Sheehy noted that "Hillary called upon her old friend [soon-to-be White House counsel] Bernard Nussbaum to counsel Wright on just how far she could legally go to staunch further 'bimbo eruptions.'"[30] After determining that Nussbaum's advice was too timid, Hillary turned to San Francisco private eye Jack Palladino, who wasn't above making physical threats, according to complaints from several women he visited.

There was more. In 2002, as part of an ongoing lawsuit by Gennifer Flowers against the former first lady and top 1992 campaign aides James Carville and George Stephanopoulos, her lawyer, Judicial Watch's Larry Klayman, told the Ninth Circuit Court of Appeals, "Anthony Pellicano was a private investigator hired by Mrs. Clinton herself."[31] Pellicano was the Los Angeles private detective who had been hired to help discredit Flowers's tapes in 1992. He later unearthed the notorious Monica Lewinsky "presidential kneepads" story in 1998 and was finally arrested in 2001 in connection with an attempt to intimidate a reporter for the *Los Angeles Times*.

Hillary's Attack on Willey

But there's one aspect of the campaign to discredit Kathleen Willey where Mrs. Clinton unquestionably played a role. In August 1997, after Willey's name started appearing in the press, the White House began gathering up correspondence she'd sent to the president in the intervening years that sounded too friendly for a sexual assault victim to have sent to her attacker. In one letter Willey described herself as Clinton's "number one fan."[32]

The letters' release prompted another lawsuit by Judicial Watch, which argued that the White House had violated the Privacy Act. In March 2000, a federal judge agreed, finding that President Clinton had committed a crime.

Though she wasn't named in the finding, Mrs. Clinton's role in the White House's Willey smear was obvious from the testimony of her top aide Sidney Blumenthal, whose lawyer explained in court documents: "Mr. Blumenthal recalls that he and Mrs. Clinton discussed Ms. Willey's letters to the President, and that the letters were inconsistent with what Willey had told '60 Minutes.' Both Mrs. Clinton and Mr. Blumenthal agreed that the letters should be released." The same court document noted that Blumenthal moved quickly to act on Mrs. Clinton's decision: "That same day, March 16, 1998, Mr. Blumenthal telephoned Ms. Jill Abramson, a reporter for the *New York Times*" to tip the paper off to the Willey letters.

And Willey wasn't the only Clinton sexual assault victim who found herself under heightened scrutiny. Three months after going public with her rape allegations against Mrs. Clinton's husband, Juanita Broaddrick told NewsMax that she believed she had been placed under surveillance around the time of impeachment by persons unknown. "There was a small gray car parked for about a day and a half up on the highway just outside my property, and when I left I noticed it would follow me," Broaddrick told NewsMax, explaining that she and her husband never got close enough to read the license plate but assumed the car belonged to a reporter. "It never really frightened me," she added. "But it's just that the person was there."[33]

> "The letters were inconsistent with what Willey had told *60 Minutes.* Both Mrs. Clinton and Mr. Blumenthal agreed that the letters should be released."
>
> *—Judicial Watch court filing*

Mob Style Intimidation

But lead House impeachment counsel David Schippers, who had sent his most trusted investigators down to Little Rock to interview Broaddrick in the fall of 1998 with an eye toward including her testimony in Clinton's impeachment trial, didn't buy the "reporter" explanation, telling NewsMax, "It was the type of stuff we ran into with the outfit [the Chicago mob]—intimidation just by watching her, making their presence known. . . . Just to let her know 'We can do what we want.'"

And there was more. "The only incident that frightened us was when our house was broken into while we were gone for a few days," Broaddrick told NewsMax, explaining that the break-in took place after word got out that she was talking to NBC's Lisa Myers. "Somebody got into the house and took the tape from my answering machine. And then they let my three cats out." While there was no sign of forced entry, there was no explanation for either the missing phone tape and mysteriously freed pets. "The last thing I did before we left was make sure the cats were in the house. And, of course, the answering machine tape just disappeared," she explained.[34]

For those who believe that Hillary Clinton's associations with her husband's scandalous past, let alone her own ethically challenged history, would keep her from reaching her goal of president of the United States, consider the following. The Broaddrick break-in and Willey intimidation stories surfaced within weeks of Mrs. Clinton's announcement that she was embarking on a "listening tour" to test the waters for a Senate bid in New York. But even with her well-documented history of hiring private detectives who specialized in witness tampering and intimidation, the mainstream media— even the allegedly Clinton-hating *New York Post*—never deemed it appropriate to ask Clinton if she knew anything about these sinister goings-on.

Indeed, while Willey's account of intimidation got some scant coverage in the *Post* and elsewhere, Broaddrick's report of having her home broken into and finding herself under surveillance around the time she was ready to go public was not reported at all by the big media. And, of course, the Senate candidate was never queried by any reporter about the substance of Broaddrick's story—that Hillary's husband had raped her.

Sexual Assault Not a Campaign Issue

In fact, before he dropped out the 2000 Senate race, Mrs. Clinton's political nemesis Rudy Giuliani was asked directly whether he would demand a response to Broaddrick's allegation from Mrs. Clinton. "No, I don't think so," the reputed GOP pit bull told NewsMax. "I don't think that's an issue that should be part of any Senate campaign or anything I should get involved with. So my answer to that is, no." Even the mayor's assertion that he would not raise the rape issue with Mrs. Clinton was deemed too dicey for mainstreamers to report.[35]

A few months later, when Kathleen Willey offered to come to New York to help get the truth about Hillary out to voters, she found no takers in either the press or the Republican Party. Similar offers from Hillary's one-time favorite bodyguard, L. D. Brown and her one-time funny-money contributor Johnny Chung likewise fell on deaf ears.

Undoubtedly, the Willey and Broaddrick stories could have had a devastating impact on women voters, especially after Rick Lazio was attacked for his performance during his first debate with Mrs. Clinton. In the most memorable episode of their three encounters, Lazio left his podium and approached her with a campaign finance reform pledge, demanding that she sign it. The mild-mannered Republican whom the Clintonistas belittled in private as "Little Ricky" was pilloried in the press for being a Neanderthal brute and bully. Women complained that he reminded them of a hectoring husband who had suddenly transformed the assertive Mrs. Clinton into a

> The GOP's decision to place Hillary's greatest vulnerability out of bounds —to ignore her husband's record of alleged violence toward women—was an unmitigated disaster.

shrinking violet and even a battered spouse. Meanwhile, the woman who hired private detectives to go after other women who had truly been battered and bruised during sexual attacks by her husband escaped unscathed.

The GOP's decision to place Hillary's greatest vulnerability out of bounds—to ignore her husband's record of alleged violence toward women—was an unmitigated disaster. Hillary achieved a stunning 12-point landslide victory over Lazio with New York State's voters overall, but she also trounced him among female voters, 61 to 39 percent.

With 2004 fast approaching and Senator Clinton leading in her party's presidential preference polls, there's no indication whatsoever that the national Republican Party—let alone the Bush White House—has learned anything from the Giuliani and Lazio campaign's critical blunder.

CHAPTER TWELVE

Barbara Olson: Hillary's "Dirty Stuff"

"Hillary takes care of the dirty stuff."
—Barbara Olson to NewsMax, January 2000

No one has written more—nor more incisively—about the dark side of Hillary Clinton than the late Barbara Olson, author of *Hell to Pay,* one of the most revealing books about Mrs. Clinton, and *The Final Days,* which details the scandals that consumed the former first couple's last months in office and was published a month after Olson was killed in the September 11 attacks. But it's less well known that Olson came by her depth of knowledge of Hillary not as any mere author researching her subject, but as the lead investigative counsel in the mid-1990s for the House Government Reform and Oversight Committee, which probed the Travelgate and Filegate scandals that swirled around the then first lady.

For two years Mrs. Olson went toe-to-toe with Mrs. Clinton and her White House legal team and learned firsthand about the real Hillary that voters in New York never got to know before they elected her Senator—and set her on a path to become president of the United States.

In a never-before-published comments made to NewsMax in an interview the year before her death, Olson shared new insights about attempts by Mrs. Clinton to fend off Travelgate investigators' questions about her intimate friend, the late Vince Foster, as well as how Hillary's transparent bid to fool probers nearly got her indicted—and even Olson's own suspicions about a secret sexual harassment lawsuit filed against Bill Clinton's 1992 campaign.

"Every time we were asking about discussions that any of the people had with the first lady involving any of the [Foster] stuff, we got cut off," the lead House investigator revealed, explaining that when it came to Foster's role in the Travelgate scandal—or in anything else connected with Mrs. Clinton—"They said 'we've already testified about this.'"

"The White House was cordoning off things they would and wouldn't answer," Olson complained. "And when we got into Vince Foster questions that went an inch beyond the part of [his suicide] note that mentioned the Travel Office and the Travel Office files, they wouldn't answer, saying it wasn't relevant." When Olson and her probers pressed the issue, Hillary's lawyers would stonewall, saying, "Look we've already been questioned on Vince Foster and all the other forums and we're not going to re-answer the same questions."

> "Every time we were asking about discussions that any of the people had with the first lady involving any of the [Foster] stuff, we got cut off."
> —*the late Barbara Olson*

Olson also revealed never-before-reported evidence that Hillary Clinton hired White House security chief Craig Livingstone, who got his hands on over 1,000 confidential FBI files on potential Clinton opponents, in a scandal that had even left-wing civil libertarians howling. The top House prober described a visit to FBI headquarters in 1996, where she learned that White House FBI agent Dennis Sculimbrene had performed the background check on Livingstone.

"In his file Sculimbrene had asked Bernard Nussbaum about Craig Livingstone coming in, just doing the typical background discussions. And that was when Bernard Nussbaum said, 'Well the reason Craig Livingstone is being hired is because Hillary wants him.'" But in a sign the FBI was still under the White House's thumb, Olson revealed "Unbeknownst to me they had shared the information [about Hillary's role] with the White House the day before." Nussbaum later testified that he had made no such admission even after other evidence tying Mrs. Clinton to the suspicious hire emerged.

If Mrs. Clinton's role in hiring Livingstone seemed transparent, if unprovable, her lies in Travelgate were of a whole different order. From the outset of her dealings with the first lady and her lawyers, Olson said, efforts to cover up her central role in that scandal were both audacious and pathetic. In her capacity as the Travelgate Committee's chief investigator, Olson drew up twenty-six questions for the first lady. Mrs. Clinton had already denied she was the instigator behind the Travel Office firings in answers to interrogatories from the General Accounting Office, but the answers weren't given under penalty of perjury.

"I wrote twenty-six questions, and Chairman Clinger sent them to [Mrs. Clinton] and she then sent them back without her signature, Olson recalled. "We sent them back and said, no, we want her to sign them. It has to be notarized under penalty of perjury." The attempt to dodge legal responsibility for her answers might have seemed pathetic to some, but Olson had been smart enough to tighten one legal loophole that could have rendered Mrs. Clinton unindictable. In one of Olson's Travelgate questions, the first lady had to swear that her responses to the GAO had been honest and truthful.

"That tied her to all of her GAO answers," the investigator turned author told NewsMax. "Before that, you could say, well, with GAO she wasn't under oath because she had another attorney, Neil Eggleston answer them. And she could always say, well, he inartfully answered. That's why I made her sign the twenty-six questions that our committee did."

The insistence that Hillary give answers under oath gave investigators a firm basis to send a perjury referral to the Independent Counsel with her name on it. "Chairman [William] Clinger [R-Pa] thought long and hard about that," Olson revealed. "But, you know, he had been in the House for many years and he just felt as though it was improper to name her." But did Clinger believe that Mrs. Clinton had perjured herself in Travelgate?

"He felt as though there was a conflict between her testimony and certain evidence," Olson explained carefully. "And if you read our White House Travel Office report on Mrs. Clinton, throughout it we talk about her deposition in which she says she did not have a hand in the firing of the Travel Office employees. Well, we had huge amounts of evidence that shows she not only had a hand but she was the driving force." Olson described another aspect of the White House Travelgate cover-up that involved probable evidence-tampering with a set of subpoenaed documents.

"What they did, the title was changed by deleting HRC (Hillary Rodham Clinton)" from the title of a 2,000-page Travel Office chronology. The title change, plus the fact that the White House was invoking executive privilege to withhold the rest of the document, made it difficult to discern how deeply Hillary was involved. But eventually the committee got its hands on a "privilege log."

"What a privilege log does," explained Olson, "is it's supposed to give the title of the document or a description of the document, you know, ten pages of chronology. And what we found out on the those 2,000 pages, practically every single document that had her name in the title." Hillary's role in the firings, however, was consistently downplayed, the chief Travelgate investigator said. "So we would see something like HRC Chronology of Travel Office events, and it would just be characterized as Travel Office chronology of events."

Some of the Travelgate documents were heavily redacted, said Olson, and the redactions, they later learned, almost always came in a place where Mrs. Clinton was mentioned. "When we saw them unredacted, and this is what really made Chairman Clinger go forward on all of the subpoenas and contempts. . . . He sat down and looked and saw that what had been redacted was not national security evidence, but was just talking about Hillary Clinton's role. And he felt as though that was a real misuse of executive privilege, which of course it was."

Olson said the Travelgate probe also gave her new insights into the way the Clintons shared power in their relationship. After first suspecting Bill Clinton as the prime mover behind the Travel Office firings, "We found out it was Hillary Clinton [behind the firings] and she was doing it because (a) she doesn't trust anybody, and (b) she wanted the slots for her friends." Olson concluded, "In their relationship Bill's the one who sort of skates on top of stuff. Hillary takes care of the dirty stuff."

One bit of dirty stuff Travelgate probers could never quite get to the bottom of was a mysterious sexual harassment lawsuit settled by the Clinton campaign in 1992. The settlement came to light in 1995, after the Federal Election Commission fined the campaign for paying the accuser off with $37,500 in federally subsidized campaign monies. As part of the deal, neither the

> Neither the accuser nor anyone else was supposed to discuss the case. In its 1995 coverage of the story, the *Washington Post* called it "one of the best-kept secrets of Clinton's 1992 presidential campaign."

accuser nor anyone else was supposed to discuss the case. In its 1995 coverage of the story, the *Washington Post* called it "one of the best-kept secrets of Clinton's 1992 presidential campaign." But when the case finally surfaced, the offending harasser was identified as David Watkins, a longtime Clinton backer from Hope, Arkansas, who was later appointed to run the White House personnel office.

"We asked David Watkins about the sexual harassment payment," said Olson. "We asked lots of people about it because we thought (a) we were questioning whether this was the person to put in charge of the administration. You know, let's get a guy that's been charged with sexual harassment to be head of personnel. And (b) it was paid off by the campaign."

Despite the shroud of silence that had descended on the case, the *Washington Post* seemed to have little trouble getting Clinton administration aides to detail the so-called secret settlement with Watkins and had no problem naming his accuser, whose identity was supposedly sealed by the courts. "The woman in the case hung up when a reporter called her and did not respond to written requests for comment," reported the paper. "But an account of how the campaign reacted to [her] allegation can be pieced together from former campaign aides, administration officials and others knowledgeable about the situation. These sources confirmed the woman's identity and described the campaign's actions on the condition that they not be named."[1]

Did it make sense that the 1992 Clinton campaign, which was so cash-strapped that aides were charging expenses on their personal credit cards, would pony up $37,500 to settle a harassment claim for Watkins, who had made millions in the advertising business and was in no need of charity? And if, in fact, it was the Clinton aide who was the harasser, what about all those accounts from campaign flight attendants about Bill Clinton's eight-mile-high friskiness aboard the plane he dubbed "Longhorn One."

"Now that we have the hindsight of the Monica Lewinsky and Paula Jones cases, that's an excellent question," Olson said. "It's one of those things now that we have a very different view of given what was going on in '92."[2]

Hillary's IRS Henchwoman?

As Barbara Olson understood better than most, Hillary Clinton became a force to be reckoned with largely because Republicans cringed at the thought of enforcing the law against a sitting first lady whose election as senator would render her even more untouchable. Still the record is clear. And that record remains the best forewarning of how the federal bureaucracy will be used and abused under a politician whose ruthlessness makes Nixon look like a choirboy. In an eight-year reign of terror conducted by the Internal Revenue Service during the Clinton administration, witness after witness in a position to testify about wrongdoing by the president—not to mention an array of conservative organizations that opposed Clinton policies—found themselves targeted by tax audits.

It started in May 1993, with a full court press against Travel Office chief Billy Dale. A nonpolitical White House worker who had served every president going back to John F. Kennedy, Dale and his six co-workers were summarily dismissed on Mrs. Clinton's orders because, as she told her personnel chief David Watkins, "We need those slots for our people." In an effort to justify Dale's dismissal, the Clinton White House hit him with everything but the kitchen sink: a federal indictment on embezzlement charges, the illegal requisition of his FBI file, and, in a move that would soon become familiar, an IRS tax audit. Dale was acquitted in less than ninety minutes on the embezzlement case by a Washington, D.C., jury, but not before the bogus Clinton probes had cost him $500,000.

Hillary's Fingerprints

As noted by conservative columnist Ann Coulter, the Dale IRS audit was ripe with evidence of a political vendetta. A White House report detailing its own version of the scandal inadvertently revealed that Associate White House Counsel William Kennedy threatened FBI probers that he would summon the IRS if they didn't immediately launch an investigation of Dale.[3] But Hillary's own fingerprints were revealed when Travelgate probers discovered a memo stating that IRS Commissioner Margaret Milner Richardson was personally "on top of" the Dale audit.[4] Richardson was an old chum from Hillary's days at Yale Law School and would later become a contributor and serve on the Clintons' 1992 transition team, a fact that IRS agents probing Dale were made "aware" of.[5]

Travelgate probers discovered a memo stating that IRS Commissioner Margaret Milner Richardson was personally "on top of" the Dale audit. Richardson was an old chum from Hillary's days at Yale Law School.

A slew of audits against Clinton administration opponents followed Dale's audit. Because the IRS doesn't make public its audit information, and targets are frequently reluctant to go public, the full range of the Clinton IRS blitzkrieg remains unknown.

But just months after the second Clinton term commenced, *Investor's Business Daily* noted, "The IRS has hit some 20 conservative groups and several of Clinton's critics with audits, audit warnings or delays in granting nonprofit status."[6]

Other targets of IRS scrutiny included:

- Hillary-care critic Kent Masterson Brown
- IRS critic Shelly Davis
- Patricia Mendoza, who confronted Bill Clinton after the 1996 terrorist attack on the Khobar Towers Air Force barracks

- Nationally syndicated radio host Chuck Harder[7]
- Elizabeth Ward Gracen, a former Miss America who was audited after admitting a long-denied sexual relationship with Clinton
- Fox News Channel's Bill O'Reilly, an outspoken Clinton critic
- Sexual harassment accuser Paula Jones, who received her audit notification a few months after she beat Mr. Clinton in the Supreme Court
- The *National Review* and the *American Spectator*, two conservative publications hostile to the Clintons
- Conservative groups including the Christian Coalition, Citizens for a Sound Economy, Oliver North's Freedom Alliance, the Heritage Foundation, the National Rifle Association, the Western Journalism Center, the National Center for Public Policy Research, Fortress America and Citizens Against Government Waste[8]

CHAPTER THIRTEEN

Bill's Sex Accusers Audited

"You should really keep your mouth shut about Bill Clinton and go on with your life. You could be discredited. You could have an IRS investigation."
—anonymous caller to Elizabeth Ward Gracen

The women on the Clinton audit list offered some of the clearest evidence that the IRS was being used as a political weapon. Paula Jones, for instance, who had filed her sexual harassment lawsuit against Clinton in 1994, was hit by an audit in late 1997 after she rejected an offer to settle from the Clinton White House. With a household income of $37,000, Jones's income group was among the least likely to be singled out for IRS scrutiny. But after the Supreme Court ruled unanimously in May 1997 that her sexual harassment case against Clinton could proceed, the White House was growing desperate.

White House press spokesman Mike McCurry vehemently denied that the Clinton IRS had been directed to audit Paula

Jones's tax returns. "We do dumb things from time to time," said McCurry, "but we're not certifiably crazy."[1] Indeed the news that the woman who'd been a thorn in the president's side for more than three years had received an audit notice just five days after she'd turned down an offer to settle her sexual harassment claim seemed too bizarre to be true.

But the press by and large bought McCurry's alibi. Even some of the most viscerally anti-Clinton conservatives argued, at least initially, that the move was simply too transparent, too audacious, too over-the-top in its outrageousness to have been cooked up even by the Clintons. No president, the thinking went, would dare audit his most celebrated accuser, calling down a world of suspicion on his head. Certainly not seasoned and clever damage controllers like the Clintons. The sheer brazenness of such an act, coming only a generation after Watergate, seemed to place any conspiracy theory beyond the realm of plausibility.

Years later, however, as the pattern of audits against political opponents grew, it became apparent that the White House had managed to con even its harshest critics, at least on the initial batch of audits targeting Clinton critics and witnesses. But the circumstances surrounding the Jones audit made plain this was anything but a coincidence, and it should have set off smoke alarms in every newsroom across America, not to mention the Office of Independent Counsel.

Jones's Tax Return Made Public

Yet the press stayed silent as details from Paula Jones's confidential IRS return began to turn up in Clinton-friendly media organs. Writing for the *New York Daily News,* the late Lars-Erik Nelson argued that Jones was selected for an audit because her legal defense fund was set up as a for-profit business. And just where did Nelson stumble across that information? From a source privy to the Jones family's confidential tax return, Nelson unabashedly admitted. "Now one of Jones' supporters has let slip the fact that Jones has reported this defense fund to the IRS on a Schedule C: 'Profit or Loss From Business (Sole Proprietorship).'. . . Filing on Schedule C means that Jones can count contributions to the fund—reportedly between $200,000 and $300,000 this far—as personal income. In addition, Schedule C allows a taxpayer to claim deductions for advertising, auto expenses, insurance, office costs, rent, travel, meals and, oh yes, legal fees."[2]

Never mind Nelson's transparent attempt to resurrect the gold-digger defense for Clinton, which became increasingly nonsensical as Paula Jones rejected one lucrative settlement offer after another. The real news was that one of the most Clinton-friendly members of the media had obtained secrets from the Jones family's personal tax return, which—and this point cannot be stressed too many times—the law deems in no uncertain terms to be a private matter between the taxpayer and the IRS. What's more, Nelson's alibi—that one of Jones's "supporters" decided to share the tax secrets with him—only compounded the problem. Asked a few days after Nelson's column appeared whether the Joneses were in the habit of sharing their tax returns with supportive friends, the Clinton sex accuser's adviser at the time, Susan Carpenter-McMillan, told me, "No. How many people carry around their tax returns?" She suggested instead that a more likely source for the illegal leak would have been someone with direct access to the Clinton IRS.[3]

Still, reporter Nelson was equally emphatic about his source being a Jones supporter, insisting in a follow-up interview, "That's absolutely correct." When asked if his source was indeed privy to Jones's return, Nelson replied, again—"Absolutely." However, specific questions about his source's identity prompted this disclaimer: "I can't give you any more details than what I put in the paper. I can't give you any more help on the source, I'm sorry."[4] Despite the fishy story—and the obvious illegality of having the tax secrets of the plaintiff in the world's most celebrated sexual harassment case published in the nation's largest-circulation daily newspaper—the establishment press didn't bat an eye.

Beauty Queen Cites Audit Threat

Even stranger was the case of Elizabeth Ward Gracen, who would eventually be audited after jumping through hoops trying to avoid testifying in the Paula Jones case and doing her best to dispel rumors that Clinton had raped her. The former Miss America, who became a TV actress, denied in 1992 that she had had sex with Bill Clinton during an encounter nine years earlier, only to reverse herself at the end of March 1998, two days before the Paula Jones case was dismissed. What prompted Gracen's change of heart were persistent stories based on the account of her friend Judy Stokes, who told reporters that Gracen had tearfully complained that sex with the then governor was "something I did not want to have happen." Gracen was coming forward now, she told the *New York Daily News,* to dispel any notion that Bill Clinton had raped her and thereby assert that Stokes got it wrong.

However, in 1999, private detective Rick Lambert, who had been retained by Paula Jones's Dallas law firm, Rader, Campbell, Fisher, Pike & Holmes, to track down women whose accounts might back Jones's sexual harassment claim, told NewsMax that Stokes was not the least bit ambiguous in the account she gave him, undermining Gracen's rape denial.

"I talked to Judy Stokes for an hour and a half. At first, she was reluctant to burn her bridges with Liz," Lambert said. "But I finally asked, 'Do you believe Clinton raped her?' She said, 'Absolutely. He forced her to have sex. What do you call that?' Stokes was totally convinced it was rape."[5]

Lambert had contacted the beauty queen's friend in December 1997 after Gracen herself refused to talk to him. "I called Liz at her stepfather's house on Christmas Eve," he explained.

"She answered the phone but pretended to be somebody else. She told me Liz was in Paris. I said, 'Liz, why won't you talk to me?' At that, she hung up on me." Lambert said he got a call from Gracen's Hollywood agent Miles Levy fifteen minutes later. I said, 'Boy, the phones sure work fast overseas, don't they? Why won't she talk to me?'"

Levy told Lambert, "Look, that would be career suicide for Liz and you know it."

As for Stokes's account of rape, four weeks after Gracen's *Daily News* tell-all, the beauty queen again insisted—this time to NBC—that her friend had gotten it wrong. "I never had that conversation with [Judy], no. No. . . . It was not true that I was ever harassed or coerced or pressured or manipulated into having sex with Bill Clinton."[6]

Newsweek's Michael Isikoff, however, added a new wrinkle to the murky tale in his 2000 book *Uncovering Clinton.* "According to Gracen's later account, Clinton flirted with her—then invited her to the apartment of one of his friends at the Quapaw Towers. They had sex that night. It was rough sex. Clinton got so carried away that he bit her lip, Gracen later told friends. But it was consensual."[7]

Since Gracen managed to elude both Paula Jones's lawyers and Independent Counsel Ken Starr's Monica Lewinsky probe, she has never told her story under oath, perhaps prompting fears at the White House about which version the former beauty queen would endorse under penalty of perjury. Whatever the reason, her very public attempt to get the president off the hook on the rape accusation only served to make her the target of somebody who obviously preferred that she stay out of the spotlight. Six months after her *Daily News* bombshell, Gracen told the *New York Post* that her Caribbean hotel room had been broken into while she was on a vacation (this during the time she was on the run from Paula Jones investigators). "Some friendly calls telling me to get out of town to dodge a subpoena from independent counsel Kenneth Starr. Some nasty calls saying my character was about to be assassinated," the ex–beauty queen revealed. "Luckily, I had work and a boyfriend who travels a lot, and really, who wants to talk about something you regret in 1982."

Gracen told the paper that she felt the heat being turned up. "My friends were being asked mystery questions about tapes. Believe me, I don't tape people, and no tapes existed." But the threatening phone calls continued, both to her and her parents. It was during a getaway with her boyfriend to the island of St. Martin that things began to get truly scary. They decided to go for a jog on the beach, leaving behind in plain sight on the coffee table a Rolex watch and $2,000 in cash.

"When we came back," said Gracen, "the place was ransacked. The $2,000 and the Rolex watch were still there. Nothing was stolen. They were looking for tapes that did not exist." Hotel workers told her that they thought the intruders—three men "in suits"—were her friends. One stood watch in the hallway outside while the others took care of business combing through Gracen's personal effects. The threatening calls continued, always with the same message but now more intense: Get out of town before you get hit with a subpoena. "I was physically scared," said Gracen. "We are talking about the presidency of the country here, and between the friendly calls on one hand telling me to get out of town for my own good and then talking about smear tactics on the other, I got scared. Yes, physically scared."[8]

Although Gracen had been denying that Clinton raped her, for Hillary Clinton's attack machine, Gracen's latest version of events may have contained an unintentional warning. Describing her encounter with Clinton early in the interview, she said, "To use the word rendezvous would give the impression it was romantic, but it was far from romantic." In the next breath Gracen seemed to catch herself, "It was consensual. I was married at the time, and so was he. No, I am not proud of it." Then, as she began to describe the prelude to her Clinton encounter, the *Post* noted, "At that stage in the interview, tears well in her eyes, and she says to her boyfriend, an investment banker: 'I really should not be saying these things.'"

Apparently the Clinton White House agreed. In January 1999, Gracen revealed through her attorney that around the time of the break-in, she began to get calls warning of an IRS audit. "They say, 'You should really keep your mouth shut about Bill Clinton and go on with your life. You could be discredited. You could have an IRS investigation,'" attorney Vincent Vento recounted to the *Post*.[9] The call came just weeks after Gracen had reiterated her fears about the man she said she regretted having consensual sex with. "I think Clinton is a very dangerous, manipulative man and I've had to be very careful," Gracen said from her hideaway at the time in Canada.[10]

The timing of the IRS threat was curious on a number of levels, particularly since Gracen had done everything she could not to corroborate Jones's sexual harassment claim. But just weeks earlier, the Starr report had been released—complete with some particularly lurid accounts of kinky cigar sex and even a footnote alluding to "oral and anal contact" between Clinton and Lewinsky, a practice apparently detailed in impeachment materials still under seal. Was Hillary's bimbo-eruption SWAT team afraid that an account from Gracen detailing what Isikoff would later describe as "rough sex" that included biting end up branding her husband as some sort of sexual pervert? And perhaps even raise questions about her own private peccadilloes?

Gracen Audit Threat Follows Broaddrick Rape Report

Gracen's account could be problematic on another count as well. The month before the audit threats to Gracen began, Starr's investigators had traveled to Van Buren, Arkansas, to interview Juanita Broaddrick. News accounts in late August 1998 reported—erroneously, it turned out—that Broaddrick's FBI interrogators had found her story "inconclusive." But Starr himself personally contradicted that claim more than a year later, telling reporters, "The investigators found her entirely credible."[11] Like Gracen, Broaddrick had previously insisted that reports of a sexual encounter—coerced or otherwise—that had swirled throughout Arkansas since 1992 were false. What would happen to Hillary's own presidential hopes, the White House surely wondered, if Gracen became the second woman to publicly accuse her husband of rape?

Whatever the reason for the audit threats, Gracen felt she had been targeted because of the Clinton connection. "She pays her taxes, she's really square," said the lawyer Vento. "She just feels it's completely unfair. . . . The only person who would benefit would be the president of the United States, unless there's some other agenda out there," he contended. A few weeks after the threats began, the Clinton IRS indeed decided to swing into action, Vento said, when letters notifying Gracen to get ready for an audit began arriving at her parents' house, which was not listed on her tax filings.

Trashing Juanita

Of all the sexual allegations lodged against Bill Clinton, none was more potent—and potentially more damaging to Hillary's political future—than Juanita Broaddrick's rape accusation. America could accept Mrs. Clinton in the role carved out for her by the press—the aggrieved woman, standing by her man "like Tammy Wynette," as the hound dog she was married to relentlessly chased skirts. But any hint that Mrs. Clinton had a larger role in Mr. Clinton's personal misbehavior—as enabler, facilitator, or co-conspirator of the "nuts and sluts" defense strategy—was never much discussed in the press. Reporters knew that she had hired the likes of Palladino and Pellicano, that she had threatened to "crucify" Gennifer Flowers, that she was the one who decided not to settle with Paula Jones and then later signed off on a despicable attempt to trash Kathleen Willey after she accused Bill of sexual assault. Somehow, the press was flummoxed by all of it.

> What would happen to Hillary's own presidential hopes, the White House surely wondered, if [Elizabeth Ward] Gracen became the second woman to publicly accuse her husband of rape?

If reporters accepted the clear implications of all the evidence pointing to Hillary Clinton's involvement in trashing her husband's accusers, then she could no longer be depicted as a long-suffering victim. And with the element of rape thrown into the equation, the possibilities were just too dark to contemplate. Instead of an icon and a role model who had been betrayed by a spouse with an out-of-control libido, Mrs. Clinton would be a de facto accomplice of the worst order: someone who should have known what was going on and acted to prevent the further victimization of her sisters, but for reasons still unexplained, did not. No one in the media, and few in the general public, wanted to believe that Mrs. Clinton had sold out her sex as part of a Faustian bargain with a predatory rapist on the chance that she might one day become president of the United States.

Still, the question continues to hang in the air. It's that inability to cope with the notion that the nation's feminist icon had nurtured, supported, and guided toward power not just a philandering husband but the worst kind of sexual deviant that most clouds Hillary Clinton's political future. If you believed Juanita, then you either believed that Hillary's state of denial was so extreme as to suggest some sort of psychological impairment—or you were forced to accept the possibility that she was an accomplice at some level to rape.

Struggling with a Rape Charge

Perhaps that explains the lengths to which the press—and even Republican senators then conducting Mr. Clinton's impeachment trial—went to bury the Broaddrick story. It wasn't a Democrat, after all, but instead Republican Senator Ted Stevens of Alaska who told lead House impeachment counsel David Schippers that Clinton's Senate trial would be rigged for acquittal, explaining, "I don't care if you can prove he raped a woman and then stood up and shot her dead—you are not going to get sixty-seven votes."[12]

The sentiment was more or less the same in most newsrooms, though expressed a good deal less bluntly. Consider the way PBS anchor Jim Lehrer had ballyhooed Anita Hill's allegations against Clarence Thomas, which were tawdry enough, but not so jarring to the national psyche that they couldn't be believed. On October 7, 1991, Lehrer introduced his newscast with these words: "Our lead story is the sexual harassment charges against Clarence Thomas. We have excerpts from the press conference by his accuser, Anita Hill." But when it came to Mrs. Broaddrick, Lehrer sounded almost sheepish on February 19, 1999, the day her account hit the national media. "We are part of this process," he explained. "We made the very clean editorial decision not to do this story, but we are talking about it tonight in a media context, because it is media news."

The reluctance to discuss the Broaddrick story was particularly apparent at NBC, the network that had secured the exclusive. As the weeks dragged on past January 20, 1999, when Broaddrick first told all to reporter Lisa Myers, expecting NBC to rush its big scoop on the air as soon as possible, the network instead circled the wagons. Two weeks into the controversy, Washington bureau chief Tim Russert had a tough time explaining the delay to radio host Don Imus, with the NBC newsman comparing his own network's bombshell to discredited videotapes accusing the Clintons of murder.

IMUS: Does a taped interview exist between Lisa Myers and this woman?

RUSSERT: Ah, er, ah, I'm not going to get into where we are. It's a work in progress about a whole lot of things.

IMUS: In other words, the answer is yes. Thank you.

RUSSERT: Well, ah, er, all right Mr. Falwell.

IMUS: (laughing) No, I just wondered.

RUSSERT: I mean, you know—there's a videotape available if you want that says President Clinton murdered people. I mean, put it on the screen.[13]

Still, at least Russert would discuss the Broaddrick controversy. *NBC Nightly News* anchor Tom Brokaw refused to so much as mention it during his broadcast, let alone devote serious coverage to this exclusive bombshell interview.

The press's visceral distaste for the Broaddrick story wasn't entirely due to the media's pro-Clinton bias. As noted by Pulitzer Prize–winning reporter Dorothy Rabinowitz, who scooped NBC with her own Broaddrick print exclusive five days before the broadcast, the network had no problem covering news about Monica Lewinsky. "I just think it's a story that NBC [*Nightly News*] refuses to promote or air the very night it's supposed to be on *Dateline,*" Rabinowitz told a seminar on the controversy in June 1999. "However, a couple of days later, they spend five full minutes promoting Barbara Walters's interview with Monica Lewinsky, which is on the competing channel. So you have to say to yourself, something's really interesting about the depths of this repression."[14]

Dan Rather: Broaddrick Part of Organized Campaign

CBS news anchor Dan Rather seemed equally eager to repress any discussion of Broaddrick, when Imus broached the topic with him more than a year later. And in a May 2001 interview with Fox News Channel's Bill O'Reilly, Rather said he "barely remembered" the Clinton rape allegation, despite the key role it played in the first impeachment of an elected president in American history. He then offered, "When the charge has something to do with somebody's private sex life, I would prefer not to run any of it."

After O'Reilly refreshed his memory on the case, Rather accused the Arkansas businesswoman of being a member of an organized conspiracy to destroy Clinton. "Just stop right there," the anchor interrupted. "Let's see—what you've got is, you have the Republicans trying to bring down Bill Clinton. . . . Sure, I think it was an organized campaign."[15]

"When the charge has something to do with somebody's private sex life, I would prefer not to run any of it."
—*CBS News anchorman Dan Rather*

Broaddrick herself, who had largely retreated from the scene after telling her story to Rabinowitz, was none too pleased by the CBS anchor's characterization of her ordeal. "It really sickens me to think that Mr. Rather would think what happened to me should be relegated to the category of Bill Clinton's private sex life," Broaddrick wrote in answer to a request for comment by a member of the FreeRepublic.com Web site. "I have to live with the fact that I did not come forward 23 years ago. But it becomes more difficult when someone such as Dan Rather makes such frivolous statements about the most horrific event of my life."

A Private Matter

The "private sex life" excuse seemed to be a favorite with males of a certain age who were reluctant to address the full implications of Broaddrick's accusation. Just a few months before he switched from Republican to Independent, Vermont Senator Jim Jeffords tried to dismiss the rape charge as "a private matter" and ended up suggesting that the Clinton accuser got what she deserved. "I think things like that are supposedly a private affair that should stay that way unless they get into the public domain by the abuse of the use of the office of the president," Jeffords told a Vermont radio station two years earlier. "But other than that, I'm not interested in what people did 21 years ago." Digging himself in deeper, Jeffords then added that if Broaddrick had invited Clinton to her hotel room as she claimed, "and was not happy with what happened, I don't know why that's not a private matter."[16] Jeffords was forced to issue an apology after NewsMax reported his comments and shared an audiotape of the WKDR Vermont broadcast with Fox News Channel's *Hannity & Colmes*.

It would have been bad enough if men alone had exhibited such insensitivity to Broaddrick's plight. But even women whose expressed mission it was to fight for women like Juanita Broaddrick were remarkably unsympathetic.

NOW MIA

After NBC finally broadcast its Clinton rape exclusive, Patricia Ireland, then president of the National Organization for Women, tried to put the best face possible on the inconvenient scandal. Saying that the truth about the rape accuser's claim would be impossible to prove, the closest she came to criticizing Clinton was to urge him to forswear the "nuts or sluts" defense. She then accused Broaddrick's supporters of waging a vendetta against the White House and feminist causes in general. "Unlike most of the voices raised on Ms. Broaddrick's behalf," Ireland contended in a statement the next day, "NOW has been working to improve women's rights on the job for more than three decades. Ultraconservatives are using this case to advance their long-standing political interest in weakening the president, undermining equal opportunity laws and discrediting the movement to strengthen women's rights."

A year later, Ireland's successor Kim Gandy showed how truly uninterested the NOW gang was in Broaddrick's claim, insisting, erroneously, to WABC Radio's Steve Malzberg that the allegation had been fully investigated by Arkansas law enforcement.

GANDY: I assume the district attorney's office did [the investigation]. They were investigating it at the time.

MALZBERG: Which district attorney? The DA's office was investigating Juanita Broaddrick's claims?

GANDY: They said that they were. Absolutely.

MALZBERG: And how did that turn out?

GANDY: I don't know.[17]

Undoubtedly some of the self-imposed ignorance about Broaddrick's claims sprung from an unwillingness to confront a basic truth about the Clintons' marriage. Contrary to the media's ongoing mythologizing about the once and future first couple, there was little Hillary could not have known about her husband's wild ways, going all the way back to the good old days in Arkansas. Even a spouse without Mrs. Clinton's resources would have picked up on the rumors of rape, which, by the time Clinton had announced for president, were whispered in political circles all across Arkansas.

Author Roger Morris, for instance—the first Clinton biographer to detail an allegation of forced sex ("a young woman lawyer in Little Rock")—told me that the story first came to him via another reporter covering Clinton in the early 1990s. The reporter had declined to pursue the story, as had so many others before him. But the story, and more than a few like it, was out there—as were Mrs. Clinton's private detectives, whose job it was to keep her apprised of the political minefield her husband had laid for the two of them before sweeping it clean by whatever means necessary.

In that context, Broaddrick's story of Mrs. Clinton's approach three weeks after her attack, where the rape victim sensed that Hillary was trying to pressure her into silence, seems all the more plausible. And if that wasn't an attempt to intimidate the rape accuser, what about the break-in of her home in December 1998, when she said nothing of value was stolen except her answering machine tape? It just so happens that around that time, Broaddrick was communicating with NBC, as well as several House impeachment managers, about whether she'd come forward with her story. A year later, with Broaddrick's story relegated to footnote status in the impeachment drama by a press corps that deemed it too hot to handle, further evidence revealed that the White House had been preparing to discredit the Arkansas businesswoman in much the same way it had tried to discredit Kathleen Willey.

Juanita's FBI File

During an appearance on Fox News Channel's *Hannity & Colmes,* former White House counsel Lanny Davis began talking about what sounded like Broaddrick's confidential FBI file. "It is a public fact that the FBI first interviewed her, and she denied that [the rape] had ever taken place," Davis insisted.[18] The only problem was, nothing of the sort was on the public record. Instead, Independent Counsel Starr and his assistant Robert Bittman had recently revealed that agents who grilled Broaddrick found her entirely believable.

Davis's slip had Broaddrick concerned. "When Lanny Davis alluded to some information that he was privy to, it just made me feel like, well, there's something he's seen," she told NewsMax three days later. "He kept referring to my lying to the FBI. I never lied to the FBI." The Clinton accuser was adamant and had gone so far as to retain the Washington, D.C.–based public interest law firm Judicial Watch to file suit on her behalf. "I just want my FBI file," she said. "You know, the White House has refused to turn it over, and I want to know what's in it. I want to know what information they have on me."[19]

At the time, Hillary Clinton was in the midst of her "listening tour," crisscrossing New York ostensibly to gauge whether the locals would warm to the proposition of turning her into the first of the first ladies ever elected to the Senate. In theory, Broaddrick wasn't on Clinton's radar screen. However, two days before Davis publicly alluded to the rape accuser's FBI testimony, something happened that undoubtedly sent chills down Mrs. Clinton's spine. In a televised New Hampshire town hall meeting, audience member Katherine Prudhomme had challenged Vice President Al Gore on whether he believed Juanita Broaddrick was telling the truth. While Broaddrick was anxious to stay out of the spotlight and had rejected numerous requests to return to TV and tell her story, the Clinton administration continued to act as if she posed an ongoing political threat. In truth, she did—or at least she would have, if the establishment reporters had ever confronted the Senate hopeful about the explosive accusation against her husband.

Broaddrick Audited

Even after the Clinton IRS had audited scandal witness after scandal witness, from Gennifer Flowers to Billy Dale to Paula Jones to Liz Ward Gracen, the news that the woman President Clinton had in all likelihood raped twenty-three years earlier was now the subject of an IRS audit had jaws dropping from coast-to coast. "How can this be a coincidence?" Broaddrick complained to NewsMax, in her first public comment on the outrageous development. "I do feel like there's certainly a connection to me coming forward." Broaddrick speculated that the White House was hoping an audit might turn up evidence that could be construed as a possible payoff for telling her story. "In 27 years in business I've never been audited," she insisted, explaining that there had been no change in the financial circumstances of her nursing home business that might have triggered IRS scrutiny.[20]

> "I just want my FBI file . . . the White House has refused to turn it over, and I want to know what's in it. I want to know what information they have on me."
>
> *—Juanita Broaddrick*

By the time of Broaddrick's audit, it was pretty much a foregone conclusion in the minds of those monitoring the Clinton scandal trail that the IRS had engaged—and would continue to engage—in a blatant pattern of illegal audits against Bill and Hillary's political enemies. The press, by now overwhelmed with revelation after revelation of White House perfidy, did its best not to notice that even impeachment hadn't mitigated the Clintons' penchant for outrageous abuses of power. The Congress, having aborted one Clinton impeachment trial despite smoking-gun evidence of multiple felonies, was in no mood to start down the path toward another. In a very real sense, executive branch oversight had been thrown to the winds for the last two years of the Clinton administration. In Hillary's Senate race, there was the unspoken sense among more than a few in the press that the Clintons were so corrupt it was impossible to know where to begin. And that once the scandal talk began, it would never stop, obscuring "the real issues."

There would be one more scandal-related audit before the Clinton administration would draw to a close. And while most of the other suspicious IRS actions had been directed at people who threatened Bill's political career, this one zeroed in on the woman who had vowed publicly to press Mrs. Clinton on the question that the media had refused to ask: Do you believe Juanita?

In August 2000, with less than three months to go before the election, a group calling itself "Friends of Juanita Broaddrick" traveled to Manhattan to protest outside Mrs. Clinton's Senate campaign headquarters. Its goal was simple: get Mrs. Clinton to react for the record to the rape charges lodged against her husband. Heading up the small knot of protesters was Katherine Prudhomme, the twenty-nine-year-old Derry, New Hampshire, woman who had stopped Vice President Al Gore dead in his tracks when she questioned him about Broaddrick at a town meeting in her home state nine months earlier. After arriving on the scene, Prudhomme delivered a moving speech that began with her own acknowledgment that, like Broaddrick, she was a rape survivor. Then she quoted Mrs. Clinton's own complaints about the outbreak of sexual violence two months earlier at the city's Puerto Rican Day parade.

"We all looked on in horror at the videotapes because we know these women," Clinton proclaimed at the time. "They are wives, and sisters, and daughters. They are friends and neighbors. We know that if it could happen there—in broad daylight—it could happen anywhere. This is a crime against all women—everywhere. And so we have to say enough is enough. This violence is unacceptable and it must stop."

Prudhomme countered, "Well, Hillary I feel your pain. Because I too have a videotape, a videotape of Juanita Broaddrick telling her story to Lisa Myers that I will give you today. It is a videotape that I have looked upon in horror. And when it told a tale of disgusting violence committed against a woman in broad daylight . . . a woman who could have been my sister, my daughter or my mother . . . I too have to say 'enough is enough—this violence is unacceptable and must stop.'"[21] With that, the New Hampshire housewife marched inside Clinton's campaign headquarters and gave the Broaddrick videotape to an aide to the first lady.

But what made this event newsworthy wasn't what happened on that Manhattan street corner but, instead, a decision by the Clinton administration a few days earlier.

Broaddrick Defender Audited

"My husband got the IRS's letter yesterday," Prudhomme told NewsMax.com the night of the Broaddrick rally. "They looked at our records from 1998 and decided we have to pay more money." Prudhomme said she'd never been audited before and that there had been no dramatic changes in her family income, which she described as "middle class."

"I feel like we're being harassed," said the feisty crusader. "My husband went over our return last night and couldn't find any red flags that might have triggered an IRS investigation."[22] Along with those who heard her announce news of the IRS scrutiny outside Clinton's campaign headquarters, Prudhomme said she suspected that the audit might have been triggered by a different kind of red flag: her determined questioning of Gore about Juanita Broaddrick the previous December—and her announced intention to get Hillary Clinton to address the same issue.

The rally outside Mrs. Clinton's headquarters had been publicized on the Web site FreeRepublic.com for weeks beforehand, giving the Clinton administration plenty of time to alert its tax enforcers. At least that's what Prudhomme suspected, telling NewsMax, "I think the timing is pretty suspicious, coming the very day before we had this demonstration." If she was right, it would have been the first political audit inspired by Hillary's political career rather than Bill's. Ten days before the election, Prudhomme received notice from the IRS acknowledging it had erred and that she was in the clear.

Hillary IRS Crony Defiant

Besides Dale, Jones, Gracen, and Broaddrick, pioneer Sexgate accuser Gennifer Flowers and Chinagate whistleblower Johnny Chung also found themselves in the crosshairs of the IRS. With the Dale, Flowers, and Jones audits under her belt by November 1997, Hillary crony Margaret Milner Richardson resigned as IRS commissioner—just as Congress began taking note of the suspicious pattern among high-profile auditees. But Richardson was defiant. In a February 1997 letter to House Ways and Means Committee Chairman Bill Archer, she insisted: "Recent media reports have alleged politically targeted examinations of tax exempt organizations by the Internal Revenue Service. These reports are inaccurate and misleading and suggest incorrectly that the IRS is enforcing the internal revenue laws for partisan political purposes. Such unfounded reports erode public confidence in the integrity of the IRS, thereby undermining the self-assessment compliance system."

The one-time Hillary campaign aide told Archer she could prove her agency's audit targets had nothing to do with politics: "I am writing to you to express our willingness to provide the Ways and Means Committee, as authorized by section 6103(f), information relating to these allegations. I am certain that information will demonstrate the IRS' fair, impartial, and nonpartisan enforcement of the internal revenue laws in the exempt organization arena."[23]

But according to author James Bovard, when it came time for Richardson to put up, she instead chose to clam up: "The Landmark Legal Foundation was another conservative nonprofit hit by an IRS audit. After being cleared by the IRS, the foundation filed a Freedom of Information Act request to find out who initiated the charges that led to its audit and the audit of other conservative organizations. The foundation's lawsuit quoted IRS officer Terry Hallihan, who stated, according to an attendee at an IRS meeting, 'that documents identifying the names of members of Congress and their staffers as the source of audit requests had been, or were being, shredded.'" Bovard also claimed that Hallihan also described "ways to disguise future requests so that they did not appear to be coming from Congressmen."

Bovard continued: "After losing two separate lawsuits over its stonewalling, the IRS provided the Foundation with roughly 8,000 pages detailing who made the accusations that led to audits. But most of the information on the pages was blacked out. . . . The IRS claimed that it could not find 114 key files relating to possible political manipulation of audits of tax-exempt organizations. The Justice Department sought to block Landmark Legal Foundation from even questioning the IRS official who allegedly suggested shredding, but federal judge Henry Kennedy overruled the government's ploy."[24]

While there was no way to prove that the first lady was ultimately behind the audits, some of Mrs. Clinton's allies were sometimes astonishingly frank about their involvement. Before the IRS began targeting groups with ties to then House Speaker Newt Gingrich, Hillary ally Charles Rangel, the Democratic congressman who would later be the first to suggest she run for Senate, issued a press release virtually boasting that the Gingrich organizations would be audited. During a January 1997 TV appearance, Rangel confirmed that he had been "in touch with the IRS on this issue" and the investigation was going ahead.[25]

Hillary ally Charles Rangel, the Democratic congressman who would later be the first to suggest she run for Senate, issued a press release virtually boasting that the Gingrich organizations would be audited.

Cynics say that political audits have been the rule rather than the exception in Washington since the days of FDR. But during Watergate, when it was revealed that Nixon had tried to audit his enemies, civil libertarians went wild. Democratic Party investigators, among whom was twenty-six-year-old Yale Law School graduate Hillary Diane Rodham, made Nixon's abuse of the IRS part of the articles of impeachment they prepared against him.

Abuse Nixon Never Dreamed Of

Though the biased media have pounded away over the years at the image of Nixon as the world's all-time champion of politically motivated tax audits, lawyer Ann Coulter argued that the thirty-seventh president was a piker compared to the Clintons. Noting that the Nixon IRS impeachment article was carefully constructed to accuse him of merely trying, as opposed to actually succeeding, "to cause" IRS audits, Coulter wrote: "Poor Tricky Dick could never actually get the IRS to audit one of his enemies. He couldn't even get them to back off from auditing him while he was president. . . . he was completely ignored by the IRS. . . . Still, he asked. Technically, Nixon stormed around his office bellowing about it, and a low level functionary took him at his word and asked, but even that was once an alarming fact in this country."[26]

CHAPTER FOURTEEN

Hillary's Path to the Presidency

Most political observers acknowledge that the 2004 Democratic Party presidential nomination is Hillary Clinton's for the asking. But the conventional wisdom holds that since she and her husband deem George Bush unbeatable, Mrs. Clinton will keep her powder dry until 2008, when she won't have to face an incumbent with the power of the White House behind him.

But this much, at least, is beyond dispute. When Bill Clinton threw his hat into the ring in October 1991, he had zero name recognition, no national fund-raising network, and almost no hope of just securing the nomination, let alone winning the White House. In 2003, with the presidential contest heating up and the election just a year away, Hillary Clinton has all three, plus a stellar poll rating that ranks her first among presidential hopefuls in her party. In other words, at this point in the campaign, Hillary Clinton now stands a far better chance of becoming president of the United States than her husband did in 1991, when, as governor of Arkansas, he too assured the voters of his state that he wouldn't run for president in the next election.

Hillary's Scheme

In fact, it's astonishing that anyone believes Mrs. Clinton's denials that she'd consider running in 2004, given the wealth of evidence that she's planning for just that contingency. Given the scope of the former first lady's activities since assuming elective office in January 2001, the operative question should be, What would Hillary be doing differently if she were indeed running for president? The answer: Very little, if anything.

Consider, for instance, her rapid rise within the Senate—a remarkable trajectory even for someone supposedly as smart and ambitious as she is. Within the span of two years, Clinton has elbowed her way to the head of the Senate Democratic Steering Committee, a post she unabashedly uses to craft her party's attacks against the Bush administration.

Shortly before taking the position, Clinton warmed up by delivering her party's response to the president's weekly radio address. Her topic: the extension of unemployment insurance, the kind of economic issue Bill and Hillary used to make mincemeat out of Bush's father during the 1992 presidential campaign. "In the recession of the early 1990s, we increased benefits five times," Clinton told a nationwide radio audience. "Today, our unemployment rate has soared to 6 percent, and Congress and the president have extended benefits only once—and once is not enough."[1]

A few days later she turned in a masterful performance on the Senate floor, pulling the rug out from under newly crowned Senate majority leader Bill Frist, who thought Hillary had signed on to a deal for a new unemployment relief package. But suddenly Clinton announced she wanted to extend unemployment insurance six months beyond the agreed-upon limits, a move that threw the Senate into chaos.

MSNBC's Chris Matthews was watching the scene unfold from the Senate press gallery. "You know what's impressive?" the TV talker asked radioman Don Imus the next day. "Sitting in the Senate press gallery and looking down and realizing that Hillary Clinton is the leader of the U.S. Senate Democrats. . . . She's the boss. Everybody was circling around her when they were having that big dispute over unemployment benefits. Hillary was calling the shots," he continued to gush. "Hillary looks to me like the number one Democratic senator right now. She's intellectually and ideologically the center of the Democratic Party."[2]

Frist finally carried the day, managing to get the unemployment benefits package passed in its agreed-upon form. But the New York senator had instantly torpedoed his debut as a Senate majority leader in full control—and sent the clear message that the GOP would have to go through her to get any legislation passed.

> She's the boss . . . Hillary was calling the shots. Hillary looks to me like the number one Democratic senator right now."
> —*Chris Matthews*

Since taking over as her party's chief Senate strategist, Clinton has continued to hone the Democrats' economic message while carefully playing both sides of the issue on national security matters. In late March 2003, as war clouds loomed large and the nation focused on the just-launched U.S. attack on Iraq, she took to the Senate floor to complain that the Bush defense budget would threaten America's economic security for generations to come.

"Under any objective assessment of where we stand in the world right now, this budget should be a nonstarter. It should be withdrawn from the floor," she demanded. Then, in an attempt to make her criticism of Bush sound patriotic, she added, "Every one of us should be saying, 'My goodness, we have higher obligations. How can we keep faith with those young men and women who are on the front lines for us?'" In a twist on her husband's 1992 campaign mantra about "the worst economy in fifty years," Senator Clinton warned, "We are in danger of being the first generation of Americans to leave our children worse off than we were. No generation of Americans has ever done that. We are about to do that. We are about to load onto the backs of our children and those lucky enough to have grandchildren, the unknowable costs of military action that may be necessary to protect our freedom [and] the unknowable costs of ongoing security to protect us here at home. . . ."[3]

General Rodham

Even more revealing than Clinton's role as one of her party's leading White House critics is her attempt to garner credibility on defense issues: This speaks volumes about her plans for the future. Hillary watchers see this move as crucial résumé building for a politician long regarded as weak on defense even by Democratic Party standards. It's worth noting that Mrs. Clinton acquired a coveted spot on the Senate Armed Services Committee after just two years in office. After winning the appointment, Clinton told the *New York Post* that she was "very excited" about the post, acknowledging that it would give her a louder voice to "criticize or praise" President Bush. "As I learn more about the operations of our various military services, what I have to say may be better grounded," Clinton predicted. The move left some in the defense establishment doing double-takes.

"I am deeply concerned that Hillary Clinton serving on the Senate Armed Services Committee represents a clear and present danger to our national security," one retired Air Force weapons engineer told NewsMax.com a week after the appointment was announced. Speaking on condition of anonymity, the former high-security military insider worried, "While she and her husband were in office, my colleagues and I were outraged about the people we were directed to 'read in' to our military's most secret programs. Many of these people were not fit to receive SECRET clearances."[4]

In fact, Hillary's efforts to acquire defense credentials dates back at least to her Senate campaign. In an incident that went largely unnoticed by the national press, she bumped U.S. Navy Secretary Richard Danzig from the May 2000 graduation program at the U.S. Merchant Marine Academy at Kings Point, New York; he had been scheduled to deliver the commencement address after the then first lady turned down the invitation. "An invitation did go out to Mrs. Clinton in the fall," a spokesman for the institution confirmed after relatives of midshipmen began calling talk radio to complain about the snub. "The Academy hadn't heard anything [from Clinton] for a number of months. We called her office to find out if she was going to accept or going to turn down the invitation. At the time, we received word that it looked like she wouldn't be able to attend, that her schedule wouldn't permit it." The Academy spokesman said that at that point, "we went to plan B, which was to invite the Secretary of the Navy."

However, as Secretary Danzig was preparing to do the honors, Mrs. Clinton changed her mind. "We received a call from Mrs. Clinton's office telling us that she could serve as commencement speaker," the school spokesman explained. "The Secretary of the Navy had already been contacted and had accepted. So the Academy called him and explained the situation and he graciously said, 'Fine.'" Mrs. Clinton's address went off without incident, although several midshipmen interviewed later made it plain they were unhappy that Danzig had been deep-sixed so that Clinton could use their graduation to burnish her military credentials.[5]

The Clintons' Moneyman

Another sure sign that Hillary intends to make her move sooner rather than later is the pivotal role played in Democratic Party politics by the Clintons' one-time chief fund-raiser, Terry McAuliffe. The former first couple went to great lengths to see that McAuliffe was installed as Democratic National Committee chairman after Vice President Al Gore lost the 2000 election. Some felt McAuliffe's appointment was a snub to the party's most loyal constituency, African Americans, many of whom were hoping to see the post go to one of their own—former Atlanta mayor Maynard Jackson. Instead of being treated honorably, Jackson, some felt, had been "archly dismissed" in a way that might leave resentments simmering.[6] Making matters worse, just before beating out Jackson for the top spot, McAuliffe referred to blacks as "colored people" in a speech complaining about the Florida election controversy. He later explained that he meant to say "people of color."[7]

Still, despite his ruffling the feathers of a key constituency, McAuliffe's history as the Clintons' fund-raiser-in-chief trumped all. This native of upstate New York had never held elected office or a job in government. Yet for twenty years he built a career in fund-raising and finance that brought him elbow to elbow with some of the Democratic Party's biggest movers and shakers in and out of government. McAuliffe is nothing if not a survivor, a remarkable accomplishment in and of itself given some of the controversies he's been involved in over the last few years. The party's 1996 fund-raising scandal—especially swirling accusations that McAuliffe played a key role in a securing the support of corrupt officials at the Teamsters Union—seemed like it might sink the Democrats' then finance chairman. For average Americans, McAuliffe was a relative unknown until his name burst upon the scene in connection with schemes to rent out any bit of White House property that wasn't nailed down. Sleepovers in the Lincoln Bedroom and rides aboard Air Force One for fat-cat contributors were among the fund-raiser extraordinaire's most effective techniques. Average Americans may have been offended, but for Democrats struggling to overcome the GOP's traditional advantage in squeezing campaign cash from the affluent, McAuliffe's success was the stuff of legend.

McAuliffe helped bankroll everything from the Clinton's New Year's Eve Millennium Celebration to the William Jefferson Clinton Presidential Library, where the man with the golden touch had pledged to raise $125 million to memorialize the Clintons' presidency. But there was no better example of the first family's personal reliance on the renowned moneyman than the help he extended with the purchase of their Chappaqua, New York, home. After eight years of Whitewater legal bills, a $90,000 contempt-of-court fine, and an $850,000 payout to Paula Jones, the Clintons were ostensibly broke. Into the breach stepped McAuliffe, who personally guaranteed their $1.35 million mortgage—at least until a firestorm of criticism forced Bill and Hillary to make other arrangements.

Still, despite his years as the nation's number one political fundraiser, McAuliffe's greatest achievement was that he escaped being sacked after the Democrats' 2002 election debacle. He had boasted that the end was near for GOP control of the House and that the Democrats were certain to increase their margin of control in the Senate—not to mention publicly vowing to unseat Florida governor Jeb Bush. But as the Election Day returns were tallied, it became clear that McAuliffe had guessed wrong on all three counts.

Some grumbled it was more than just a little bad luck. Questions were raised, for instance, about the Democratic moneyman's decision to pour millions into the Florida race at the last minute. Meanwhile, with control of the U.S. Senate hanging in the balance, Democrats in several key races were facing stiff challenges from Republican opponents and needed every dime they could get from the Democratic National Committee.

McAuliffe's 2002 Debacle?

In a development that was largely overlooked during the campaign, McAuliffe's father-in-law, Richard Swann, served as finance chairman for Jeb Bush's Democratic challenger, Bill McBride. Some suspected it was no coincidence when McBride's campaign was showered with record-breaking infusions of DNC cash during the closing weeks of the race. "While the national party poured millions into a fruitless effort in Florida, other Democrats nationally could have used more last-minute money to avoid narrow losses that shifted control of the U.S. Senate to Republicans," noted Florida's *Bradenton Herald* as Democrats nationwide licked their wounds. The paper went on to report that McAuliffe's relative was "heavily involved in pushing McBride's candidacy—even when the Tampa lawyer was virtually unknown and still battling to upset former U.S. attorney general Janet Reno in the primary."

At least one Democrat, New York gubernatorial candidate Carl McCall, who ostensibly had the Clintons' backing, publicly complained he was being shortchanged. Meanwhile McAuliffe poured $15.7 million in soft money into the doomed McBride campaign. "The fundraising total during that final period was a record for Democrats in such a short period of time, even outpacing the state Republican Party, which pulled in $14.7 [million]," the *Herald* noted. *Newsweek* reporter Howard Fineman claimed that behind the scenes, Bill and Hillary had actually encouraged McAuliffe to pour more resources into the Florida race as part of a plan to "humiliate" the Bush family.

But on Election Day Jeb Bush crushed McBride by 14 points. "Obviously with the vision of 20/20 hindsight, it wasn't a good investment," lamented Democratic Party fund-raiser Mitchell Berger. Referring to Senate Democrat Jean Carnahan's excruciatingly narrow defeat, which ushered in GOP control of the Senate, Berger added, "A little bit of money would have gone a long way in Missouri."

Democratic Party insiders weren't the only ones blaming McAuliffe for the loss. Just days after the election, outspoken New York City reverend and soon-to-be-presidential candidate Al Sharpton was calling for the DNC chair's head, telling

MSNBC's Chris Matthews, "I think [McAuliffe is] a nice guy, but I think we need a new coach." Criticizing McAuliffe for relying on nostalgia for the Clinton years to carry the party to victory in the midterm elections, Sharpton complained, "The strategies did not work. There was no voter registration. There was no voter mobilization. I remember I was in five or six states, and their strategy for labor wasn't there." The civil rights activist continued to grumble, "We lost the mayor's race last year. We lost the governor's race this year in New York. . . . We lost Mondale. We lost McBride. We lost Hawaii."

> "I think [McAuliffe is] a nice guy, but I think we need a new coach."
>
> — *Rev. Al Sharpton*

In fact, Sharpton's point was well taken. Even under the best of circumstances, party chairmen seldom survive a defeat like the one suffered by Democrats in November 2002. On the other side of the aisle, Republican National Committee chairman Jim Nicholson even stepped down after a campaign that saw his candidate, George Bush, win the White House. His successor, Virginia governor James Gilmore, was pressed into retirement before he could even test his skills in the midterm election. For McAuliffe to last as party chairman until 2008, when Hillary Clinton will need his fundraising expertise more than ever, would be remarkable. But if the DNC chairman can't win back the White House in 2004, Sharpton won't be the only one calling for his scalp.

Almost no one disputes the fact that Bill and Hillary still control the Democratic Party—and they will probably continue in that role until another Democrat wins the White House. The fact that McAuliffe survived the 2002 midterm with his chairmanship intact serves as ample testimony that the Clintons want him to remain in that position. The question is, Why? If he's unlikely to be around in 2008, one good reason would be to keep McAuliffe in control of party purse strings should other Democrats be unwilling to step aside in the event Mrs. Clinton decides to get into the race in 2004.

Hillary's Presidential Hope Chest

Even absent any presidential announcement, Mrs. Clinton has been working hard to master the fine art of political fund-raising and now has one of the richest PACs of any elected Democrat in Congress. According to conventional wisdom, it was all in a good cause, helping other Democrats get elected by handing out favors that wouldn't be redeemable until the former first lady herself sought higher office in 2008. But it turns out that Senator Clinton's political altruism might not be all it's cracked up to be.

According to a February 2002 study done by *The Hill* newspaper, the nation's most popular elected Democrat spent most of her massive HILLPAC political-action committee's jackpot on herself rather than donating it to other Democrats. Commenting on *The Hill*'s analysis, the *New York Post* observed, "Clinton (D-N.Y.) has the biggest federal PAC of any Democrat in Congress and spent $3.3 million last year but gave only 31 percent to other candidates."

> "Clinton's PAC spending is more like 2004 Democratic presidential candidates Rep. Dick Gephardt (Mo.), Sen. Joe Lieberman (Conn.) and Sen. John Edwards (N.C.) . . ."
>
> —New York Post

"It looks like she's building a national network," Larry Noble of the Center for Responsive Politics told the paper. "The assumption on the part of many people is that this is the beginning of laying the groundwork for a presidential campaign for the future."

Compare Clinton's relative stinginess with that of another prolific Democratic Party fund-raiser, newly crowned House Minority Leader Nancy Pelosi. Turns out the California Democrat gave away 70 percent of her PAC war chest—more than twice the percentage Hillary dispensed. Then again, there's no one beating down Pelosi's door to get her to run for president. "Clinton's PAC spending is more like 2004 Democratic presidential candidates Rep. Dick Gephardt (Mo.), Sen. Joe Lieberman (Conn.) and Sen. John Edwards (N.C.), whose PACs are all giving a small share to other candidates," noted the *Post*. Another telltale tidbit includes the fact that Clinton was much more generous when it came to bankrolling candidates in the state of Iowa, where caucuses in January 2004 will be the nation's first presidential proving ground. HILLPAC gave $10,000 apiece to the Iowa Democratic party, the state's Democratic governor, and U.S. Senator Tom Harkin.[8]

The Reluctant Front-Runner

Also working to Senator Clinton's advantage in 2004 is her tremendous name recognition—not just as a celebrity politician, but also as the symbol of what many Democrats would argue was eight years of unprecedented peace and prosperity. That's what keeps her at the top of one Democratic Party presidential poll after another. It also makes it unwise for her to announce her presidential intentions much before her party's Boston convention in July 2004.

If Clinton were to throw her hat into the ring in fall 2003 or enter the race during the early primaries of 2004, she and her husband would become the immediate target of some of the same criticism that dogged them throughout the 1990s. The former first family have enjoyed a respite from the political attacks of the past largely because they were deemed to be finished as a national political force after January 2001. With Bill Clinton out of the Oval Office, late-breaking scandals like the pardons-for-sale imbroglio, the trashing of the White House complex, and the missing White House furniture that later turned up in Hillary's Chappaqua home—not to mention some of the post-impeachment controversies like Juanita Broaddrick's rape allegation—quickly faded from the media's radar screen.

Still, these and other unresolved questions about, for instance, the former president's decision to turn down a deal for Osama bin Laden's extradition to the United States, could cause trouble. Though a compliant mainstream media is likely to let sleeping dogs lie, the growing conservative alternative press could throw sand in the gears of the former first family's media machine. Mrs. Clinton knows that the less time she is exposed to public scrutiny as a presidential candidate, the less time her critics have to revisit lingering questions left over from her husband's presidency. Better to let the Democrats slug it out till convention time, when, if Bush looks weak, Hillary can ride to her divided party's rescue.

The Sharpton Factor

One of those divisions could be particularly problematic for Democrats, so much so that by March 2003, it had already generated a genuine "Draft Hillary" movement. Americans in the heartland largely regarded the presidential candidacy of Reverend Al Sharpton as a joke. But in the Democratic strongholds of the nation's urban centers, party stalwarts knew they had a problem on their hands. A year before the 2004 New Hampshire primary, the *New Republic,* long considered the journalistic home base of the New Democrat wing of the Democratic Party, began sounding the alarm.

"Well aware of the havoc wreaked by the bomb-throwing reverend in many a New York election, party strategists are exceedingly nervous about Sharpton taking his racialist political theater to the national stage. . . . Dems worry about what will happen if their party gets too snuggly with the reverend. . . . With Sharpton in the race, warns one Democratic player, 'the question is whether he will destroy the national party the way he did the Democrats in New York.'"[9]

Others began to mutter about the presidential primary in South Carolina, the second major contest of the campaign season where average citizens will get to cast their votes. With its large black population, the state could actually make Sharpton the Democratic Party's national front-runner in terms of the delegate count, at least until Midwestern primary voters begin to weigh in a few weeks later.

Sharpton's long-shot bid for the White House got another shot in the arm with the release of a March 2003 Zogby International poll that said he was the number one choice for president among New York City Democrats. "In New York City, Sharpton was the strongest [Democrat] with 13 percent of the vote, followed closely by [Senator Joseph] Lieberman (12 percent) and [Representative Richard] Gephardt (11 percent)," the respected pollster claimed. What's more, in New York State overall, Sharpton trailed only two other Democrats—again, Lieberman (14 percent) and Gephardt (13 percent). Among black Democrats nationwide, however, Sharpton was the out-and-out presidential front-runner, garnering 20 percent of their support, according to a *Time*/CNN survey conducted around same time. While the Zogby and *Time* polls received next to no mainstream media attention (*Time* covered its Sharpton results only in a press release), within days a "Draft Hillary" movement emerged. According to at least one report, the draft idea was floated with the single purpose of rescuing the party from Sharpton.

"If a favorite other than Sharpton doesn't become obvious by late fall, look for a strong effort to draft Sen. Hillary Rodham Clinton," reported *U.S. News & World Report.* "The Iowa Democratic Party," said the magazine's "Washington Whispers" column, "is already thinking that. We hear it wants Clinton as the featured speaker at an annual fall event—an invite that's irked Sen. John Kerry."[10] A source close to Sharpton's campaign confirmed to NewsMax a few days later that there was rampant speculation "about the Democratic party making a strong effort to draft Hillary Clinton."

No wonder. The Democratic Party doesn't have a prayer of recapturing the White House—let alone winning back control of the House and Senate —without strong black support for the party's 2004 candidate. However, in little-noticed comments in his own October 2002 presidential campaign manifesto, "Al on America," Sharpton threatened to break the party's lock on black voters. "To this day, I feel the Democratic Party had to be taught a lesson and still has to be taught one nationally," the radical reverend announced. "A lot of 2004 will be about what happened in New York in 2001."

That last comment is sure to send shudders down the spines of Democratic party strategists everywhere, who remember how Sharpton torpedoed what was considered the all but certain election victory of New York City Democratic mayoral hopeful Mark Green two years ago. And unlike most black leaders, Sharpton has sent the signal that if officials don't heed his advice to move the party leftward, certain consequences can be expected to follow. "The Democratic Party acts like we [black people] are their mistress that they have to hide, like we're some political scarlet whore rather than their respected partner," the firebrand reverend complained. "Either we're going to have a healthy marriage or we're getting a divorce and marrying someone who will respect us. We will no longer allow ourselves to be screwed by the Democrats."

Sharpton's remarks were not off-the-cuff, impromptu comments by the radical minister, who sometimes lets his racial grievances eclipse his sense of political discretion. No, these are the words Sharpton carefully chose to include in a book designed to pave the way for his presidential campaign, a message so potentially devastating to Democratic election prospects that the party's friends in the mainstream press have helpfully declined to discuss the quotations. More from presidential candidate Sharpton:

- "The [Democratic Leadership Council] was led by folks like Bill Clinton, Al Gore and Joe Lieberman and was set up as the anti-Rainbow Coalition. . . . I am running to take out the DLC, which I call the Democratic Leisure Class, because that's who it serves—the leisure class and the wealthy."

- It's about dignity. Blacks, Latinos and Progressives have voted in unusual numbers for Democrats. Ninety five percent of the black vote went for Al Gore in 2000. And we don't have a black in the United States Senate? We don't have a black governor. The Democrats won't take a strong stand on affirmative action. They won't deal with the disproportionate number of blacks and Latinos in jail."

- "People, especially many black people, got duped by Clinton. There are some who even refer to him jokingly as the first black president. . . . [Clinton's] style ingratiated him with blacks and the media. But in many ways his style betrayed black America because his substance and his policies really did not serve our needs."

- "How can we continue not to challenge the party that got 95 percent of our vote? We can't as long as they continue to take us for granted. . . . This is the message for the Democratic Party in 2004: Don't take us for granted."

- Defending his role in the Tawana Brawley rape hoax imbroglio: "We've had all kinds of people leading in this party who had extramarital sexual relationships with young girls or had questionable relations, like Ted Kennedy, Gary Condit and Bill Clinton. So when people say, 'Do you have hesitations about running (for presi-

> dent) because of Brawley?' I say, 'No!' That makes me want to run even more so they can compare what they consider my baggage to the trunks some of the leaders of the Democratic Party are carrying."[11]

The prospect that Sharpton may be willing to air the dirty laundry of other Democrats is sure to cause party officials many a sleepless night as they wrestle with his challenge. For while names like Mary Jo Kopechne and Juanita Broaddrick have long been expunged from the Democrat lexicon, they know Sharpton not only has the chutzpah to take these unresolved episodes out of the party's scandal closet, but also has the media savvy do so in a way that would guarantee significant press coverage. In a sign that the Harlem presidential wannabe continues to view the Democratic Party's scandal card as one of his most potent weapons, he broached the topic again in a January 2003 interview with *Newsday*'s Jimmy Breslin. "The next time anybody wants to know about Tawana Brawley," he warned, "I'm going to ask them, 'Do you ask Teddy Kennedy about Chappaquiddick? Do you ask Hillary Clinton about her husband?'"

> "The next time anybody wants to know about Tawana Brawley, I'm going to ask them, 'Do you ask Teddy Kennedy about Chappaquiddick? Do you ask Hillary Clinton about her husband?'"
>
> —*Rev. Al Sharpton*

If Sharpton can't be neutralized by convention time, the Democratic Party will need a standard-bearer who can retain the enthusiasm of African American voters without alienating white Democrats—or face the prospect of having the 2001 New York City mayoral election debacle replayed on the national stage. Will Senator Joe Lieberman be able to fill the bill? Not likely, especially considering the suspicion with which many black Democrats viewed his selection as Gore's vice presidential running mate in 2000. At the time, for instance, Sharpton himself referred to the Lieberman pick as "political racial profiling."[12]

As for the two other leading Democratic presidential contenders, Senators John Kerry and John Edwards, neither has demonstrated enough appeal with African American voters to rescue the party's presidential prospects from any Sharpton-generated rift. Only one Democrat has the power to overcome a threat like that—Bill Clinton, who has been revered by African Americans since his 1998 impeachment. And while the ex-president can't run again, his wife certainly could—a prospect many would view as the chance for the third Clinton term Democrats were denied because of so-called GOP treachery in the 2000 Florida presidential race.

The Path to the White House

In 2004, the road from the opening presidential primary to the election in November will be fraught with unpredictable twists and turns. Beyond the swirling currents within the Democratic Party, the success or failure of President Bush's war on terrorism, whether or not his economic program jump-starts the economy in time, and the aftermath of the U.S. military campaign in Iraq will all play a decisive role. Another critical factor will be the press, whose amply documented love affair with the Clintons is by now beyond dispute.

Against this backdrop, Hillary Clinton will have to decide whether this election cycle is the right time to make her move. Should she try to repeat her husband's success in defeating President Bush's father in 1992 under conditions that, in more than a few respects, mirror that time? Or would the former first lady do better to wait till 2008, when memories of Clinton-era triumphs will have faded and other Democrats may have supplanted her in the national political spotlight? Indeed, if Hillary sits out 2004 and events erode Bush's popularity during the fall campaign, a Democrat other than Clinton could reclaim the

White House for his party, leaving Bill and Hillary out in the cold till 2012.

Eight years is a long time to hold a party hostage to one's presidential ambitions. In Hillary's scheme to retake the White House, rebuild the tattered Clinton presidential legacy, and make history as the first female president of the United States, timing will be critical. For Senator Clinton, the timing will never be better than it is in 2004.

Notes

Chapter 1

1. NBC News Special Report: The Inauguration of George W. Bush, NBC News Transcripts, 20 Jan. 2001.
2. *Newsday,* 21 Jan. 2001.
3. Associated Press, 16 Aug. 2002.
4. *Chicago Sun-Times,* 12 Dec. 2001.
5. Senator Hillary Clinton, interview with NBC's *Meet the Press,* NBC News Transcripts, 9 Dec. 2001.
6. Terry McAuliffe, interview with NBC's *Meet the Press,* NBC News Transcripts, 4 Feb. 2001.
7. Interview with author, 15 Nov. 2002.
8. *The Economist,* U.S. Edition, 11 Nov. 2000.
9. George Stephanopoulos, "Memorandum to Mrs. Clinton From: George Stephanopoulos Re: Why You Shouldn't Run," *Newsweek,* 1 Mar. 1999, p. 31.
10. *San Antonio Express News,* 22 Feb. 1999.
11. *San Antonio Express News,* 22 Feb. 1999.
12. David Maraniss, *First in His Class* (New York: Simon & Schuster, 1995), p. 311.
13. *Newsday,* 6 Jan. 1999.

14. Tim Russert on NBC's *Meet the Press,* 3 Jan. 1999, NBC News Transcripts.

15. John Zogby and Dick Morris, interviewed on Fox News Channel's *The O'Reilly Factor,* 6 Nov. 2000; NewsMax.com transcription.

Chapter 2

1. Hillary Clinton, interviewed on WLIE Radio's *Mike Siegel Show,* 24 Jan. 2003.

2. *New York Post,* 6 Apr. 2001.

3. *Newsday,* 2 Mar. 1994.

4. *Arkansas Democrat-Gazette,* 1 Jan. 1998.

5. David Maraniss, *First in His Class* (New York: Simon & Schuster, 1995) p. 456.

6. Carl Limbacher, "Hillary's Presidential Slip Showing," NewsMax.com report on ABC Radio Network news audio, 19 July 2001.

7. Hillary Clinton, interviewed on WLIE Radio's *Mike Siegel Show,* 24 Jan. 2003.

8. *The Telegraph* (London), 22 Dec. 2002.

9. Limbacher, "Dick Morris Says Hillary Will Be America's Next President," NewsMax.com, 8 May 2002.

10. Gail Sheehy, *Hillary's Choice* (New York: Random House, 1999) p. 197.

11. *New York Post,* 9 Nov. 2000.

12. Sheehy, p. 198.

13. Limbacher, "Dick Morris Says Hillary Will Be America's Next President."

14. Beth Harpaz, *The Girls in the Van* (New York: St. Martin's Press, 2001) p. 202.

15. Gail Collins, "The Rudy Chronicles," *New York Times,* 6 May 2000.

16. *New York Post,* 22 May 2000.

17. Dana Blanton, "Bush Bests Gore in Rematch," Fox News.com, 22 Nov. 2002.

18. *The Columbia Journalism Review,* Sept./Oct. 1993.

19. Dan Rather, interviewed on *Imus in the Morning,* 7 Feb. 2002.

20. Harpaz, p. 283.

Chapter 3

1. Author's interview with Meredith Oakley, 10 Jan. 2003.

2. Author's interview with Larry Nichols, 29 Jan. 2003.

3. Author's interview with Susan McDougal, *Washington Post* Online chat, 15 Jan. 2003.

4. Author's interview with Susan McDougal, 2 July 2000.

5. Author's interview with Susan McDougal, WLIE Radio, 17 Jan. 2003.

6. Author's interview with John Doggett, 8 Jan. 2003.

Chapter 4

1. *New York Daily News,* 25 Mar. 2001.

2. Hillary Clinton, interviewed on WABC Radio's *John Gambling Show,* 5 Sept. 2002.

3. *New York Post,* 8 Aug. 2002.

4. *New York Daily News,* 30 July 2002.

5. *New York Daily News,* 10 July 2002.

6. *Washington Post,* 15 July 2002.

7. Questioned by author, 29 Apr. 2000.

8. *New York Daily News,* 29 Apr. 2000.

9. *New York Daily News,* 4 Nov. 2000.

10. Carl Cameron, Fox News Channel, 2 Nov. 2000.

11. Senator Simpson, interviewed on MSNBC's *Hardball,* 2 Nov. 2000.

12. *National Review Online,* 15 Nov. 2000.

13. *Arkansas Democrat-Gazette,* 30 Oct. 1992.

14. *Boston Globe,* 31 Oct. 1992.

15. *Minneapolis Star-Tribune,* 31 Oct. 1992.

16. *The Guardian,* 3 Oct. 2002.

17. PR Newswire, 28 Oct. 2002.

18. Bill Schneider, CNN, 27 Dec. 2002.

19. Scripps Howard, 31 Dec. 2002.

20. *This Week with George Stephanopoulos,* ABC News, 29 Dec. 2002.

21. *Weekly Standard, 22 July 1996.*

22. *New York Daily News,* 11 Dec. 1996.

23. Associated Press, 15 Dec. 1993

24. Bill Clinton, interviewed by CNN, 20 Dec. 2002.

25. Paul Alexander, *Man of the People: The Life of John McCain* (Hoboken, N.J.: Wiley, 2002) p. 264.

26. Senator John McCain, interviewed on *Imus in the Morning,* 6 Jan. 2003.

Chapter 5

1. *New York Post,* 14 Feb. 2001.

2. *Washington Times,* 25 Jan. 2001.

3. Carl Limbacher, "Columnist Stands By Air Force One Looting Story," NewsMax.com, 15 Feb. 2001.

4. *New York Times,* 4 Aug. 2000.

5. Limbacher, "O'Reilly: Bush Insider Claims Clinton Deal Torpedoed Pardongate," NewsMax.com, 21 Jun. 2002.

6. Limbacher, "Bush and Hillary Paired Up for Air Force One Big Apple Trip," NewsMax.com, 10 July 2001.

7. Limbacher, "Bush's Impeachment Sought by Clinton-Connected Group," NewsMax.com, 22 July 2002.

8. Limbacher, "DNC Spokesgal Claims to Be 'Appalled' at Bush Impeachment Drive," NewsMax.com, 25 July 2002.

9. Hillary Clinton, interviewed on CNN, 10 Nov. 2001.

10. *New York Post,* 9 Nov. 2001.

11. *Albany Times-Union,* 23 Dec. 2001.

12. Limbacher, "Hillary: Tax Hike Needed to Fight Iraq," NewsMax.com, 5 Sept. 2002.

13. L. D. Brown, *Crossfire: Witness in the Clinton Investigation* (San Diego, Calif.; Black Forest Press, 1999) p. 71.

Chapter 6

1. *New York Times,* 18 May 2002.
2. Carl Limbacher, "Hillary Demands 'Immediate' Answers on Bush 9-11 Heads-Up," NewsMax.com, 16 May 2002.
3. Limbacher, "Hillary: National Security My New Top Priority," NewsMax.com, 17 May 2002.
4. Limbacher, "Hillary Panned for Sour Demeanor During Bush Speech," NewsMax.com, 21 Sept. 2001.
5. *Sunday Oklahoman,* 26 May 2002.
6. *Boston Herald,* 25 June 2000.
7. United Press International, 30 Aug. 2000.
8. Limbacher, "Lou Dobbs: Clinton SEC Turned Blind Eye to Enron," NewsMax.com, 21 July 2002.
9. *Crane's New York Business Weekly,* 9 Oct. 2000.
10. *New York Daily News,* 14 Mar. 1999.
11. *New York Post,* 14 Mar. 1999.
12. *New York Post,* 16 Mar. 1999.
13. *Ethnic News Watch,* 29 Mar. 2000.
14. *New York Daily News,* 19 Apr. 2000.
15. *Washington Times,* 24 Mar. 2000.
16. Rothstein Catalog of Disaster Recovery, www.disastercenter.com/crime/uscrime.htm

Chapter 7

1. Associated Press, 22 Dec. 1999.
2. Gail Sheehy, *Hillary's Choice* (New York: Random House, 1999) p. 11.
3. Sheehy, p. 139.
4. Ronald Kessler, *Inside the White House* (New York: Pocket Books, 1995), p. 231.
5. Joyce Milton, *The First Partner* (New York: William Morrow, 1999) p. 259.
6. *Star,* 21 Feb. 2000
7. Barbara Olson, *Hell to Pay* (Washington, D.C.: Regnery, 1999) p. 5.
8. Dee Dee Myers interviewed for PBS's Frontline *The Clinton Years,* Jan. 16, 2001, www.pbs.org/wgbh/pages/frontline /shows/clinton/interviews/myers.html
9. *New York Daily News,* 19 July 2002.
10. Jerry Oppenheimer, *State of a Union* (New York: Harper-Collins, 2000) p. 153.
11. *New York Daily News,* 17 July 2000.
12. Carl Limbacher, "Hillary Slurred Jews 10 to 20 Times, Used 'N' word Too: Bodyguard," NewsMax.com, 17 July 2000.
13. Dick Morris, interviewed on *Hannity & Colmes,* the Fox News Channel, 4 Nov. 1999.
14. *NBC Nightly News,* NBC News Transcripts, 17 July 2000.

Chapter 8

1. *New York Daily News,* 13 Nov. 2000.
2. *New York Post,* 15 July 2000.
3. *New York Post,* 15 July 2000.
4. Author's interview with Rick Lazio, 2 Aug. 2000.
5. Author's interview with Rick Lazio, 15 Nov. 2002.
6. Byron York, *The American Spectator,* "'Our Guy' in the White House," April, 1997
7. Associated Press, 17 June 1999.
8. Author's interview with Rick Lazio, 15 Nov. 2002.
9. Adam Dickter, interviewed by WABC-NY Radio's Steve Malzberg, 20 July 2000.
10. Associated Press, 25 July 2000.
11. *New York Daily News,* 8 July 2000.
12. *Jewish World Review,* 7 Nov. 2000.
13. Ibrahim Hooper, interviewed by WABC Radio's Steve Malzberg, November 15, 2002.
14. Barbara Olson, *Hell to Pay* (Washington, D.C.: Regnery, 1999) p. 37.
15. *New York Times,* 8 May 1998.
16. *New York Daily News,* 12 Nov. 1999.
17. *Newsday,* 13 Nov. 1999.
18. Limbacher, "Hillary Booed off Stage in Wake of Mideast Violence," NewsMax.com, 12 Oct. 2000.

19. Beth Gilinsky, interviewed on WOR-NY Radio's *Bob Grant Show,* 12 Oct. 2000.

20. Noach Dear, interviewed on WABC-NY Radio's *Sean Hannity Show,* 12 Oct. 2000.

21. *Jewish Forward,* 26 May 2000.

22. *New York Post,* 4 Nov. 2000.

23. Limbacher, "'Hezbollah Hillary' Caught Red-Handed—Again!," NewsMax.com, 4 Nov. 2000.

24. Limbacher, "Hillary Caught in Pro-Arafat Fund-Raising Cover-Up," NewsMax.com, 27 Oct. 2000.

25. *New York Daily News,* Oct. 28, 2000.

26. United Press International, 29 Oct. 2000.

27. Olson, p. 20.

28. Gail Sheehy, *Hillary's Choice* (New York: Random House, 1999) p. 345.

29. Limbacher, "Clinton Admits: I Nixed Bin Laden Extradition Offer," NewsMax.com, 11 Aug. 2002.

30. Hillary Clinton, interviewed on *Meet the Press,* NBC News transcripts, 15 Sept. 2002.

31. Hillary Clinton, interviewed on WLIE-NY Radio's *Mike Siegel Show,* 24 Jan. 2003.

32. Knight Ridder News Service, 20 Sept. 2002.

33. Hillary Clinton, interviewed on WLIE-NY Radio's *Mike Siegel Show,* 24 Jan. 2003.

34. Hillary Clinton, interviewed on WLIE-NY Radio's *Mike Siegel Show,* 24 Jan. 2003.

Chapter 9

1. *Seattle Post Intelligencer,* 21 Aug. 1992.
2. *Los Angeles Times,* 23 Sept. 1992.
3. Senator Hillary Clinton, video clip aired on *Hannity & Colmes,* the Fox News Channel, 23 Mar. 2000.
4. Beth Harpaz, *The Girls in the Van* (New York: St. Martin's Press, 2001) p. 115.
5. *Albany Times Union,* 17 May 2000.
6. Limbacher, "Hillary's Letter of 'Apology' for Convention Cop-Spitters," NewsMax.com, 2 June 2000.
7. Limbacher, "Giuliani: Arrest Hillary's Delegates for 'Assault' on Police," NewsMax.com, 26 May 2000.
8. Limbacher, "Hero Fireman Slams Phony Hillary," NewsMax.com, 23 Oct. 2001.
9. *New York Post,* 27 Dec. 2001.
10. Beth Harpaz, interviewed on *The O'Reilly Factor,* the Fox News Channel, 28 Nov. 2001.
11. Barbara Olson, *Hell to Pay* (Washington, D.C., Regnery, 1999) p. 55.
12. Gail Sheehy, *Hillary's Choice* (New York: Random House, 1999) p. 201.
13. Olson, p. 55.
14. *The Atlanta Journal and Constitution,* Aug. 29, 1992.
15. Horowitz, interviewed on *The Right Perspective* radio show, WCBQ, 15 Nov. 1999.

16. Limbacher, "No Apology from Hillary for Still-Injured Cop," NewsMax.com, 30 Oct. 2001.

Chapter 10

1. Carl Limbacher, "'Clinton Report Cost Me My Show': TV Talk Host," NewsMax.com, 13 Sept. 1999.
2. Hillary Clinton, interviewed on *Breakfast with Bauerle,* WGR-AM Buffalo, 19 Jan. 2000.
3. Limbacher, "Buffalo Talk Host Who Grilled Hillary Is MIA," NewsMax.com, 20 Jan. 2000.
4. *Reliable Sources* transcript, CNN.com, 23 Jan. 2000.
5. Patrick Halley, *On the Road with Hillary* (New York: Viking, 2002) p. 38.
6. Fred Dicker, interviewed on MSNBC's *Hardball,* 8 June 2000.
7. Fred Dicker, interviewed on WABC-NY Radio's *The Buzz* with Steve Malzberg and Richard Bey, 9 June 2000.
8. Glenn Schuck, interviewed on WABC Radio's *The Sean Hannity Show,* 17 Mar. 2000.
9. WOR-NY radio's *The Bob Grant Show,* 29 Mar. 2000.
10. *Washington Times,* Oct. 25, 2000
11. *San Francisco Examiner,* 31 Jan. 1999.
12. Mary Matalin on *The Mary Matalin Show,* WRC Radio in Washington, D.C., 1998.
13. Christopher Andersen, *Bill and Hillary: The Marriage* (New York: Morrow, 1999) p. 185.
14. Author's interview with Lucille Bolton, 16 Aug. 1998.
15. *New York Daily News,* 23 Nov. 2002.

Chapter 11

1. David Gergen, interviewed for PBS *Frontline* "The Clinton Years," 16 Jan. 2001. http://www.pbs.org/wgbh/pages/frontline/shows/clinton/interviews/gergen.html
2. *Washington Times,* 19 July 2002.
3. Associated Press, 5 Dec. 2002.
4. *New York Post,* 21 Mar. 2002.
5. Hillary Clinton, interviewed on *Today,* NBC News transcript, 27 Jan. 1998.
6. Hillary Clinton, interviewed on *Good Morning America,* ABC News transcript, 28 Jan. 1998.
7. Christopher Andersen, *Bill and Hillary: The Marriage* (New York: William Morrow, 1999) p. 150.
8. Gail Sheehy, interviewed for NBC's *Dateline,* NewsMax.com transcript, 19 Nov. 1999.
9. *New York Daily News,* 19 Jan. 1998.
10. L. D. Brown, *Crossfire: Witness in the Clinton Investigation* (San Diego: Black Forest Press, 1999) p. 62.
11. Kathleen Willey, interviewed on CBS's *60 Minutes,* CBS News transcript.
12. *New York Times,* 19 Mar. 1998.
13. Michael Isikoff, *Uncovering Clinton* (New York: Crown, 1999) p. 256.
14. Isikoff, p.162.
15. Carl Limbacher, "Broaddrick Blockbuster Set to Run Friday—Before NBC Panicked," NewsMax.com, 29 Jan. 1999.

16. Roger Morris, *Partners in Power* (New York: Holt) p. 238.

17. Juanita Broaddrick, interviewed on NBC's *Dateline,* NBC News transcript, 24 Jan. 1999.

18. *Wall Street Journal,* 5 Mar. 1999.

19. Andersen, p. 164.

20. George Carpozi, *Clinton Confidential* (Del Mar, Calif.: Emery Dalton, 1995) p. 90.

21. Gail Sheehy, *Hillary's Choice* (New York: Random House, 1999) p. 121.

22. Andersen, p. 147.

23. *New York Times,* 29 Apr. 2002.

24. Limbacher "Juanita Broaddrick Slams Hillary's Anti-Rape Hypocrisy," NewsMax.com, 30 Apr. 2002.

25. *Hannity & Colmes,* the Fox News Channel, Media Millworks transcript, 16 Dec. 1999.

26. Webster Hubbell, *Friends in High Places* (New York: William Morrow, 1997) pp. 191–92.

27. Hubbell, p. 298.

28. *The Nation,* 17 May 1999.

29. *New York Post,* 2 Feb. 1999.

30. Sheehy, *Hillary's Choice,* p. 201.

31. Limbacher, "Hillary's Lawyer Calls Attack on Gennifer Flowers 'Political Speech,'" NewsMax.com, 24 Feb. 2002.

32. Sue Schmidt and Michael Weisskopf, *Truth at Any Cost* (New York: HarperCollins, 2000) p. 121.

33. Limbacher, "New Broaddrick Shocker: 'I Was Followed,'" NewsMax.com, 19 May 1999.
34. Limbacher, "New Broaddrick Shocker: 'I Was Followed.'"
35. Rudolph Giuliani, questioned on WABC Radio's *Ask the Mayor* program, 24 Sept. 1999.

Chapter 12

1. *Washington Post,* 15 Feb. 1995
2. Author's interview with Barbara Olson, January 1999.
3. Ann Coulter, *Washington Times,* 8 June 2000.
4. *Washington Times,* 8 June 2000.
5. Ann Coulter, *High Crimes and Misdemeanors* (Washington, D.C., Regnery, 1998) p. 132.
6. *Investor's Business Daily,* 2 October 1997.
7. Joyce Milton, *The First Partner: Hillary Rodham Clinton* (New York: William Morrow, 2000) pp 324–327.
8. *Washington Times,* 8 June 2000.

Chapter 13

1. Associated Press, 16 Sept. 1997.
2. *New York Daily News,* 17 Sept. 1997.
3. Carl Limbacher, "The Washington Weekly," 22 Sept. 1997.
4. Limbacher, "The Washington Weekly," 22 Sept. 1997.
5. Limbacher, "The Jane Doe Case Files," NewsMax.com, 24 Feb. 1999.

6. Elizabeth Ward Gracen, interviewed on NBC's *Dateline,* NBC News transcripts, 24 Apr. 1998.
7. Michael Isikoff, *Uncovering Clinton* (New York: Crown, 1999) p. 256.
8. *New York Post,* 27 Sept. 1998.
9. *New York Post,* 13 Jan. 1999.
10. *Toronto Star,* 19 Sept. 1998.
11. Cox News Service, 3 Dec. 1999.
12. David Schippers, *Sell Out* (Washington, D.C.: Regnery, 2000), p. 23.
13. Tim Russert, interviewed on *Imus in the Morning,* 3 Feb. 1999.
14. Julia Malone, "The Juanita Broaddrick Charges: Too Hot for the Press to Handle," NewsMax.com, 24 June 1999.
15. Dan Rather, interviewed on *The O'Reilly Factor,* the Fox News Channel, Media Millworks transcripts, 15 May 2001.
16. Limbacher, "Republican Senator Says Rapegate 'A Private Matter,'" NewsMax.com, 26 Feb. 1999.
17. Kim Gandy, interviewed by WABC-NY Radio's Steve Malzberg, 8 July 2001.
18. Lanny Davis, interviewed on *Hannity & Colmes,* Fox News Channel, Media Millworks transcript, 16 Dec. 1999.
19. Limbacher, "Juanita Broaddrick Sues Clinton White House," NewsMax.com, Dec. 20, 1999.
20. Limbacher, "Broaddrick: 'Audit Connected to Me Coming Forward,'" NewsMax.com, 30 May 2000.

21. Katherine Prudhomme, speech delivered outside Hillary 2000 campaign headquarters, FreeRepublic.com transcript. http://www.freerepublic.com/forum/a399fc65c1a92.htm.

22. Limbacher, "Prudhomme Audited on Eve of Clinton Rape Protest," NewsMax.com, 19 Aug. 2000.

23. The EO Tax Bulletin, Subject: 1997-8:(3) "Political" Audits?; IRS Issues Art Advisory Board Report, www.tax.org/taxa/tadiscus.nsf/8525624b005f29198525624a0064a42b/4825a450c4ff28628525644b005890d4?OpenDocument

24. James Bovard, *Feeling Your Pain* (New York: St. Martin's Press, 2000).

25. *Sunday Times* (London), 2 Feb. 1997.

26. Ann Coulter, *High Crimes and Misdemeanors* (Washington, D.C.: Regnery, 1998), p. 134.

Chapter 14

1. Associated Press, 28 Dec. 2002.

2. Chris Matthews, interviewed on *Imus in the Morning,* 9 Jan. 2003.

3. Senator Clinton's speech as broadcast on C-SPAN, 20 March 2003.

4. Carl Limbacher, "'Black Program' Vet: Hillary a Security Risk on Armed Services Committee," NewsMax.com, 4 Feb. 2003.

5. Carl Limbacher, "Hillary Bumps Navy Secretary at Merchant Marine Commencement," NewsMax.com, 10 May 2000.

6. The *New Republic,* 17 Feb. 2003.

7. *New York Post,* 7 Nov. 2002.

8. *New York Post,* 24 Feb. 2003.

9. The *New Republic,* 17 Feb. 2003.

10. *U.S. News & World Report,* 17 March 2003.

11. Al Sharpton, with Karen Hunter, *Al on America* (New York: Kensington, 2002).

12. *USA Today,* 14 Aug. 2000.

Index

C

D

H

L

M

Q

R

S